CHINA

and the Legacy of Deng Xiaoping

CHINA
and the Legacy of
Deng Xiaoping

From Communist Revolution to
Capitalist Evolution

Michael E. Marti

Brassey's, Inc.
Washington, D.C.

The views expressed in this book are those of the author and do not reflect the official policy or position of the U.S. Department of Defense or any agency of the U.S. government.

Library of Congress Cataloging-in-Publication Data

Marti, Michael E.
    China and the Legacy of Deng Xiaoping/Michael E. Marti.—Ist ed.
        p. cm.
    Includes bibliographical references and index.
    ISBN I-57488-416-6 (alk. paper)
        I. Deng, Xiaoping, 1904—Views on economic policy. 2. China—Economic
    policy—1976–2000. I. Title: Legacy of Deng Xiaoping. II. Title.

    DS778.T39 M37 2002
    951.05'8'092—dc2I

                                                    2001037842

ISBN I-57488-416-6 (alk. paper)

Printed in the United States of America on acid-free paper that meets the American National Standards Institute Z39-48 Standard.

Brassey's, Inc.
2284I Quicksilver Drive
Dulles, Virginia 20I66

First Edition

I0 9 8 7 6 5 4 3 2 I

DEDICATION

To my parents, Henry and Patricia
and my wife, Sharon

CONTENTS

PREFACE

A number of books have been written about Deng Xiaoping and his reforms. The purpose of this book is to document Deng's master plan by which he hoped to institutionalize those reforms and to make China into a rich and powerful nation by the year 2049, the centenary of the People's Republic of China.

Deng's reforms valued the economy over ideology, replaced failing Marxist economics with capitalist market mechanisms, replaced ideologues with technocrats, and in the process opened China to the world, but to effect these changes, he needed to break the hold of the Marxist central planners. By offering the Army a greater role in policymaking and funds for modernization, he secured the "power of the gun" to force a grand compromise that ties the fate of all elements of society—the party, army, public security forces, and regional authorities—to the success of his reforms and goals. As a result, the imperative that guides China's foreign and domestic policies is economic growth, and understanding this has strategic implications for American policymakers in the years to come as the United States tries to come to terms with China's rising economic and military power in Asia and on the international scene.

This book would not have been possible without the assistance of Professor Richard C. Thornton of George Washington University. I would like to thank him for his guidance, encouragement, and thoughtful suggestions. I would also like to thank Mr. Richard M. Valcourt, my agent, for his efforts on my behalf. A special thanks also goes to Don McKeon, publisher of Brassey's, for the opportunity to present my views in a public forum, and to Christina Davidson and Dorothy Smith for their assistance in editing the manuscript. Finally, I would like to express my gratitude to my wife, Sharon, for her continuous support, encouragement, fortitude, and inspiration during the time it took to bring this book to fruition.

INTRODUCTION

Modern Chinese history is inexorably linked with that of the Chinese Communist Party (CCP), beginning with the founding of the party in 1921. Established with the assistance of the Comintern, it was heavily influenced by Moscow during its early years. Only when Mao Zedong successfully purged the Moscow-oriented Politburo members at the historic Seventh Party Congress in July 1945 did the CCP come under the control of Mao and his supporters, who would dominate Chinese politics for the next fifty years. Though there were many internal policy disputes, such as the "anti-rightist movement," the "Great Leap Forward," and the "Cultural Revolution," Mao remained final arbiter until his death in 1976.

Subsequently, Deng Xiaoping made his successful comeback at the Third Plenum of the Eleventh Party Congress in 1978, after having been purged by Mao in the Cultural Revolution in 1965 and again in 1976. Upon his return to power, Deng began the process of reversing Mao's disastrous economic, political, and social policies, opened China to the outside world, launched an economic modernization campaign, and reformed the party.

It is my contention that Deng set China on the path of modernization, and that to ensure that the process survived him, he actively manipulated the inexorable generational change under way within the party, government, and army. Daily operational control of these institutions has been transferred to a "selected" successor generation that, for the most part, has had no experience of the Long March, the wars, and the revolution that engulfed China between 1919 and 1949. The process to establish the successor generation to the "Long Marchers" began in earnest in 1978 with Deng's return to power; it was finalized at the Fourteenth Party Congress in October 1992, and it was "blessed" by the remaining Long Marchers.

It is my thesis that following his resignation from his last official office in November 1989, following the Tiananmen Massacre, Deng gradually came to realize that his "selected" generational transfer process was in mortal danger of being totally aborted by the conservative reaction within the party to the collapse of communism within the Soviet Union and worldwide. Deng's modernization policy, strategically linked to an activist party intervention in the economy, was also in mortal danger. If the "selected" generation was usurped by the conservatives Deng had labored since 1978 to replace or neutralize in the modernization process, then all his efforts would have been for naught. Deng therefore resolved to take direct action to reverse the trend and put his modernization and generational selection process back on course. This he did in late 1991 and 1992, when he effected a "Grand Compromise" among the party factions: elders, conservatives, liberals, regional leaders, technocrats, and the People's Liberation Army (PLA).

The Grand Compromise consisted of three key components: (1) the PLA would support Deng's reforms, the primacy of the party, and the unity of the state; (2) in return, the provincial party chiefs would ensure that revenues would be remitted to the central government; and (3) the central government, in turn, would finance the Army's continued modernization. Thus, the elders and conservatives would be ensured party control of a unified state and the funds to support it, but would have to compromise with reformers on the issue of central economic planning. The technocrats would be free to pursue capitalist economic policies and modernization without hindrance from "leftist" ideologues, but would have to submit to party discipline. The PLA, which has been undergoing a process of professionalization and depoliticization since 1985, would be guaranteed funds for continued modernization and would have a voice in party policy, but would have to submit to the party's authority.

It must be emphasized that the thread connecting all of the parties to this compromise was and is economics. Deng's desire was to create an economic system that would allow China to become a rich and powerful nation by the middle of the twenty-first century. It was the motivation behind all of his policy maneuverings, and he pursued his agenda with a single-minded determination. Any analysis of Chinese politics under Deng's tenure that fails to take his economic motives into consideration will fall short in attempts to explain the politics of the period.

Power in this new arrangement is currently centered on a "core group" within the Politburo Standing Committee, consisting of Jiang Zemin, Hu Jintao, Li Peng, Zhu Rongji, Li Lanqing, and Li Ruihuan. These individuals, however, are not as important as the constituencies they represent: Jiang and Hu, the elders and party rank and file; Li Peng, central ministries and conservatives; Zhu and Li Lanqing, new technocrats, liberal economic thinkers or closet capitalists, and regional leaders. Under Deng's new power equation, the party general secretary wields no significant power, but with PLA and Public Security support and the informal power of the few remaining elders, the team will implement the terms of the compromise. Deng had sought to ensure continuity of his policies by restructuring the Leninist, single-party state through selective replacement of the authoritative power structure to ensure a broad-based institution. Supporting this is a modern PLA, ready to enforce the will of majority at the "core" of the arrangement.

The purpose of this book is to document the Grand Compromise. I will show that it was Deng's own miscalculation that forced him to construct a Grand Compromise in 1991. Deng had placed himself in the position of a retired emperor, similar to Mao after the failure of the Great Leap Forward in 1959, when, in the aftermath of the Tiananmen riots in June 1989, he had allowed Zhao Ziyang and his faction of economic reformers to be purged from the party and government. Zhao, representative of the young technocrats with provincial experience and success owing to the policies of economic liberalization, had been handpicked by Deng. However, because of Zhao's tendencies towards political liberalization, Deng had assented to his ouster. In doing so, however, Deng seriously limited his ability to control policy. He had miscalculated the depth of his support. Thus, having resigned all official positions, as he had been urging other elders to do, he had lost direct control over policy formulation. With the purge of the Zhao faction, the central planners under Li Peng initiated a three-year economic retrenchment in late 1989.

Initially, Deng believed, despite his break with the reformers under Zhao and his subsequent siding with the conservatives, that retrenchment would be no more than a temporary pause, after which his economic policies would be reinstituted. The conservatives, or hard-liners, while they felt that Deng's policies had merit, were more concerned with the scope and pace of implementation and the more important and related issue of party survival.

As early as the mid-1980s, the hard-liners had expressed concern over the specters of inflation, corruption, and graft. Devolution of economic decision-making to the provinces often resulted in capital expenditures that had not been budgeted in the central plan. Subsequent shortfalls had to be covered by printing more money, which produced inflation. This in turn resulted in price increases for consumer goods and demands for wage increases. By 1989, the level of inflation had risen to 30 percent, the highest in recent memory. Civil protests had already occurred throughout the provinces. Corruption, which seemed to thrive and grow under Deng's reformist policies, was the major charge leveled by the students against the party and government in 1989. These factors, combined with the collapse of the Communist Party of the Soviet Union in 1991, spurred the hard-liners to take action to ensure what they felt was no less than the survival of the party. Thus, they ignored Deng's instructions in 1991 to return to the more liberal economic policies, and continued retrenchment. They also initiated steps to ensure that the new Congress, to be chosen in the fall of 1992, would have a "selected" membership more representative of their views than those of the modernizers associated with Deng's policies.

For the reformist provincial leaders, the issue was social stability and economic survival. Many had adopted Deng's policies as the only way to improve the lot of the people and provide employment for their growing populations. But when the banks stopped providing funds and backing loans in 1989, private ventures employing thousands failed or could not meet payrolls. The result was local unrest—strikes, work stoppages, protests, and violence. For the reformers, the 1991 decision to continue retrenchment presented them with an unacceptable situation. They believed the failure to revert to Deng's more liberal policies would lead to economic collapse and rebellion, threatening not only the party but their own survival.

For the PLA, the issues were modernization and political neutrality. Included in Deng's Four Modernizations, the PLA had been in the process of transformation since 1985. In exchange for its voluntary depoliticization, it was equipped with modern weapons and its officer corps professionalized. However, continued modernization depended on the availability of funds from the central government, which in turn relied upon remittances from the provinces, all of which was threatened by retrenchment. Furthermore, the PLA was being asked to arbitrate the internal party debate, thus threatening its neutrality. By marching on Tiananmen to restore order, the PLA clearly enhanced the hard-line, or conservative, position.

Fueling the debate during this period was the collapse of the Soviet Union and its Communist party in 1991. The hard-liners blamed Gorbachev's political liberalizations. They were convinced that Deng's economic liberalization (reform and opening) was leading China down the same path, and would result in the party losing control. The solution was to reassert and strengthen party discipline and central control.

Deng, on the other hand, viewed these events as an opportunity rather than a threat. Simultaneous with the collapse of the Soviet Union, the remaining superpower, the United States, was in the process of withdrawing from the western Pacific. Deng realized that conditions might never again be as favorable for China to reassert hegemony over Southeast Asia and to acquire the foreign investment capital that might otherwise go to rebuild Eastern Europe and Russia. However, to take advantage of this historic opportunity, Deng realized that he had to regain control of policy, foreign and domestic, which meant he had to reassert his authority over the party. Thus, he took a page from Mao.

After the disastrous Great Leap Forward of 1959, Mao had been forced into semiretirement by the party, effectively silencing him. To regain control, he had to bypass the central party apparatus in Beijing. He turned to his supporters in Shanghai to gain access to the press, which he used to mobilize the students in an assault on the party leadership. The resulting

Cultural Revolution, supported by the PLA, spread nationwide and propelled him back into power.

Deng, likewise, bypassed the central party apparatus in his return when, in 1992, he appealed to his supporters in the economically powerful southern provinces, who owed their prosperity to his policies, and who consequently had the most to lose if they were reversed. But rather than the force of the students, Deng cut a deal in December 1991 with the PLA, whose modernization was linked to his economic reforms. Thus, through the alliance of the PLA and the leaders of the economically powerful southern provinces, Deng was able to reassert his influence over policy and force the party hard-liners in Beijing to compromise. From there, he pushed through policy and institutional changes that gave the regional party leaders and a younger, "selected" generation of members control of the party apparatus, and he replaced an entire generation of military leaders with a new, younger, more educated military class that had sworn allegiance to the party.

It may be asked what motivated Deng, in frail health and retirement, to return to the fray to arbitrate the party debate. It is my contention that Deng had a larger goal, an agenda, that drove him—his desire to make China a rich and powerful nation on a par with the West by the middle of the twenty-first century. As my research will show, it was never his intention to liberalize China politically. Indeed, he gambled that the people were more concerned with their economic welfare than personal freedoms. The compromise he worked out, the "Grand Compromise," was to ensure the success of a very practical and nonideological agenda: economic modernization through the use of proven capitalist methods, and party primacy and a centralized state sustained by force of arms and a mutual binding of the major players into codependency. The significance of this book is that it is the first to postulate and document the theory and components of the Grand Compromise.

Like the other watersheds in Chinese history, only with the passage of time will the significance of Deng's actions in 1992 become evident. As for Deng, his health was failing him and after 1994 he gradually withdrew from politics and left it to his chosen successors to carry on. He died in 1997. History will now debate his legacy.

ABBREVIATIONS

CAC   Central Advisory Commission
CCP   Chinese Communist Party
CMC   Central Military Commission
CPSU   Communist Party of the Soviet Union
ETO   Economic and Trade Office
FBIS   Foreign Broadcast Information Service
GDP   gross domestic product
GPD   General Political Department
GSD   General Staff Department
KMT   Kuomintang Party (Taiwan)
MFN   Most Favored Nation
MITI   Ministry of International Trade and Industry (Japan)
MMT   million metric tons
NATO   North Atlantic Treaty Organization

NPC	National People's Congress
PAP	People's Armed Police
PBOC	People's Bank of China
PLA	People's Liberation Army
ROC	Republic of China (Taiwan)
SEC	State Economic Commission
SEZ	special economic zone(s)
SPC	State Planning Commission
WTO	World Trade Organization

1 | Reform and Opening

◇ Return to Power

Since his second political rehabilitation in 1977, Deng had one purpose in mind. . . . to realize his desire for the future of China, which he set out in his keynote address to the Third Plenary Session of the Eleventh Party Congress in December 1978: "The Central Committee had put forward the fundamental guiding principle of shifting the focus of all Party work to the four modernizations . . . a great and profound revolution . . . our new Long March . . . to change the backward condition of our country and turn it into a modern and powerful socialist state."[1]

Deng did not, however, anticipate the extent and depth of his opposition. His rehabilitated comrades, especially Chen Yun, while desiring to move away from Mao's disastrous social, political, and economic policies, did not necessarily agree with Deng's economic formula. Although they, like Deng, had suffered during the Cultural Revolution, many still retained faith in Marxist ideology and economics, Leninist single-party rule, and Stalinist state capitalism. Consequently, almost as soon as they were rehabilitated, several of his longtime colleagues started questioning his economic policies and his seeming disregard of Communist ideology. So too did Hua Guofeng and those in the leadership who had benefited under Mao and were not willing to give up power. These diverse groups quickly divided into factions, which would form much of the opposition to Deng's economic policies for the remainder of his days.

Thus, in 1978, Deng had to battle not only Hua Guofeng, Mao's chosen successor, and the Maoists, but his erstwhile colleagues as well. While he had apparently assembled a bloc of support on the Standing Committee to out-vote Hua, in 1978 (see chart below) Deng could not actually consolidate his position vis-à-vis Hua until he assembled a majority faction on the Politburo and Standing Committee at the Fifth Plenum in February 1980 (see chart below).[2] By that time, Deng had succeeded in rehabilitating all the members of the Eighth Party Central Committee, elected in 1956 and purged by Mao during the Cultural Revolution, with the exception of those who had died or shifted allegiance to Mao.[3]

Thus, the period between 1978 and 1989 was one of constant struggle for Deng and his supporters to implement his agenda. Of necessity, he made many tactical shifts in policy, but in general his strategic goal, outlined in his speech at the Third Plenum, was his guiding principle.

It was under these turbulent conditions that Deng began his efforts in 1979 to transform the economic structure. To do so, he had to reform the party and change old ways of thinking. He advocated free thinking by "pathbreakers" who dared to go against popular thinking and break old taboos to venture into new areas, especially foreign economic thinking and practices; devolution of power to the provinces and local authorities to allow them to make their own economic decisions; and the adoption of Western models and technology. To implement his policy, he recommended:

> We must learn to manage the economy by economic means. If we ourselves don't know about advanced methods of management, we should learn from those who do, either at home or abroad. These methods should be applied not only in the operation of enterprises with newly imported technology and equipment, but also in the technical transformation of existing enterprises. Pending the introduction of a unified national program of modern management, we can begin with limited spheres, say a particular region or a given trade, and then spread the methods gradually to others.[4]

This policy of selective experimentation became known in the party lexicon as "the strategic principle of opening to the outside world."[5]

Deng's objective, in measurable terms, was to quadruple the per capita
income of China's 1.05 billion people from $250, established as the
benchmark in 1981, to approximately $1,000 by the year 2000.[6] This was
to be quadrupled again to $4,000 by the year 2050, at which time China
would be the center of an East Asian trading bloc similar to the European
Community or the North American Free Trade Area.[7] However, this trading bloc would encompass 70 percent of the world's population, produce
more than 50 percent of the world's commodities, consume 40 percent of
the world's production, and account for 70 percent of the world's trade.[8]
China would then truly rank among the most economically advanced
nations of the world, a powerful socialist country, capable of playing a
major role in maintaining world peace and stability.[9] Deng had clearly set
off on a bold new Long March.[10]

Deng was restored to the Standing Committee at the Third Plenum of
the Tenth Congress in July 1977, and to his posts as military chief of staff
and State Council vice-chairman, as part of the succession agreement
worked out following Mao's death that included Hua Guofeng's official
appointment as Party Chairman.[11] He was subsequently reelected to the
Standing Committee of the Eleventh Congress in August of the same year.[12]
At the Third Plenum of the Eleventh Congress, in December 1978, Chen
Yun was added to the Standing Committee as a Deng supporter. Along
with Ye Jianying and Li Xiannian, already on the Standing Committee,
Deng had a majority vote of four to one against Hua. In addition, the Polit-
buro was expanded to twenty-six members which, like the restored Central
Committee, consisted of a majority of Deng's rehabilitated associates
and allies who could be expected to support him against Hua and the
Maoists.[13]

While Deng had not yet achieved complete control as a result of the
Third Plenum, he was able to garner sufficient support for a number of
initiatives. He normalized relations with the United States in December
1978, launched a punitive invasion of Vietnam in February 1979 to punish
it for invading China's client state Cambodia, and attempted to open a dialogue with Moscow in April of 1979. He also began his initial opening to
the world as he scaled back Hua's economic plans and developed "special
economic zones" (SEZ).[14]

With the addition of his protégés Hu Yaobang and Zhao Ziyang to the

Standing Committee at the Fifth Plenum in February 1980, Deng's paramount position in Chinese politics was secured. The outnumbered Hua, totally isolated, faded from sight and resigned as premier of the State Council in September 1980 and as Party Chairman at the Sixth Plenum in 1981.[15]

POLITBURO STANDING COMMITTEE, THIRD PLENUM[16]

Deng Xiaoping	Chen Yun
Ye Jianying	Hua Guofeng
Li Xiannian	

POLITBURO STANDING COMMITTEE, FIFTH PLENUM[17]

Deng Xiaoping	Hua Guofeng
Ye Jianying	Zhao Ziyang
Li Xiannian	Hu Yaobang
Chen Yun	

FIFTH PLENUM POLITBURO[18]

Hua Guofeng	Deng Xiaoping	Ye Jianying
Li Desheng	Chen Yun	Li Xiannian
Chen Yungui	Zhao Ziyang	Xu Xiangqian
Ni Chifu	Hu Yaobang	Nie Rongzhen
	Xu Shiyou	Yu Qiuli
	Wei Guoqing	Fang Yi
	Geng Biao	Zhang Tingfa
	Peng Chong	
	Wang Zhen	
	Deng Yingchao	
	Ulanfu	
	Liu Bocheng	
	Peng Zhen	

The new power structure, however, did not ensure smooth sailing for Deng's agenda. Although he was adamant about maintaining the party's control of Chinese politics, he was willing to scrap the old economics and experiment with new ideas to modernize China. Many of the rehabilitated cadre however, especially Chen Yun, had only visions of tinkering around the edges of the old system. They attributed economic problems to excesses in the past—in other words, the system was not broken. Deng failed to anticipate the tenacity of old ideas among his veteran colleagues. Chen Yun, Peng Zhen, Li Xiannian, Bo Yibo, Wang Zhen, and many others rehabilitated by Deng were old-line Marxists, schooled by Moscow, who believed in central planning and a centralized, Stalinist state as the best way to manage a socialist economy, and each had his own base of support from which to challenge Deng.[19]

Likewise, the new government and party organs quickly developed their own interest groups that did not always endorse Deng's economic and social policies. Among those rehabilitated and the holdover Maoists were many who had the same revolutionary credentials as Deng and were unwilling to concede to his leadership or ideas.

One such group, the restored Eighth Congress veterans, now much older and many too old and feeble to return to their former posts, quickly evolved into an "elders" faction. Their power was concentrated in the Central Advisory Commission (CAC), set up by Deng in 1982 with Chen Yun as director to coax the rehabilitated Eighth Central Committee members to move aside. It grew in power and size over the years as more retired to the informal status as "elders." They all had revolutionary credentials to match Deng's and younger protégés within the party and government that they continued to sponsor, much to Deng's consternation. The elders developed an informal advisory power over government and party policy, like the Genro of late nineteenth-century Japan. The elders included, in addition to Deng, Chen Yun, Peng Zhen, Bo Yibo, Wang Zhen, Yang Shangkun, Li Xiannian, and many others. Thus, Deng was only the "first" among "equals"; he had to respect their views and authority.

Another faction developed within the central ministries. Their political power and importance had grown under the economic policies of Mao and his successor, Hua. Leaders like Kang Shien, a State Council vice-premier, and Li Xiannian, a Standing Committee member as well as State Council vice-premier, opposed Deng's policies that would strip them of their bureaucratic power over segments of the economy. This group often allied with Chen, who also opposed Deng's overall weakening of the role of the central government.[20]

The hard-line ideologues were another influential faction that formed a symbiotic alliance with Chen Yun and the central planners to foster a Marxist society and oppose the influx of Western political ideas that came with Deng's economic experimentation. But of most concern to this group, who were mostly rehabilitated cadre like Peng Zhen, Wang Zhen, Chen Xitong, Wang Renzhi, Hu Qiaomu, and Deng Liqun, was the spread of "bourgeois liberalization" which, they feared, would ultimately undermine the position and power of the Communist Party and its ideology. This faction could be expected to side with any other opposing Deng.

The Public Security and Internal Security forces also formed a significant faction with which Deng had to contend. Their nominal leader, Peng Zhen, was also an "elder," who, as the former mayor of Beijing and a Politburo member, had supervised party legal and political affairs. Once restored to the Politburo in 1980, he sought to regain power. Thus, he often opposed Deng's policies, not on the basis of their merit, but as part of a calculation to trim Deng's power. Consequently, Peng frequently allied with Chen Yun, but his patronage of those in the internal security administration, like Qiao Shi, gave him leverage over Deng as a faction leader who could not be ignored.[21]

It was Chen Yun, however, who was ultimately the major source of opposition to Deng, and a rallying point for the other factions vying for power. Deng had appointed him head of the ad hoc Financial and Economic Group formed in 1980, and had assigned him overall responsibility for China's economic and financial policy in recognition of his success in orchestrating economic recovery after Mao's disastrous Great Leap Forward. However, he believed in only limited economic activity outside of the central plan. According to his "bird cage" theory of economics, the local, or free market, was the bird in a cage. Outside of that cage was the realm of the central plan. The bird's cage could be enlarged, but the bird could never be freed.

As a consequence, Deng found it necessary to maneuver around him and the central planners, to replace them whenever possible, and to institute extralegal organizations, such as the Commission for Restructuring the Economy, to implement his policies. Chen Yun's own economic organization was a primary example of an ad hoc entity established to get around the bureaucracy. Many such organizations were established, or would be, to support Prime Minister Zhao and later Vice-Premier Zhu Rongji, but

Deng went one step further to secure support. Reminiscent of Mao, he bypassed the center by going directly to the provinces, where he had his loyal supporters, to implement the radical, capitalist, free-market policies drafted by the State Council and its advisors: Hu Qiaomu, Xue Muqiao, Sun Yefang, and Huan Xiang.[22]

The SEZ: Beginnings

Deng also turned to the provinces for ideas about implementing foreign economic practices. At a Central Committee work conference in April 1979, Deng met with Xi Zhongxun and Yang Shangkun. These two Guangdong leaders had impressed him with the favorable economic conditions enjoyed in their province, which were the result of being adjacent to the British Crown Colony of Hong Kong and being able to adapt capitalist economic methods to a socialist environment. Taking their example, he suggested that "we can delimit an area called a special zone. Was Shaanxi-Gansu-Ningxia not a special zone?[23] Since the central authorities lack funds, we call on you (the local governors) to find a way out."[24]

Following his directive, the Central Committee and State Council sent Gu Mu, a state councilor, to study the areas of Guangdong and Fujian and discuss the running of special economic zones. Based on his study, the Central Committee and State Council issued a document in July 1979 delineating the areas of Shenzhen, Zhuhai, Shantou, and Xiamen as special economic zones. Throughout the summer and fall of 1979, additional edicts were issued to formalize the trial zones as places to draw foreign capital. In 1980, the National People's Congress formally approved the "special economic zones." Over the next two years additional regulations were established to regulate and define the SEZ.[25]

According to these regulations, the SEZ were special economic zones, not political zones. Their function was to implement special economic policies and a particular economic management system. In theory, the SEZ were to rely on foreign capital. Their products were to be manufactured for export within the framework of the socialist economy, that is, while the area was under the political control of a Marxist government which practiced a Marxist, centrally-controlled economic system, allowance would be made for the local, limited practice of capitalist economic methods. These local capitalist initiatives of diversified economic components were mainly characterized by joint ventures and enterprises run by foreign businessmen as sole proprietors.

The economic activities of the SEZ were to be based on market conditions, as opposed to centralized planning, and foreign businessmen who invested in the SEZ were to receive preferential treatment in taxation and other matters. In all, the SEZ were to implement a management system totally different from the one prescribed for the interior. This was known as "exceeding the bounds of the current system."[26] In other words, the SEZ were designed to attract foreign investors who, in turn, would bring technology and modern management methods to China to produce exports for hard currency, encouraged by tax holidays, lower tax rates, reduced tariffs, modern infrastructure, flexible wage and labor policies, and less bureaucracy.[27]

It was during this period that Deng managed to elevate Zhao Ziyang to the premiership. Zhao had been successful in Sichuan between 1976–79 in reforming agriculture. Thus, in elevating Zhao to premier in September 1980, Deng was placing a "pathbreaker" in charge of the economy.[28] He needed people like Zhao to implement his new policy of opening to the world, since there were bound to be growing pains.

Indeed, it did not take long for the adverse effects of opening to be felt. The temptations created by exposure to the West and relaxed political controls in the SEZ spawned rampant criminal activity—smuggling, illegal trading, corruption, bribery, and theft of state property. Within two years, it had created a serious problem for the leadership in that it provided ammunition for the opponents of Deng's policies. Chief among the opposition was Chen Yun, who regarded this criminal activity as the inevitable by-product of a flirtation with capitalism.

Thus, the center was forced to respond. In January 1982 the Politburo issued new regulations calling for a crackdown on illegal economic activity, the real purpose of which was to curtail the experiment. As a defensive measure, Deng and his faction, headed by Zhao as premier, sent a team of noted economists from the Chinese Academy of Social Sciences to

Guangzhou to review progress within the SEZ. Their reports, drafted to negate calls for ending the experiment, stressed Marxist support for attracting foreign capital and the need for the "Open Door." They pointed out that, while capitalism was being practiced in the SEZ, that China was actually the beneficiary, since it had sovereignty over the territory and it was not being exploited as it had been during the nineteenth century. While they conceded the need for better planning and training of cadre, they affirmed that the concept of the SEZ and opening up to the outside world "is an unchanging policy."[29]

The Politburo met again in April 1982 under the prodding of Chen Yun and the conservatives to further discuss the "serious" deterioration of the SEZ. Chen charged that "the SEZ had sparked illegal and criminal activities that were the worst in thirty years."[30] Chen could not be ignored. In addition to his role as czar of economic policy, he was the head of the Discipline Inspection Commission, the ad hoc organization to enforce party discipline, a powerful base from which to launch attacks on "corrupt" party members who did not toe the correct policy line.

Deng was forced to concede that "a number of cadres have been corrupted in the brief year or two since we adopted the policy of opening to the outside world and stimulating the economy. Quite a few are involved in economic crimes."[31] Deng also acknowledged that investigations had uncovered many cases of abuse involving both individuals and groups. Some had smuggled gold and silver to Hong Kong, others had lined their pockets with bribes, and still others had appropriated state property. Deng called for action, but in a country still recovering from the last political purge, the closing of "Democracy Wall," Deng refused to launch a "movement." Rather, he called for a "continuous struggle against economic crime until the day the four modernizations are achieved."[32]

By the fall of 1982, Deng had completed his consolidation of power, as well as the restoration of the old status quo from prior to the Ninth Party Congress of 1969—that is, restoration of Eighth Party veterans removed during the Cultural Revolution.[33] Deng was now in charge. With a new Politburo and Central Committee favorable to his policies, Deng could expect to move forward with little opposition. The new Standing Committee consisted of Deng, Zhao, and Hu leading the market socialists, Chen Yun and Li Xiannian speaking for central planning and control of the economy, and Ye Jianying spokesman for the military and internal security. Thus it was that a confident Deng announced in his opening speech to the Twelfth Party Congress in October 1982 that the policy initiated at the Third Plenum (the SEZ) would continue. However, he stressed that while the modernization program would continue to draw upon the expertise and experience of foreign models, the process would be integrated with the universal truths of Marxism and the concrete realities of China. Thus would China blaze a path of its own and build "socialism with Chinese characteristics."[34]

Again acknowledging the corruption that had crept into the SEZ experiment, Deng faced down the criticism and boldly reaffirmed that "we shall unswervingly follow a policy of opening to the outside world and actively increase exchanges with foreign countries on the basis of equality and mutual benefit."[35] While trade with the West, especially technology transfers from the United States, would continue to grow, corruption would not be tolerated. "We shall keep clear heads, firmly resist corruption by decadent ideas from abroad and never permit the bourgeois way of life to spread in our country."[36]

Normalization with the United States

Deng also recognized that his program would not succeed if China remained the implacable enemy of the Soviet Union and failed to normalize relations with the United States, which was necessary to increase trade with the West in the major technologies that Washington controlled through the Coordinating Committee on Export Controls (COCOM), NATO's organization for limiting technology transfers from the West to the Eastern Bloc Communist nations, including China. Normalization was necessary to access Western sources of finance, credit, and developmental assistance, which were also subject to American vetoes or political pressure.

The Soviet Union, on the other hand, with its troop buildup along China's northern border, forced spending for the military, which Deng had placed last in his "four modernizations" of agriculture, industry, science and technology, and national defense. However, when Hua Guofeng spurned Moscow's attempts to open a dialogue on the eve of the Fifth National People's Congress (NPC) in February 1978, he put an end to the early attempts by Deng to normalize relations. Thus, when Hua's rejection of Moscow's overtures was followed by the Soviet-supported Vietnamese invasion of China's client state, Cambodia, in December 1978, Deng was faced not only with a foreign policy and national security crisis, but with a threat to his economic plans as well.

Deng thus urged that normalization with the United States be completed as quickly as possible, by tabling the sticky issue of U.S. support of Taiwan. Perhaps he hoped that normalization would result in American political support, neutralizing a Soviet threat to China's northern border in the event of a Chinese invasion of Vietnam. While he did not get that support, he did get access to American markets, which were essential for economic modernization.[37]

In any event, Deng seized control of the People's Liberation Army (PLA) with Ye Jianying's assistance, and launched the invasion of Vietnam, in February 1979. While the Soviets did not attack China's border, which Deng could argue was a result of his opening to the United States, the PLA performed badly, demonstrating to the world their lack of modern combat capabilities. This only confirmed in Deng's mind the need to expedite his modernization program.

However, the failure of the United States to offer unqualified support of Deng's invasion of Vietnam, its failure to follow through with trade in advanced technologies, and its continued military support of Taiwan caused Deng to back away from the newly established relationship in 1979.[38] Instead, he pressured the United States for more concessions as the price for trade with China and support against Soviet expansion in Afghanistan and the Middle East. In addition, he demanded a resolution of arms sales to Taiwan, previously overlooked in his rush to normalization. It was a bold gamble, since he had to have foreign access and trade to modernize the economy, and his attempts at reconciling with Moscow in late 1979 had fallen apart in the wake of Moscow's invasion of Afghanistan on Christmas Day 1979, but he also needed to placate his domestic critics.[39]

Fortunately, as a result of his political machinations, Deng had assembled a majority on the Politburo and the Standing Committee. This gave him a free hand to play hardball with the new Reagan administration that had pledged, during the 1980 election campaign, to restore recognition of Taiwan. As a result, Reagan's advisors, convinced of the need to gain access to China's emerging market and the value of the "China Card" in the triangular Washington-Moscow-Beijing geopolitical relationship, pushed to reach an agreement with China.[40] After protracted negotiations, a communiqué was signed on 17 August 1982 in which the United States stated that it did not intend to carry out a long-term policy of arms sales to Taiwan, that future sales would not exceed past quantitative or qualitative levels, and that it would gradually reduce its arms sales to Taiwan. The Chinese, in turn, stated their peaceful intent toward Taiwan.[41] Thus, Deng had completed his normalization process with America.

Determined to achieve normalization with Moscow as well, Deng again attempted a rapprochement. However, internal Soviet politics associated with Brezhnev's death cut short the opening.[42] Spurned again by Moscow, Deng announced at the Twelfth Party Congress in October 1982 China's "independent" policy of not aligning with any foreign power against another. With this statement he intended to "inform" Moscow that "normalization" had been achieved as far as China was concerned. In combination with his "Three Worlds" theory from 1974 that placed China in the Third World, the two superpowers in the First, and western Europe in the Second, the "independent" policy permitted China to pursue its own international policy.[43] Deng had maneuvered China to a position equidistant from the superpowers.

> China's affairs should be run in the light of China's specific conditions and by the Chinese people themselves. Independence and self-reliance have always been and will always be our basic stand. While we Chinese people value our friendship and co-operation with other countries and other peoples, we value even more our hard-won independence and sovereign rights. No foreign country can expect China to be its vassal, nor can it expect China to accept anything harmful to China's interests. We will unswervingly follow a policy of opening to the outside world and actively increase exchanges with foreign countries on the basis of equality and mutual benefit.[44]

Thus, Deng could cut military spending and concentrate on the domestic economy.[45] However, with no opening to Moscow, he was forced to pursue economic development through the West, and the United States in particular. This would have disastrous political results later on, when he actually began to normalize relations with Moscow.

The SEZ:

Problems Develop

The SEZ continued to prosper despite corruption and the dangers of bourgeois ideas. In 1983 Hu Yaobang, secretary general of the party, told the local authorities in the SEZ that "you have accomplished the tasks assigned by the central authorities remarkably. Since the special economic zone is a new emerging thing, we must be bold in exploring and blazing new trails; the special and new emerging aspects of the special zones should be run in a special and new manner."[46]

After an inspection tour of southern China in 1984, Deng came away convinced that the SEZ should be expanded and run in a "quicker and better way."[47] Upon his return to Beijing in early 1984, Deng convened "a conference with senior comrades of the central authorities" to discuss expansion of the original four SEZ and the extension of the "Open Door" policy to selected port cities.[48] While these cities were not to be called SEZ, they were to operate under the same principles. These discussions were "heated," meaning that not all cadre agreed, but Deng was able to convince a sufficient number to push a favorable decision through the Secretariat of the Central Committee and State Council to go forward. Fourteen coastal cities, including Tianjin, Shanghai, Dalian, Qinhuangdao, Yantai, Qingdao, Lianyungang, Nantong, Ningbo, Wenzhou, Fuzhou, Guangzhou, Zhanjiang, and Beihai, were opened to the world for the purpose of importing foreign technology, obtaining knowledge, and learning management.

Zhao Ziyang, in summing up Deng's thoughts for the new direction in policy, stressed

it was a great and far-reaching decision to demonstrate the
superiority of the policy and to accelerate the development of
the coastal areas, and in promoting the modernization program throughout the country; the trend is to open more areas;
three different forms will be developed: SEZ, economic and
technical exploitation zones, and coastal cities, which will be
granted greater self-decision power in utilizing foreign capital
and carrying out technical transformation and cooperation;
the coastal opening will rely on central policy for support, but
no funds will be available; that policy is to ensure that our taxation and markets are attractive to foreign capital and businessmen, and self-decision power is granted to the coastal areas in
carrying out foreign economic and technical cooperation.[49]

The plans for opening more cities were part of a major new initiative by
Deng and his modernizers. The policy was adopted as part of the new
plans worked out at the Party's Third Plenum of the Twelfth Congress,
held in October of 1984. At that meeting, it was determined that the policy for agriculture had been a success. First of the Four Modernizations,
agricultural reform had been laid out at the Third Plenum of the Eleventh
Congress in December 1978. By elevating Zhao to premier in 1980, based
on his success between 1976–79 in transforming the agrarian economy
in Sichuan, Deng had placed his man in charge of a nationwide radical
reordering of agriculture, which Zhao had proceeded to do with much
success.[50] The communes were dismantled, and the peasant household was
made responsible for production quotas. Agricultural output increased 50
percent between 1978 and 1984,[51] and peasant per capita income rose.
Thus, by 1984 Deng had completed his basic reorganization of rural
China, and its success permitted him to move on to the next priority, modernization of industry.

In 1984, the Plenum declared "the necessity and urgency of speeding
up reform of the structure of the entire national economy with the focus on
the urban economy."[52] The program adopted spelled out all of Deng's plans
for modernization, and specifically addressed the "opening to the world"
policy. It called for continued flexibility in economic policies, reform of the
foreign trade structure to allow more local initiative, expansion of foreign

ventures, greater development of both overseas and domestic markets, and more emphasis on developing international economic relations.[53]

Thus, Deng had been successful in pushing through his economic modernization with emphasis on reform, devolution of power, and adoption of market-driven economics. Central planning had been curtailed. But the processes set in motion had a downside that was to be a continuing problem for modernization efforts. As the planned portion of foreign trade was reduced and shifted to the hundreds of provincial and local trading companies, the loss of income to Beijing, coupled with the devolution of its investment authority, meant that the center lost its control of the economy. The result was uncontrolled local investment and the shortage of tax revenues, requiring the center to print money to cover its shortfalls and leading to much-dreaded inflation. Deng had an economic nightmare on his hands that only hardened the opposition of Chen Yun and the die-hard central planners.

To further complicate matters, Deng's modernization policies had also produced an all-time high foreign trade deficit, $14.9 billion, by 1986.[54] The central government had intervened in an attempt to cut back uncontrolled imports by borrowing locally retained foreign exchange, which it never repaid. This reduced the deficit, but only temporarily. Acknowledging the seriousness of the deficit problem, Deng launched a significant new direction in his policy of "opening to the world." The SEZ would begin to emphasize an export-oriented economy.[55]

This new direction was also motivated by Deng's realization that primary commodities like oil and coal could not finance modernization, particularly in view of the drop in oil prices in 1985. He therefore encouraged the SEZ and coastal cities to imitate Japan and finance modernization by exporting consumer goods. Thus, after 1985 the composition of Chinese exports changed drastically. Where in the early 1980s they had been almost equally divided between primary products and manufactured goods, after 1985 primary products dropped to approximately one-third of the total, while manufactured products jumped to over two-thirds. The change was due to the rapid growth in exports of light industrial goods and textiles, though it was not until 1987 that the deficit was turned into a surplus.[56]

Deng next turned his attention to the problems of agriculture and political restructuring. Regarding agriculture, Deng was quite explicit: China had to increase grain production by 5 million tons annually to avoid a major set-back in meeting the needs of the people. He stated that merely modest investments in that sector would not forestall stagnation as population growth outstripped productivity. He warned that China's managers had to continuously give priority to agriculture in order to ensure that, by the year 2000, China would be producing 480 million tons of grain. (See chart below.) Only with that level of production could China avoid importing grain, which would retard the economy.[57] Recent statistics would seem to indicate that the Chinese would reach the necessary production figure, as output reached 460 million tons in 1995.[58]

PRC AGRICULTURE HARVEST, 1979–92[59]

Year	Grain Output (Million Tons)
1979	332.12
1980	320.56
1981	325.02
1982	354.50
1983	387.28
1984	407.31
1985	379.11
1986	391.51
1987	402.98
1988	394.08
1989	407.55
1990	446.24
1991	435.29
1992	442.29
1995	460.00

Addressing the need for political restructuring, one of the two basic points of his "one center and two basic points" policy line, he noted that the current political superstructure was not adapted to economic reality. Political restructuring had to be considered a part of reform, indeed the hallmark of reform. This meant "streamlining the administration, delegating real powers to the lower levels and broadening the scope of socialist democracy."[60] All of which were meant to bring into play the initiative of the masses and grass-roots organizations. However, what was happening was in fact just the opposite, according to Deng. As new powers were delegated, "the government invented new organs to reclaim that power. The net result was organizational overlapping, overstaffing, bureaucratism, sluggishness, and unreliability."[61]

The issue of "bourgeois liberalization," the unwanted influx of Western political ideas that followed Western technology, finance, and talent, was another problem that would not go away. According to Deng, its advocates worshipped the "democracy" and "freedom" of the Western capitalist countries and rejected socialism. He would not allow this. While it must modernize, China would not liberalize nor take the capitalist road. Those who advocated bourgeois liberalization had to be dealt with severely. Failure to do so would lead to chaos. Thus Deng made it a principle to check any liberalization trends.[62]

However, major party members, some of whom were also intellectuals, such as Fang Lizhi, Liu Binyan and Wang Ruowang, deliberately misinterpreted Deng's ideas on reform of the party as authority for political change. They took advantage of the generally relaxed social norms of the boom years and Hu Yaobang's hands-off policy regarding intellectual debates to add Western political ideas to the domestic debate. This provided ammunition for a growing student protest movement, which erupted in riots in December 1986. Deng, of course, had long ago, in 1979, ruled on the inappropriateness of Western liberal democratic ideas. His Four Cardinal Principles that grew out of his decision to close "Democracy Wall" in 1979 drew a line that intellectuals understood. While he had used the open, democratic views of the democracy wall protesters to cut the ground out from under Hua Guofeng, once the protesters turned on him, their value was gone.[63]

Nevertheless, the intellectuals continued to take advantage of Hu's relaxed approach. They were aware that they were pushing the envelope, but with Deng silent, they presumed approval. However, with the student outburst in late 1986, Deng was forced to remind everyone that he would not permit political liberalization. As a result, at the Sixth Plenum of the Twelfth Party Congress, Deng demanded that measures be taken against anyone who violated the law, and that party members take a clear-cut stand against the demonstrations as well as the liberalization trend.[64]

Opening to the
Soviet Union

Since his return to power in 1978, Deng's long-term international geo-political strategy had been to position China midway between the two superpowers, the United States and the Soviet Union.[65] However, Hua was able to stop Deng's efforts to normalize relations with Moscow in 1978, and Moscow's invasion of Afghanistan in December 1979 forced Deng to terminate his own initiative. Tentative efforts by Moscow at normalization flagged in the waning days of Brezhnev's reign in 1981 and 1982. Thus, Deng was forced to "tilt" to the West, more precisely to the U.S., in his efforts to modernize China.[66] This led to a faction within the leadership that favored pursuing the "American Card."[67] This faction included those whom Deng had brought to power on his return in 1978, most promi-nently Hu Yaobang and Zhao Ziyang.

All of this changed, however, in 1985, when Mikhail Gorbachev came to power in Moscow. Gorbachev, like Deng, intended to institute economic reform, but to do so he needed secure borders, so he offered an olive branch to China in his speech at Vladivostock in July 1986.[68] Ironically, this offer from Moscow was to lead to a showdown within Deng's faction.

Discussions between Chinese leaders and ex-President Richard Nixon in 1985 revealed the extent of differences among Deng and his lieutenants, Hu and Zhao, regarding rapprochement. Hu Yaobang, then-party secretary general, was wary of Moscow. He felt that, while Gorbachev's words were different, the policy was the same. He was very adamant about his views on the Soviet Union, stating "for China to move toward the Soviet Union would be a repudiation of China's whole independent policy over the past thirty years. China's 'honor' would be questioned all over the world. China will never again be a puppet! If we submit to Moscow, we would give up all that we have gained over the past thirty years."[69] Clearly, any decision by Deng to reconcile with Moscow would force a split with Hu.

Then-Premier Zhao Ziyang likewise expressed his opposition to Deng's movement towards Moscow. Zhao told Nixon that China's economic re-forms were irreversible, that there could be no turning back, and that no major opposition to the reforms existed. He argued that the economic

difficulties brought on by reform had been exaggerated and would be reme-
died through controls on excessive growth.[70] Zhao, echoing Hu, stated that
China would never again be closely allied with the Soviet Union. "What
possible advantage could there be in such an alliance for us?"[71]

Deng, on the other hand, stated that the Soviet Union and the U.S.
represented equal threats to China. He too was wary of Gorbachev, whose
policies, according to Deng, were "loud thunder and little raindrops."[72]
According to Deng, the U.S. did not have to fear closer Sino-Soviet relations. U.S. technology transferred to China would not end up in Soviet
hands. He went on to say: "We have far more differences with the Soviet
Union than with the U.S., but we don't want to tie ourselves to one char-
iot."[73] Deng clearly wanted to use the Soviets to balance the "American
Card."

Regarding basic economic policy, differences also existed among them.
Deng, in discussing China's new economic reforms with Nixon, stated
"China would try them out and, as long as they worked, would continue
with them. But if they fail we will drop them. In three to five years we
decide our future course. *The reforms are irreversible in their direction, but tactics
could change.*"[74] As for opposition to his reforms, he acknowledged that it
existed: "China, after all, is a big country. But opposition would remain
insignificant as long as reforms worked."[75] Thus, by 1985, the divisions
were already apparent, not only between Deng and the conservatives, but
within Deng's camp as well.

Deng accepted the Soviet olive branch and began to cultivate improved
trade and political relations with Moscow and the Warsaw Pact countries of
Hungary, Czechoslovakia, Poland, and East Germany. Under his direction,
China signed a major economic agreement with Moscow in late 1986,
signaling a major policy change as well as sending a favorable signal to
Chen. Trade with the Soviets and Eastern Europe was regarded as "safe,"
with less chance of liberal bourgeois ideas creeping in. Trade with the
Soviets would not compete with the SEZ, since Soviet trade would most
likely be barter deals, involving Soviet refurbishment of aging industrial facilities in exchange for consumer goods, and would thus reinforce
central planning and controls. The economic agreement called for increasing the then-U.S.$2 billion trade between China and the Soviet Union to
U.S.$10 billion by 1990. It also gave the central planners a major new stake
in policy.

Hu could not accept the turning away from the "American Card" to the "Soviet Card." The initial showdown came in late 1986 over the issue of including political reform in expanding economic reforms.[76] He supported student protests calling for democracy. He had apparently believed that he could coax Deng into some measure of political liberalization, which would limit the opening to Moscow and thus block a revival of the powers of the central planners over the economy.

But Deng had never envisioned importing Western political freedoms. He had constantly placed his modernization and opening policies under the umbrella of his "Four Principles." When Hu argued for continued expansion of the "American Card" to include political reforms to free up the energy to achieve greater economic results on a model seen throughout the West, he had overplayed his hand with Deng and was ousted for his efforts.

Hu had allowed the generally permissive intellectual environment to flourish, and when he linked it to stopping Deng's plans to make an opening with Moscow, he was blamed for the disturbances. Deng admonished him for failing to take a strong stand against bourgeois liberalism, despite several personal warnings. He also charged him with failing to uphold the Four Cardinal Principles of keeping to the socialist road, upholding the people's democratic dictatorship, upholding the leadership of the Communist Party, and upholding Marxism-Leninism and Mao Zedong Thought. Deng had no intention of abandoning party control and his brand of socialism. Thus, in an expanded meeting of the Politburo and Central Committee in January 1987, Hu was replaced by Zhao.[77]

Deng had thought that this change in party leadership would in no way affect the policies of "opening," both domestically and internationally, and reform of the economic and political structures.[78] However, in the SEZ there was concern that Hu's ouster and the campaign against bourgeois liberalization would negatively affect economic policy. Gu Mu, the state councilor responsible for the opening to the outside world, was sent to Shenzhen in early February to reassure a nervous foreign community as well as local officials. In response to the question of how the struggle would affect the SEZ and coastal zones, Gu responded that policy would not change. He noted that Deng himself had recently reassured foreigners on that subject.[79] Gu announced that the State Council had drafted some new regulations that the SEZ would be required to implement later in the year, but they were based on regulations already operating in the open coastal cities to offer even more attractive incentives to foreign investment. He stressed that the country would continue to open to the world under the aegis of the Four Cardinal Principles.

Thus, neither the creeping invasion of bourgeois capitalist ideas, nor the large foreign trade deficit, nor the challenge from within his own faction over the opening to Moscow had derailed Deng's process of opening to the world and economic modernization. In fact, by mid-1987 he was advocating speeding up economic reform. As he saw it, "our achievements in the last few years have proved the correctness of our policies of reform and opening to the outside world . . . therefore we must not abandon these policies or even slow them down."[80]

The Thirteenth Congress

At the Thirteenth Party Congress held in October 1987, Zhao Ziyang, promoted to party secretary general to replace the fallen Hu, still gave the work report to the Congress, instead of the new premier, Li Peng. Zhao praised Deng's economic policies. In addressing the recurring problems of inflation, budget deficits, money supply, and bourgeois liberalization, he concluded that they were rooted in the contradiction between the growing material and cultural needs of the people and the backward means of production.[81] In light of Hu's dismissal and the student riots, Zhao reiterated that the basic line of the Party would continue to be "one center and two basic points," that is, the pursuit of economic development coupled with adherence to the Four Cardinal Principles and the policies of reform and opening up.[82] He went on to reassure his domestic and foreign audiences, who feared another policy reversal. He concluded with the pronouncement that China was in the initial stage of socialism, as defined in Marxist lexicons, and that stage would last at least one hundred years, at the end of which, modernization would be mostly complete.

However, Deng also felt it necessary to placate the conservatives. He intended to pursue his economic reforms, but realized that the economy needed to be cooled down and the reformers counterbalanced. Thus, Deng sided with Chen at the party congress in 1987 to promote Li Peng, a Chen protégé, to premier. He could allow Li to do the necessary tightening up of the economy without having to share in the fallout from slowed growth, which was inevitable in any attempt to rein in inflation. Thus, he was protecting his economic policies from criticism by the masses. If the conservatives under Chen Yun and Li Peng throttled the economy too much, Deng would allow Zhao to intervene.

The Thirteenth Congress also marked the beginning of a Deng-engineered transformation of the party. Whereas the Eleventh and Twelfth Congresses had merely been a reestablishment and then a continuation of the Yenan generation of leaders, at the Thirteenth, Deng pushed the revolutionary generation to retire from office. Thus, the Thirteenth Congress had over 65 percent new, younger, more educated members. The overwhelming majority, 93 percent, had not been on the Central Committee prior to 1982, the result of a total rebuilding effort begun in earnest in 1982 by Deng and Hu. The Standing Committee—Zhao, Hu Qili, Li Peng, Yao Yilin and Qiao Shi—contained no one from the Yenan era, while on the Politburo, only two, Hu Yaobang and Yang Shangkun, had participated in the Long March.[83]

By the conclusion of the Thirteenth Congress, however, with the resignation of the old guard, the contending factions within the party had coalesced. Zhao and Hu represented the market socialists, or reform faction, who had little concern for ideology. So long as the cat caught mice, it made no difference what color it was. Li Peng and Yao Yilin represented the Marxist central planners, the conservative faction. They were concerned with Marxist economic purity, and were not above using leftist ideologues who stressed the virtues of Maoism to neutralize the reformers. Finally, Qiao Shi represented the law-and-order group, centered around Peng Zhen and the other party elders who, above all else, wanted the party to survive and abhorred the possibility of another round of internal instability. As Deng still spoke for the PLA, it did not as yet constitute a faction. Ultimately, it was Deng's mistake to ignore each faction's basic concerns. For while Deng was a practical, organization man; the others were committed to an ideology.

Although Deng pushed the revolutionary generation to retire, he had no intention of retiring, nor had his opponents, especially Chen Yun. Deng resigned from the Politburo Standing Committee, but continued to control the military as chairman of the Military Commission, which made him the most powerful individual in the party. Chen Yun likewise resigned, but continued to head the Central Advisory Commission, along with vice-chairmen Bo Yibo and Song Renqiong. Thus, Chen continued to have a major say in all economic affairs, since his commission sat in on all Politburo discussions and used its informal power to push his agenda.

Deng also moved to concentrate power in a small group of party leaders, to ensure not only his policies but also the dominance of the party over all aspects of society. To that end, he engineered a rewrite of the constitution to resubordinate the Party Secretariat to the Standing Committee.[84] Under Hu, it had been responsible to the Central Committee, not the Standing Committee, and it had had a larger membership. It had also been more independent, especially when, according to Zhao, the State Council and the Secretariat handled the day-to-day affairs of the party and government during the mid-1980s. The Politburo and the Standing Committee had not met regularly then, leaving routine business to Zhao and Hu.[85] This meant that the senior leadership, the Politburo and the Standing Committee, lacked the ability to monitor daily party affairs. This was unacceptable if Deng wanted to exercise ironclad control over policy. He was clearly taking steps, as he grew older, to ensure that he had a tighter grip on policy and that his supporters, on his death, would prevail through dominance at the apex of an ever narrowing circle of power.

The chart below gives a general factional lineup of the Politburo in 1987 as a result of the Thirteenth Congress.[86] While it is clear that Deng was in charge, it is also clear that economic activity was subject to Chen's influence by virtue of his supporters on the Standing Committee, Li Peng and Yao Yilin, who managed economic policy on a day-to-day basis.

POLITBURO (STANDING COMMITTEE)

Market Socialists	Marxist Socialists	Law and Order
Zhao Ziyang	Li Peng	Qiao Shi
Hu Qili	Yao Yilin	

POLITBURO

Market Socialists	Marxist Socialists	Law and Order
Zhao Ziyang	Li Peng	Qiao Shi
Hu Qili	Yao Yilin	Jiang Zemin
Tian Jiyun	Song Ping	
Hu Yaobang		
Wu Xueqian		
Li Ruihuan		
Li Tieying		
Wan Li		
Li Ximing		
Yang Rudai		
Yang Shangkun		
Qin Jiwei		
Ding Guangen		

In spite of the glowing reports at the Thirteenth Congress, the economy was getting out of hand. Retail prices, which had risen an average of 7.4 percent annually between 1984–87, had shot up by 18.5 percent in 1988. State enterprises were overextended in investments, the money supply was growing, and inflation had risen from 10 percent at the start of the year to a record of nearly 30 percent by year's end. As inflation grew, entrepreneurs reduced production. Laborers complained and reduced their output. Across China, panic buying had set in. Consumers withdrew their money from savings and rushed to purchase goods. One survey indicated that the number of urban and rural workers, whose real income had been eroded by inflation, had doubled between 1986 and 1987 from 20 percent to 40 percent.[87] Rising prices and inflation led to worker resentment and charges of corruption. In late 1988, the government attempted to rein in runaway inflation and uncontrolled growth, but as power had been allowed to devolve to the provinces and local enterprises, efforts to increase the amount of retained earnings that the provinces had to turn over to Beijing to reduce credit drastically, to ban certain imports, to expand import substitution restrictions, and to recentralize many trade decisions had limited success. Custom duties were doubled on washing machines, radios, and cassette players; controls over silk and pesticide imports and exports were recentralized; and imports of luxury cars, cigarettes, and liquor were banned.[88] Inflation was eventually stemmed, but so was the economy. Hundreds of thousands were put out of work and living standards fell. These issues were in no small measure behind the disturbances at Tiananmen in the summer of 1989.[89]

With the dismissal of Hu, the promotion of Zhao, and the compromise with the Chen faction, the liberals recognized that Deng had set new limits. Chen Yizi, a key Zhao advisor and director of the Institute for the Reform of the Economic Structure under the State Commission for the Restructuring of the Economy, confirmed to foreign journalists that a battle had raged for over two years over the direction of reform.[90] He and other reformers took their cue from Deng's elevation of Zhao in late 1987: "They could not count on the full support of paramount leader Deng Xiaoping."[91]

Tiananmen

To understand the explosion at Tiananmen in 1989, one must recall the fundamentally different positions held by Deng, Hu, and Zhao as revealed in the Nixon interviews in 1982 and 1985 and confirmed later in party documents. Hu was replaced as much for his political ineptness as for his political liberalism, but many believed that it was Zhao who was the driving force behind economic liberalization, even arguing that Zhao favored seizing all control at Deng's expense in order to carry out economic reform.[92] Whether or not Zhao advocated a break with Deng over economic policy, it was over political reform that they parted company. Deng acknowledged as much when he returned to power at the end of his southern tour in early 1992. According to him, "they [Hu and Zhao] had stumbled on the issue of opposing bourgeois liberalization."[93] Indeed, Zhao verified this in his self-confession in 1989: "I have more and more deeply realized that reform of the political structure can neither surpass nor lag behind economic structural reform. . . . In the past, I thought that as long as economic structural reform was successful and the economy developed, then the people's living standards would be enhanced and the people would be satisfied and society would be stable. I later found that this was not the case in reality. With the enhancement of peoples' living standards and cultural attainments, they will have a stronger sense of political participation and will long for democracy more strongly."[94]

The issue that had forced the showdown, however, was over the direction and pace of economic reform. By the Party Plenum in late 1988, inflation had reached an all-time high of approximately 30 percent. Even Deng could not ignore the psychological effect that inflation had on the Chinese people. Many had lived through the last years of the Nationalist regime and remembered how hyperinflation had wiped out their savings. Thus, Deng became convinced of the need to take strong measures to cool off the economy. That decision was implemented at the September Plenum, where he allowed Chen and Li to rein in most of Zhao's prized programs. Capital investment was reduced by 20 percent and state investment was cut for 1989. Credit was restricted; ceilings were placed on credit limits for domestic banks and interest rates were raised on bank loans to discourage investment outside the state plan; and a halt was ordered on loans to private and rural enterprises. Interest rates were raised for individual savings accounts, but the amount that could be withdrawn was restricted. Zhao's planned reform of price controls, with which he had intended to break the hold of the central planners, was shelved. Instead, price controls on steel, copper, aluminum and other production materials were reimposed, as were the monopoly controls on many raw and finished farm inputs and fertilizers. Procurement prices for grain, sugar, and oil-seed crops were raised to stimulate the sagging agriculture sector, and restrictions were placed on foreign trade firms to reduce their numbers and the kinds of goods that could be imported.[95] In a final act, Zhao was stripped of his role over economic activity, which now passed to Li Peng and the central planners. While the Standing Committee had not changed, Li's faction actually had the votes to control the economy, since Zhao was neutralized and Qiao not involved in economics.

By the end of 1988, retrenchment of economic reforms was well under way as the party leaders made arrangements for Gorbachev's visit the following spring. Zhao, unwilling to stand by while his economic programs were strangled and a rapprochement with Moscow that would strengthen the Li-Chen faction loomed, turned to the student protest movement to recapture Deng's support and undercut the centralists.

The Tiananmen protests of 1989 began obstensibly as a tribute to

Hu Yaobang, who had died suddenly on April 15. Students, who regarded him as a sympathetic force within the party for political reform, marched to Tiananmen Square to lay wreaths in his honor. They also took the opportunity to present to the senior party leadership at Zhongnanhai, the leadership compound located just off the square, a petition listing seven demands: (1) affirm as correct Hu Yaobang's views on democracy and freedom; (2) admit that the campaigns against spiritual pollution and bourgeois liberalization had been wrong; (3) publish information on the income of state leaders and their families; (4) end the ban on privately run newspapers and permit freedom of speech; (5) increase funding for education and raise intellectuals' pay; (6) end restrictions on demonstrations in Beijing; and (7) hold democratic elections to replace government officials who made bad policy decisions.[96] However, when the government refused to meet with the students, much less accept their petition, the students initiated a sit-down protest.

Zhao Ziyang assured Deng and the leadership that the students were harmless, and that once the funeral was over on April 22 they would return to their campuses. Convinced that he had the situation under control, he left Beijing on a planned visit to North Korea. In his absence, however, Li Peng, as acting head of the Standing Committee, pushed for a harder line. He saw in the protests a hidden agenda to topple the party. Indeed, the students had formed independent unions and were increasing their demands daily for greater democracy and reform. They were also attracting the support of the masses.

With the decline in the economy, both industry and agriculture suffered. Government production had decreased, subsidies had been increased, and overall productivity had dropped. While inflation had been cut to 6 percent for the year, down from the 27 percent in 1988, industrial growth had shrunk from 17 percent to only 7 percent, and real GNP had grown only 4 percent, down from 1988's growth rate of over 12 percent. As a consequence, industrial workers, who had been laid off or paid only a percentage of their salaries, and bureaucrats on fixed incomes who had had their savings wiped out by inflation, had found common cause with the students.[97] As a result, Li Peng was able to convince Deng and the elders that the threat to order and stability was real. They agreed to a harshly worded article in the *People's Daily* that labeled the student protest a "turmoil," which only served to further incite the protestors.

Upon his return to Beijing, Zhao attempted to mediate the situation. He argued that the stand represented by the editorial should be softened. After all, the students had "put forward slogans, such as supporting the constitution, promoting democracy and opposing corruption. These demands were basically in line with the position of the party and the government, and we could hardly turn them down."[98] However, when he was unable to persuade the students to clear the square, the Standing Committee met to decide on martial law. The vote on May 17 was split: Li Peng and Yao Yilin voted for it, Zhao and Hu Qili against, and Qiao Shi abstained. With a split decision, Deng and the elders—Chen Yun, Li Xiannian, Peng Zhen, Deng Yingchao, Yang Shangkun, Bo Yibo, and Wang Zhen—took control of policy from the Standing Committee and for the remainder of the crisis made the decisions. Yang Shangkun issued the order declaring martial law in Beijing on May 20. Zhao, who could not support the action, was relieved of his positions and placed under house arrest. The elders then made a number of changes to the Standing Committee that were not announced until the Fourth Plenum in June, following the massacre at Tiananmen.[99]

In retrospect, Zhao's mistake was trying to force Deng to side with political liberalism as part of economic expansion, which was the student position. Deng had opposed liberalism from the start, and if he sided with Zhao he would be pitted against all the party elders and his own "Four Cardinal Principles." Deng had no choice; if he wished to maintain his position, he had to make an example of the liberals and Zhao. He sided with the Li-Chen faction and agreed to the removal of Zhao as secretary general. Deng sided with preservation of one-party rule and ordered in the PLA to ensure the outcome.

The charges leveled against Zhao at the Fourth Plenum of 23–24 June 1989, were:

> At the crucial juncture having a bearing on the survival or extinction of the Party and the state, Comrade Zhao Ziyang made a mistake of supporting the turmoil and splitting the Party, and had unshirkable responsibilities for the shaping up and development of the turmoil. The nature and consequence for his mistakes are very serious. Although he did something beneficial to the reform, the opening of China to the outside world, and economic work when he held principal leading posts

in the Party and the state, he obviously erred in regard to guide-lines and practical work. Especially after taking charge of the Central Committee, he took a passive approach to the princi-ple of adhering to the four cardinal principles and opposing bourgeois liberalization and gravely neglected Party building, the building of spiritual civilization, and ideological and polit-ical work, causing serious losses in the cause of the Party.[100]

The Plenum also moved to purge others of the Zhao or "American" faction. Those dismissed from the Secretariat included Rui Xingwen, in charge of propaganda; Yan Mingfu, responsible for minority affairs; An Zhiwen, vice-minister of the State Commission for Reform of the Eco-nomic Structure; Bao Tong, director of the Committee on Reform of the Political Structure; Wen Jiabao, head of the Central Committee's General Office; Du Rensheng, director of the Rural Policy Research Center; and Wang Meng, the minister of culture. Zhao's ally Hu Qili was removed from the Politburo, its Standing Committee, and the Central Committee Secretariat. The Plenum also officially moved to elevate former Shanghai mayor and party leader Jiang Zemin to the post of secretary general. Jiang was an elderly party veteran without major political liabilities, and thus was a compromise candidate of the major factions. Li Ruihuan, the former mayor of Tianjin and a Deng supporter, was elevated as a replacement for Hu and given charge over propaganda. However, both individuals were rel-ative political lightweights. With the appointment of Song Ping, a strong central planner and an ally of Lu Feng, as head of the Organization Department, control effectively rested with the conservatives.

Deng had left himself with no active supporters on the Standing Com-mittee—a very serious and unexplainable mistake. With Chen and the other seniors still sitting on the Central Advisory Commission, supervising the work of their protégés, Deng was clearly outmaneuvered.[101]

POLITBURO (STANDING COMMITTEE)

Market Socialists	Marxist Socialists	Law and Order
Li Ruihuan	Li Peng	Qiao Shi
	Song Ping	Jiang Zemin
	Yao Yilin	

Deng had allowed control of the party to slip from his hands. His hand-picked successor, Zhao, who could have exercised control over the party and policy, had been replaced by a compromise candidate with no independent political base. Jiang would side with the majority, which in this case were the Marxists under Chen and the leftist ideologues. Thus, with Zhao gone, Deng's only supporter on the Standing Committee was Li Ruihuan, a former worker and mayor of Tianjin, who had no base other than Deng's support. He could not be expected to challenge Chen and Li Peng. Qiao Shi, who could be expected to support Deng, was still only one vote against the three central planners, Li, Song, and Yao. Since it was not necessary to summon the Politburo for daily decisions, Deng had also lost control over economic policy in the aftermath of the Fourth Plenum. Apparently, he had felt that it was not an issue, since he had told the elders over and over during meetings in May and June that any new leaders had to agree to his reform program.[102] Unfortunately, once in power, the conservatives listened to Chen and ignored Deng.

2 | Losing Control

Conservatives Seize the
◇ Economic Initiative

What Deng considered a tactical move in 1989 gradually became a strategic mistake as events unfolded in 1990 and 1991. Domestically, the economic initiative rested with Chen, while internationally, with the collapse of communism, the initiative rested with the leftist ideologues, whom Deng had allowed to take over propaganda in his efforts to punish Zhao and the liberals. Thus, we see that as the result of being maneuvered to side with Chen, Deng had lost the power to control daily economic policy. This now rested with the conservative bloc on the Standing Committee, which could issue new monetary and fiscal policies, which Li Peng and conservatives on the State Council and in the ministries would implement. This was a major mistake. This chapter will document Deng's gradual realization that he had been outmaneuvered and his often-frustrated attempts to rectify the situation, all of which forced him to act boldly in the end.

With the purge of the "American Faction" at the Fourth Plenum in June 1989, the central planners were free to go about reining in Deng's economic reforms. This they did at the Fifth Plenum in November, where the economy was the principal item on the agenda. Li Peng delivered the key address, in which he laid out a three-year austerity plan for 1989 through 1991, on top of the retrenchment program begun in 1988. The basic elements of the plan were included in a thirty-nine-point document, "Decision on further rectifying economic order and deepening reform."[1]

This plan was drafted under the guidance of the State Planning Commission (SPC), which had been inactive under Zhao. The resurrection of the SPC under the directorship of Yao Yilin, assisted by another Standing Committee hard-liner, Song Ping, marked the return to central control over the economy. Zhao's liberal think tanks and ad hoc organizations, which had directed the market reforms, were shorn of all power over the economy. Their directors were either relieved of office or simply ignored as Li Peng shifted power to other government organizations. The SPC reasserted control over the State Commission for Restructuring the Economic System and reduced its staff to the point that it no longer functioned; the Economic Research Institute and the Rural Development Research Center were closed.[2] Thus Deng, in losing the voting majority on the Standing Committee, had lost control of policy planning.

The extent of the victory of the "Soviet Faction" can be seen in the policies implemented as part of the thirty-nine-point program, which was imposed on top of the 1988 retrenchment policies that had already had debilitating effects. These included a drop of 8 percent in fixed asset investment by state enterprises, an increase in loan defaults, and a shortage of working capital, which had seriously affected the rational flow of funds to efficient industries and state sectors. Labor productivity growth had dropped from over 8 percent in 1988 to 3 percent in 1989, along with an increase in the number of loss-making enterprises and a drop in overall state productivity. While the measures had been agreed to as a compromise in late 1988, the result had already had the effect of cutting industrial growth from 16 percent to 10 percent. With Zhao out of the way, and the removal or silencing of his supporters throughout the party and government, the mood was to press for greater recentralization, as well as to continue the cool down of the economy.[3] The goal, of course, was to slow the shift towards a market economy.

The plan, adopted by the Plenum, called for cutting inflation to 10 percent by 1990 and 5 to 8 percent by 1991, for slowing Gross Domestic Product (GDP) growth to 5 percent, removing infrastructure bottlenecks, continuing the tight credit policy, and balancing the budget.[4] According to party press and statements of the SPC, agriculture growth would be limited to 4 percent, while industry would be held to 7 percent. In order to balance the central budget, which had been dropping as a percentage of the national income, from 33 percent in 1979 to 22 percent in 1988, Beijing took steps to increase that percentage. Workers and enterprises were forced to purchase bonds, and Beijing attempted to renegotiate the center's share of local revenues to increase the return from the provinces. The SPC also called for restricting local growth of rural industries for a three-year period. Local officials would be forced to shut down inefficient factories or unprofitable ones. However, no provision was made for the large numbers of workers who would be laid off during the three-year belt-tightening program. Moreover, Li Peng stated that local industries could not compete with state industries for resources, in spite of the fact that local industries had been the fastest growing sector of the economy, absorbing millions of surplus farm laborers. Finally, ignoring Zhao's arguments that price reforms could help solve infrastructure imbalances, the SPC announced it would continue the old administrative habit of preferential loans and allocation of state-supplied resources to favor state enterprises, permitting local enterprises to founder without access to credit and resources.[5]

While the Fifth Plenum announced that China was entering a period of austerity with the economic plan, it expressed a commitment to the SEZ and the open door policy. The net effect of the plan, however, with tight credit, recentralization of state control over natural resources and foreign trade, and renewed emphasis on agriculture, was to begin a process of rolling back Deng's economic liberalizations. Hardest hit would be the provinces along the coast engaging in export industries and the provincial and local industries outside the state plan that were employing the millions of otherwise wandering jobless agrarian surplus labor force. Li Peng went so far as to urge peasants to consider re-forming collectives.[6]

It was also at the Fifth Plenum that Deng resigned his one remaining official post, chairman of the Central Military Commission (CMC). His daughter has stated that Deng resigned and retired to "abolish the feudal life tenure system in China, and to promote younger people to the leading posts."[7] The elders, the Yenan-era generation rehabilitated in 1978, had grown to enjoy the perks of office and were loathe to give them up. Deng and Hu Yaobang had tried to coax them into retirement, while retaining close associates like Yang Shangkun to direct the modernization program. However, some elders, like Chen Yun and Peng Zhen, who opposed his policies, would apparently not retire until Deng did. Thus, his resignation and retirement in 1989, in the aftermath of Tiananmen, was an attempt to coax Chen and the CAC members to follow suit, and perhaps even an attempt to shoulder some of the blame for the massacre at Tiananmen.

Deng may have envisioned that he would return to power to once again press for his policies. In any event, when the Fifth Plenum accepted his resignation as CMC chairman, he in effect walked away from his economic modernization and opening policies and left them in the hands of his longtime opponents. Thus, the economic slowdown set in place for 1990 continued to strangle the provinces—the cost of curbing inflation, at least in Beijing's mind, while the favored state sectors still managed to obtain credit. But with productivity down, sales down, and interest rates on loans rising, most state-run enterprises either defaulted or soaked up the money being printed by the state to keep them afloat and their laborers paid. Ironically, priming the state industries did nothing to stimulate industrial growth; it served only to drive up inflation.[8] The provincial leaders were obviously not happy with these economic policies, but they had no one left to turn to for help.[9]

The party next met in the fall of 1990 to work on the draft of the Eighth Five-Year Plan (1991–95) and the Ten-Year Program for the Seventh Plenum.[10] Its proposals again paid lip service to the goals of opening to the outside world and reform, but the actual policies did anything but that. China's tremendous growth in the 1980s had resulted in high GDP rates; the new proposals, expressing concern for the renewed inflationary surge, recommended a steady GDP for the 1990s of only 6 percent. They also called for greater investment in agriculture, the basic industries, the infrastructure, education, science and technology, and the defense establishment, and they proposed the overhaul of state enterprises, prices, taxation, banking, labor, wages, and investment policies. They also set forth the five main tasks of reform for 1991 through 1995: development of a multi-ownership system, with public ownership being predominant; deepening of enterprise reform; acceleration of the pace of price reform to solve the dual-track price system and to set up new markets; perfection of the macro-economic control system by revamping tax distribution and by strengthening the central bank's functions; and acceleration of the reform of the social insurance and housing systems.[11]

Opening to the world was severely undercut by statements stressing the importance of self-reliance: "China must base economic construction on its own efforts. The importance of foreign capital and technology must go along with the efforts to develop China's economy and enhance its ability to self-reliance."[12] This was read by Deng and his supporters as a throwback to the charges hurled by the Gang of Four in the early 1970s as they sought to undercut Deng's reform efforts. As for the SEZ, the restrictions placed on them during the initial phases of the retrenchment were left in place. More disturbing was the call for the elimination of bourgeois liberalization, which was attributed to the SEZ. The new emphasis was on orthodox Marxism, with the media again highlighting the thinking of Mao.

The ability to implement such plans, however, was seriously limited, as the Politburo as well as the Standing Committee were split between supporters of Deng-style reforms and those who favored central controls. While Chen and his supporters had effective control of the central government, they lacked the necessary votes in any expanded meeting to initiate major changes. Thus, Deng's forces could block new actions, but could not initiate major policy changes, since the Standing Committee was controlled by the votes of the conservatives.[13]

Indeed, by late 1990 forces had emerged that began to limit the free hand that Li Peng and Chen Yun had had in politics. Although Deng had resigned from all public offices, he continued to be supplied with party documents. He had agreed with the necessity for retrenchment in 1988 to curb inflation and the excesses of the political liberals, but clearly the conservatives had gone too far in rolling back his policies. He understood the need for a rational taxation system, which was included in the proposals, but taxation that strangled new provincial and rural industries to the benefit of inefficient state enterprises did not improve China's economy or ability to compete with the new Asian economic dragons—Singapore, Taiwan, Korea, and Hong Kong. He also saw disaster in the 6 percent annual growth rate called for in the plan. It would, he warned, relegate China to continued Third World status, without a chance of its economy catching up with those of the West. However, Deng had little impact at the Seventh Plenum. Although his constituents were able to block any change in the contract system for provincial–central revenue payback, he was powerless to influence the formulation of the new Ten-Year and Five-Year Economic Plans.[14]

Deng was sidelined in retirement, and any appeal to the rank and file would not be heard since the conservatives, who controlled the media, filled the air waves and press with articles supporting Marxist central planning and socialism and criticizing anything else as being bourgeois liberalization and peaceful evolution towards capitalism. Such charges were enough to silence his most ardent supporters. Deng had committed a grave error in removing Zhao and his supporters in 1989 without ensuring replacements strongly committed to him and his policies. Clearly, Deng had to rebuild a force within the party if he was to reverse the economic trends that were emasculating his reforms.

Deng Responds

Deng lost no time in responding. Although his initial efforts were less than successful, he did identify a new standard bearer, Zhu Rongji, the mayor and party leader from Shanghai whom he eventually propelled into power in Beijing. Zhu was a graduate of the premier engineering school in China, Qinghua University. He had worked on the State Economic Commission (SEC) and taught economic management. He was elected an alternate to the Thirteenth Central Committee in 1987, and named mayor of Shanghai in 1988. With the elevation of that city's party secretary, Jiang Zemin, to the party secretary generalship in late 1989, Zhu was selected to fill Jiang's municipal party post. Zhu, who was known as a pragmatist, was renowned for his ability to cut through red tape and get things done. He had impressed Deng with his management style as early as 1989, when he was able to handle student protests without military intervention. He was the ideal candidate to pick up the mantle of the fallen Zhao and support

renewed economic liberalization. Indeed, Deng had tried to get him elevated to the Politburo during its December 1990 Plenum, but was blocked
by Li and Chen, who would only allow such a promotion if Zou Jiahua,
the acting head of the SPC, was also promoted. This Deng was unwilling
to do at the time.[15]

In January 1991 Deng went to Shanghai, ostensibly for the purpose of
reviewing the proposed development and opening of the Pudong area.
However, he used the occasion to address a major oversight in his earlier
opening of China, and thereby increase his constituency. In 1984, he had
concentrated on opening key coastal cities, but had failed to grant them
SEZ status. Now he proposed extending SEZ privileges to key provincial-
level cities like Shanghai, Tianjin, Guangzhou, and Wuhan. As the occasion
of the briefings on Pudong development lent itself to his purpose, Deng
"gave many important instructions on the issue of opening wider to the
outside world. He called for hoisting even higher the banner of reform and
opening up, for decades, and the need for faster, better and bolder reform
and opening, and for not equating the planned economy with socialism
and the market economy with capitalism."[16] The key to this was a growth
rate greater than the 6 percent called for in the Eighth Five-Year Plan, as
announced by Li at the Seventh Plenum in 1990. By putting his prestige
behind Zhu's efforts to build up Shanghai and Pudong, Deng was attempting to mobilize support for expansion of the economy.[17]

As Deng had been frozen out of the national media by Chen's leftist
ideological supporters in charge of the media in Beijing, Deng turned
to the Shanghai press, under the control of his new protégé, Zhu Rongji,
in an attempt to convey his message. This was done in a series of articles
published by the *Liberation Daily* under the pseudonym of Huangfu Ping.[18]
These articles, and various other editorials in the Shanghai press, outlined
Deng's thoughts, augmented by Zhu, on inefficient state enterprises, on
cadre selection to the Fourteenth Party Congress, and on the speed, direction, and characterization of his reforms. They also served to reflect his
displeasure at the direction in which Li was taking the economic reform
process.

Huangfu Ping was actually three people: Zhou Ruijin, a graduate of the
Journalism Department of Fudan University, who went to work for *Liberation Daily* after the Cultural Revolution and became the paper's party secretary in 1991 in charge of commentaries; Ling He, a writer of commentaries

on law and journalism, transferred to the *Shanghai Daily* following the Cultural Revolution to write what were considered leading commentaries on law, democracy, and the press; and Shi Zhihong, a longtime correspondent for the local party paper specializing in agricultural affairs, and a secretary of the municipal party's research office, where he produced and supervised commentaries.[19]

These articles declared that 1991 was to be a historical turning point in reform and opening. Two years of retrenchment had broken inflation, and any further efforts were merely strangling the new rural and provincial industries. Further funding of inefficient state industries would not work. What was called for in the 1990s was not the same as that demanded in the reform efforts of the 1980s. Reforms of the 1990s would focus on invigorating large and medium state enterprises. Rural economic reform and development of a diversified economy were now sideline issues.

Work to reform the large and medium enterprises was portrayed as a battle to storm the fortifications. Such an effort would be more difficult, have greater impact throughout the economy, and have wider coverage than the earlier rural efforts. Such an attack would demand new ideas and tactics; it simply would not do to copy methods used in the past. Thus, revolutionaries and leading cadres of the older generation, some in the vanguards of reform ten years earlier who now hesitated or stood still on the issues of pursuing more in-depth reforms, were warned by Huangfu Ping to be careful, lest they fall into ideological stagnation.[20]

Expanding on the article, Zhu argued that the state industries needed to be reformed, could be reformed, and that he would do it and avoid the dire consequences of massive layoffs.[21] In various editorials, he pointed out that the new Ten-Year and Five-Year Plans both depended on gains made in the crucial first year, 1991. To succeed, "we should concentrate on economic work and resolve prominent contradictions and critical problems, especially problems concerning invigorating state-owned large and medium-sized enterprises."[22] These enterprises, numbering more than ten thousand, had fixed assets that accounted for 70 percent of total state assets. Despite ten years of reform efforts "to expand enterprises' management power, to allow enterprises to retain a part of their earnings, to pay taxes instead of profits to the state, to implement the contract responsibility system in business management, to lift various restrictions on business operations, and to implement the share-holding system, results of these reform measures are not very satisfying."[23] The situation was such that many state industries still had not been cut free from their administrative masters and were thus not operating independently, responsible for their own profits and losses. Moreover, state enterprises were under no pressure to reform as prescribed by the directives issued from Beijing. In short, state enterprises were still being bailed out by the retrenchment policies of Li Peng that continued to pour money into them.

The state enterprises were a problem, the resolution of which, in the view of the Shanghai party, that is, Zhu Rongji, brooked no delay. The solution was to deepen reform. This would include a return to earlier efforts that had been on hold since Zhao's reform plans took a back seat to stability and normalization with Moscow in 1986. These reforms included separation of administrative and management powers, building a socialist commodity economy with fair competition, improving the enterprises' microeconomic operating mechanisms, and allowing them to operate independently, responsible for their own profits and losses, and to regulate themselves. The entire structure of the industrial economy was to be remade, from micro- to macroeconomic perspectives, to give enterprises greater internal and external freedoms to operate in a commodity economy. Specifically, Zhu was advocating deepening reform of the state enterprises to include giving plant managers independent decision-making power, improving market mechanisms for regulating production, and applying technology to transform outdated structures. He further called for these industries to raise quality, diversify, and improve efficiency.[24] Zhu's formula to reform industry redefined Beijing's policies. He offered real reform of the state enterprise system, whereas Li Peng and Chen Yun, through the Five- and Ten-Year Plans, offered only more of the same.

To manage a reformed state enterprise sector, Deng and Zhu advocated a new cadre selection process, which stressed commitment to economic modernization over ideological thinking. Zhu stated that "judging whether a cadre has both morals and talent will ultimately be based on his actual contributions to socialist construction while upholding the Four Cardinal Principles."[25] That is, the key to success in selecting new talent lay in selecting "sensible persons"—those "who uphold the Four Cardinal Principles while enthusiastically supporting reform and opening, are loyal to Marxism as well as proficient in their respective specialized field of knowledge, who are firmly devoted to socialism and thoroughly understand contemporary capitalism, who have strong principles as well as a high degree of flexibility, who have the dedication to willingly bear the burden of office as well as an inexhaustible enterprising spirit, who have a clear idea of the overall situation as well as the invaluable drive to do solid work at their own posts, and who can uphold unified centralism and have the courage to assume independent responsibility."[26] While Communists said capitalism was evil, Zhu noted that it was very good in discovering and using new talent. He praised capitalism for its lack of concern for seniority: "Whoever is qualified will be employed."[27]

Zhu also challenged the party to be bold in reforming outdated organizational and personnel systems. "We should resolutely do away with the promotion system under which a person is good when he is said to be good, even though he is not good; and a person is bad when he is said to be bad when he is not, as perceived by the masses. We should bring democracy into play and boldly promote into new leading bodies those people who are publicly recognized by the masses as having persisted in and scored political achievements in carrying out the line of reform and opening."[28]

The issue of cadre selection was critical to Deng, especially in light of the upcoming Fourteenth Party Congress. Whoever controlled the selection process would control the Congress and the direction of China's economy. Deng was clearly launching a campaign to control the party's next congress.

The Huangfu articles also took on the sensitive subject of internal stability by warning the conservative, or "Soviet," faction against trying to ignite class warfare over ideological issues as a substitute for economic reform. They recounted the history of class warfare in China following the Eighth Congress in 1956, when events in Eastern Europe—the Polish and Hungarian revolutions—had prompted the Chinese Communist Party (CCP) to adopt policies to thwart "peaceful evolution." This had led to the disastrous policy of putting class struggle forward as the main contradiction in society. Comparing that era with the events that had occurred in Eastern Europe and the Soviet Union since 1989, Huangfu Ping noted that some party members feared that another wave of "peaceful evolution" threatened the party, and that once again they stressed that the principal contradiction was the struggle of two systems, two classes, and two roads, rather than the development of productive forces. They called for economic construction to give way to the struggle against "peaceful evolution," the result of "economic pragmatism" that had been in effect since Deng's return to power. Thus, according to Huangfu Ping, their attempts to define things as "capitalism" or "socialism" was reigniting the class warfare struggles of an earlier era.[29]

These articles caused a firestorm throughout China and among party members. They launched a debate that was carried on in the party press and theoretical journals over the next year, which pitted the "American" faction and the "Soviet" faction in a struggle for total domination over the party. The party press in Beijing and throughout China was mobilized to counterattack the Shanghai articles, and Li Peng personally delivered the Party's criticism of Zhu in the fall of 1991. Deng, however, openly acknowledged his responsibility for the articles when, in early 1992, he said "these articles are well written and the points they made are all correct. I heard that some people wanted to investigate the background of these articles. If they continue to do this, just tell them that I requested these articles and I made the points. Let them investigate me."[30] The pressure wielded by Chen and the conservative press controlled by Beijing was such that Deng failed to mobilize support outside the Shanghai area. Thus, his first attempt to stop the Li–Chen team had failed. Deng had lost the initiative, but he chose not to force the issue at that time.

Although Deng had lost out to Beijing, he was clearly determined to oust the conservative "Soviet Faction" from the Politburo by seizing control of the upcoming Fourteenth Party Congress in 1992. To do so, he obviously needed more than the support of the mayor of Shanghai. He needed someone at the center in Beijing to preserve his position while he developed his counterattack. This explains why, in the spring of 1991, Deng compromised with the "Soviet Faction," and both Zhu Rongji and Zou Jiahua were promoted to vice-premierships on the State Council. Although this effectively nullified Zhu's (Deng's) influence, Deng at least had a man at the center once again.[31] In Zhu, he had a protégé who could challenge the conservative managers in Beijing over the disastrous policy of supporting inefficient state enterprises. More importantly, however, his promotion marked an end to Deng's attempts to groom an heir from within the party bureaucracy.

Deng's earlier choices, Hu Yaobang and Zhao Ziyang, had been creatures of the party, and their bases of support had resided within the party. Once under siege from within, neither had had a source of external support except for the personal prestige of Deng. When Deng withdrew his support to save himself, neither had survived.[32] Zhu lacked a strong party base. While he had some support from his various associations in the SPC and SEC as an economic manager, he was a creature of the government, with a limited base among the educated elites familiar with modern economic principles. However, as mayor of Shanghai, he had alienated even this modicum of support by attempting to reinterpret Li's economic policies and by his popularity at a time when the leadership in Beijing was being scorned locally and internationally for its actions during and after Tiananmen. Deng had chosen him because he could contend with the Marxist economic planners in Beijing and apply sound economic principles at the State Council level in opposition to those advocated by Li, Yao, and Zou. In short, he was chosen for his skill and drive in reforming the economic system. It did not matter to Deng who succeeded Zhu, so long as they were competent to manage an evolving economic system.

This philosophy was bound to infuriate as well as threaten party stalwarts, who stressed ideological purity. If cadre were selected simply by virtue of skills that could aid modernization, then soon party membership would be nothing more than a formal requirement for holding office—the substance of any Marxist thinking would be gone. Thus, in choosing Zhu, Deng forced the ideologues to align with the "Soviet Faction" in order to preserve their positions and what they viewed as their sacred trust: preserving Marxism, Leninism, and Mao Zedong Thought.

What Deng was offering was a pragmatic, mechanical approach to leadership. The goal was to reform the economic system; whatever worked would be called socialism, even if it imitated capitalism, since the party would remain in charge. Leaders would be selected on the basis of economic management abilities. Thus, along with Zhu's promotion to Beijing and the vice-premiership, Deng also paved the way for the rehabilitation of other reformers, former associates of Zhao. Hu Qili, Yan Mingfu, and Rui Xingwen were given minor posts after the spring NPC meeting.[33]

Up to this point, Deng was content to proceed at a measured pace. Nothing forced Deng to challenge policy at the Politburo level directly. Even the Gulf War did not demand immediate attention. He allowed the attacks on Zhu and the Shanghai Party, which was supporting his views, to go unchallenged. However, international events in August 1991 forced him into direct action against the ruling faction.

Ideological Response to the
Soviet Collapse

The major factor that forced Deng to take an activist role and stage a virtual coup d'état against Li Peng and Chen Yun was the collapse of the Soviet Union. Deng's goal of modernization was constructed on the premise that China could maneuver between the two superpowers without allying with either one. In Deng's "Middle Kingdom" scenario, China had international stature as the third leg or pole of a triangular relationship with Washington and Moscow. With the collapse of the Soviet Union, the United States was the sole remaining superpower, and China lost its importance. Indeed, it could simply be ignored by the United States, and worse, if the West looked to the former Soviet Union as an investment opportunity, there could be less international funding available for investment in China.

Deng's whole modernization plan was based on drawing in Western investments. Thus, any move by the party to retrench in the face of ideological catastrophe also threatened what Deng had supposed to be a general agreement of the rehabilitated cadre—that China would never repeat the mistakes of the past, as when it turned from the West in 1949. Thus, Deng was spurred to action by the sudden and unexpected collapse of the Soviet Communist Party in the aftermath of the failed August 19 coup in Moscow, and the reaction of the Chinese leadership to the event. This best explains why Deng was finally moved to action, whereas earlier he had chosen to merely relay platitudes to the leadership and to tolerate the attacks on Zhu Rongji.

In other respects, international affairs in 1991 had already taken a toll on the conservative leadership. The United States, leading the United Nations, forced Iraq to withdraw from Kuwait. The quick victory of the United States over the Soviet-equipped Iraqi forces was not lost on the PLA leadership. The technology of warfare was changing; as a consequence, Deng had no difficulty in getting the NPC to increase the PLA's budget by 11 percent over the 1990 appropriation.[34]

Although he had resigned his post as chairman of the CMC, Deng had not severed his ties. "Though I have left the army and retired as well, I will still concern myself with the cause of our party and state, as well as the future of our army."[35] Deng had also handpicked the men left in charge: Yang Shangkun, a trusted ally from their Second Field Army days and later party work at the center; his brother Yang Baibing; and Liu Huaqing, another Deng loyalist.[36] His authority was such that he could mobilize the PLA on his command, as he did at Tiananmen, and he could delegate authority to a trusted ally like Yang, who, though not on the Standing Committee, was given authority to deploy troops under his own signature, ignoring the titular leader, Jiang Zemin. This was the source of Deng's continued power and influence, and the ultimate threat behind his maneuvers to regain power. (Deng, recognizing that it would be a threat to stability in "the wrong hands," later set policy to permit only a Politburo Standing Committee member, like Jiang or Liu Huoqing, to order troop movements, thus concentrating power in the hands of a tiny circle of elders.)

At the same time that the technology of warfare was changing to the disadvantage of the PLA, the collapse of communism was having a tremendous psychological effect on the Chinese leadership. As Huangfu Ping noted, many in China wanted to shift from economic reform to combating "peaceful evolution" as a result of the changes in Eastern Europe and the Soviet Union. This faction, the "Soviet Faction," mounted an all-out attack on Zhu Rongji and his economic reforms in Shanghai as "capitalist" and dangerous and promoting "peaceful evolution."[37] Deng's response, known as the twenty-four-character directive, issued in early 1991 to calm a jittery leadership in Beijing, consisted of "observing with a cool head, securing our position, dealing with the situation calmly, hiding our capacities and biding our time, being good at defense, and never being in the limelight."[38]

Jiang Zemin went to Moscow in May 1991, officially to return Gorbachev's 1989 visit and continue the normalization process. However, part of his mission was to shore up Gorbachev's crumbling power structure and prevent Yeltsin's rise, which was seen as a threat to the Communist Party of the Soviet Union.[39] The idea that communism could collapse there, in the country of origin and the internationally acknowledged spokesman for the movement, was unnerving, and the propaganda value to the West would be inestimable. China, however, had economic as well as political motives for wanting a unified and stable Soviet Union. If its economy collapsed as well, the West would take advantage of the situation, perhaps turning a kindred ally and neighbor against them, and investment monies would certainly be diverted from China to the Soviet Union.

In his meetings with Soviet officials, Jiang stressed that the visit was meant to "continue pushing forward normal development of relations between the two countries and two parties."[40] Even though Sino-Soviet relations would never return to the level that had existed in the 1950s, he expressed the hope that his visit would solidify a friendly, mutually beneficial relationship of cooperative understanding between the two nations, based on the five principles of peaceful coexistence, (mutual respect for sovereignty and territorial integrity, mutual nonaggression, noninterference in each other's internal affairs, equality and mutual benefit, and peaceful coexistence), first espoused by Zhou Enlai at the Bangdung Conference in 1955. Such a relationship, according to Jiang, would also have positive effects on peace and stability in Asia and the world at large.[41] However, in acknowledgment of the new world order that was emerging (multipolar, reflecting the disintegration of the USSR and the Soviet Bloc), Jiang stressed that improvement in relations was not to be interpreted as being directed at any other country.[42]

Jiang and Gorbachev also exchanged views about their respective economic policies. Jiang explained the Ten-Year and Eighth Five-Year Plans and stressed the need for domestic stability to ensure success. Gorbachev explained his views on renovating socialism through adopting constructive and evolutive methods. He also thanked the Chinese for their economic support of Soviet reforms (they had lent them $700 million), and acknowledged their efforts to build socialism with Chinese characteristics.[43] At the conclusion of his visit, Jiang announced new agreements with Moscow and signaled the end of the period of estrangement.

In spite of the seemingly pleasant tone of the meeting, Jiang had been shaken by what he had seen of Gorbachev's innovative socialism. It reeked of pluralism, multiparty democracy, and "peaceful evolution." Upon his return to Beijing, he addressed those concerns to the Politburo and to the Party at large in his 1 July speech on Party Day.[44] It was a well-written defense of China's Communist Party and ideological purity.[45] In it, he defended the necessity of a strong communist party to "develop a socialist system with Chinese characteristics. . . . we must maintain the people's democratic dictatorship . . . (which) must not be weakened. . . . We should not weaken or negate Communist Party leadership, nor should we ever practice a Western-style multiparty system."[46] Feeding on "leftist" fears for the fate of communism in China, in light of events in the international communist world, Jiang came down hard on the side of the dictatorship of the proletariat. He argued that "class struggle will exist for a long time to come within certain areas of our country" and that "hostile international forces" were attempting to subvert China's socialism.[47] He pointed to "the turmoil and the counterrevolutionary rebellion which took place in Beijing in the late spring of 1989" as proof of his point, in spite of the fact that Deng had ordered a Central Committee review that had rendered the incident a "disturbance" and not a "turmoil or rebellion."[48] Jiang had apparently adopted the leftist line and switched his allegiance.[49] Indeed, he was announcing the opening of another ideological campaign, one that would certainly force everyone to recall how earlier campaigns, such as the Great Cultural Revolution, the Anti-Rightist Campaign, and others that had plagued China under Mao, had begun and unfolded.[50] This flew in the face of promises by Deng and the elders that there would be no more such campaigns. He went on to declare that "The ideological sphere is a major arena of struggle between people trying to effect peaceful evolution in China and people working against it. Bourgeois liberalization is the antithesis of the Four Cardinal Principles and the struggle between the two is, in essence, a political struggle over whether or not the leadership of the Communist Party is to be upheld and whether or not we are to adhere to the socialist road."[51] Jiang was clearly putting Deng's "economic pragmatism" at odds with party loyalty and ideological purity.[52]

Jiang's speech hammered away at the ideological issues facing China's economic modernization, equating ideology with economic reform. "The socialist economy, socialist political system and socialist culture with Chinese characteristics form an organic, inseparable whole."[53] Lest anyone missed his point, he made it quite clear that "We should bear in mind the lessons learned in recent years from our mistake of stressing material progress to the neglect of cultural and ideological progress, try to promote material progress and cultural and ideological progress simultaneously and give full play to one of our Party's strong points, which is in stressing the importance of ideological and political work, so as to ensure coordinated development of the socialist economy, socialist political system and socialist culture with Chinese characteristics."[54]

Jiang called for reinvigorating party cells in economic units down to the lowest levels in the provinces. This would reestablish the power of the party (leftists) in the domain of the provincial reformers. While the reformers had been silenced with the dismissal of Zhao and the loss of strong support at the center, they had retained control of their organizations. If the party launched a recruitment or recertification campaign, the center, in the persona of the Organization Department, could restructure the political makeup of the provincial party machines. After all, this was how Mao had toppled the party at the start of the Cultural Revolution. Deng was aware of it, and Chen was aware of it; there was room for only one victor.

Deng was later to criticize Jiang for his speech, calling it "one-sided,"[55] but this was a mild rebuke, made in private, that did not alter the results. The speech was the sign the leftists were waiting for. They took it as approval for an all-out ideological campaign against bourgeois liberalization and peaceful evolution. Jiang was leading the party into another ideological campaign.[56]

Immediately following Jiang's speech, "Four June" investigative groups, operating under the authority of the Central Committee and guided by Deng Liqun, entered the universities to review all theses written by tutors and graduates since 1986. Those found to advocate "peaceful evolution" were disqualified from their positions and expelled.[57]

It was no coincidence that Deng Liqun led the charge. Earlier in the year, he had used the Central Party School to prepare a propaganda and educational campaign against peaceful evolution. According to him, it was wrong to improve the economy first; if political power was lost, an improved economy would only benefit others.[58] He charged that "the intellectuals were the most dangerous at that time. . . . Today, the intellectuals breathe and serve as capitalism's tool for peaceful evolution."[59] Jiang's July speech, coupled with the "leftists' " control of the party propaganda organs, state culture offices, and major Beijing newspapers, was a recipe for continued emphasis on anti-peaceful evolution at the expense of Deng Xiaoping's reform and opening.

Although Jiang, Li Peng, Chen Yun, and others within the party leadership were appalled by and suspicious of what was going on in the Soviet Union, they were unprepared for the 19 August coup attempt in Moscow and its failure. This one event changed everyone's thinking about the political equation within the Chinese leadership, including that of Deng

Xiaoping. The failure of the Soviet Red Army to support the Communist Party of the Soviet Union (CPSU) in its bid to regain control threw the CCP into a panic. The Chinese leadership feared that a precedent had been established. It also raised the question of the party's control of the PLA, and whether it could be counted on to preserve the CCP. Mao's maxim had been that power grows out of the barrel of a gun, but the party controls the gun. The Soviet Red Army had stood aside, refusing to assist the hard-line Communist coup leaders.

At the formal, state-to-state level, China adopted a strict, noncritical policy of noninterference in the domestic affairs of another country, based on the five principles of peaceful coexistence. During the coup on 19 August, and after the coup, on 22 August, Foreign Minister Qian Qichen met with the Soviet ambassador to assure him that the event was viewed as a strictly internal affair, having no effect on Sino-Soviet relations.[60] But immediately after the coup failed, a Politburo meeting was convened to analyze the events in Moscow and discuss their ramifications for the CCP. The meeting produced a ten-point resolution on 24 August that laid out both the international and domestic policy positions of the CCP.

For foreign consumption, it was agreed that the Politburo would reissue Deng's twenty-four-character instruction. That instruction called for "observing with a cool head, securing our position, dealing with the situation calmly, hiding our capacities and biding our time, being good at defense, and never in the limelight."[61] But internally, the party did everything but "deal with the situation calmly." The CCP was furious with Gorbachev for allowing the demise of the Soviet Communist Party. Internal documents for party consumption, numbered One and Two, listed the criminal charges against him:

> (1) He was a careerist and opportunist who had betrayed the fundamental principles of Marxism; (2) He completely repudiated the history of the CPSU, causing it to abandon its predominance and eventually lose its ruling position; (3) He initiated a "multiparty system" and "separation of the three branches of power;" and abandoned the dictatorship of the proletariat, thus laying down the conditions for the seizure of power by anti communist and anti socialist forces; and (4) His reform deviated from the socialist direction and gradually

evolved toward the capitalist system. The net result of his actions were to allow anti communist forces both at home and abroad to connive with each other to step up infiltration of peaceful evolution.[62]

In addition, these documents charged that the coup leaders had failed to act out of concern for legality, failed to seize control of the media, and failed to use force. They further charged that "over the years Gorbachev's democratic and humanitarian ideas have seriously infected people from all aspects of the party, government, and military over the years, prompting them not to dare to use force nor to cause bloodshed."[63] Perhaps the most revealing point raised in the documents was the apparent foresight of Chinese leaders in early 1990, when Gorbachev started his liberalizations:

> When the CPSU Central Committee decided to introduce a multiparty system and political pluralism in February last year, our party central pointed out that the so-called new thinking and democratic socialism initiated by Gorbachev was in fact another version of the Second Comintern's social democracy appearing under new, modern conditions. In fact, it repudiates class struggle on a worldwide scale, changes the character of the communist party, and accepts the West's parliamentary democracy. Gorbachev's reform is not the self-perfection of socialism, but a peaceful evolution toward capitalism.[64]

Yeltsin was not spared either. He was vilified as an "adventurous henchman in the restoration of capitalism and leading representative of right-wing forces, a leader of the anti communist, anti socialist forces."[65] Chen Yun was quoted as saying that "we must never allow persons like Yeltsin to appear."[66]

Party ideologues provided the basic spin on the Soviet coup and the reasons for its failure. Their position was enunciated by Gao Di, editor of *People's Daily*, in discussions with propaganda officials on 30 August, just days after the failed coup.[67] He argued that the coup had failed because the people had become confused by Gorbachev's new thinking, that the good of mankind as a whole had replaced class struggle. Gao labeled this as democratic socialism and a denial of real socialism. He pointed out that, since the establishment of socialism, the forces of imperialism had been trying to destroy it, first through shooting wars and later through efforts to bring about "peaceful evolution of socialism" (smokeless warfare). Gao also pointed to the poor economic conditions in Russia as one of factors the West used as proof of the failure of socialism. When Gorbachev himself admitted that fact he was, according to Gao, repudiating Stalin, which amounted to a repudiation of Marxism and Leninism.[68]

Gao further argued that the leaders of the coup were not seasoned Marxists, since they were too polite to Gorbachev and Yeltsin. Had they been real Marxists, they would have arrested the two. It was a revolution, and, as such, it was either kill or be killed—"Revolution is merciless." Gao compared the Soviet coup (the 19 August incident) to China's own June the Fourth incident. China had been successful because it had mercilessly suppressed the uprising of the students. He also pointed out that, without the leadership of the Communist Party of the Soviet Union, the nation was disintegrating. Gao also argued that it would take the Soviet Union twenty years to transition to a market economy. China had to improve its system during that time to prove the efficacy of socialism.[69]

Gao maintained that China would hold the line for socialism, even as other socialist regimes were rapidly collapsing around the world. So long as the party controlled the gun and remained strong, it would not fall. The ruin of the Soviet Union lay in its betrayal of Marxism and socialism; thus, for China, it was important to learn the appropriate lesson from the Soviet example. On matters of principle, a clear line had to be drawn between what is Marxism and what is not, and between what is socialism and what is not. Gao ordered the press to be low-keyed on reporting Soviet affairs, but within China, things would be different. The necessity of maintaining the party would be stressed, and a multiparty or parliamentary system would not be allowed to develop. Control over the gun would be strengthened, bourgeois democratic freedoms suppressed. Public ownership over privatization would be maintained, and Marxism would be upheld, with no allowance for ideological pluralism, while working hard at reform and opening up.[70] Deng would agree with the need for party control, but Gao intruded on the issue of economic reform when he raised the issue of what was socialism and what was not. This was a direct assault on Deng's reforms.

Thus, the party leadership, especially Chen Yun, believed that the Soviet Union had been the victim of "peaceful evolution," which could be traced back to Khrushchev. Stories circulated that Mao had initiated the Cultural Revolution to stamp out "peaceful evolution." A parallel was drawn between the events that had occurred in the Soviet Union to those that were emerging in China as a result of Deng's policy of opening to the world. Deng's reforms were equated to economic pragmatism, which was behind "peaceful evolution" and which was anathema to the leadership in Beijing. The Politburo's response was to organize an "Anti-Peaceful Evolution Leading Group," with Song Ping as leader and Wang Zhen, a conservative hard-liner on the CAC, as adviser.[71] Chen's son was among those who authored a report critical of Deng's "romantic capitalism." Thus the "leftists" were poised to conduct socialist education campaigns throughout China, and through their dominance of the Organization Department, they were prepared to verify the ideological credentials of delegates to the Fourteenth Party Congress. In short, the "leftists" had seized control of the party apparatus. They had found common ground as a result of events in Moscow. The elders could not ignore the fact that this was how the Cultural Revolution had started under Mao, and they had to consider what would happen if the current campaign got out of hand.

Internal documents, numbers One and Two, provided the justification for a campaign against "bourgeois liberalism" or "capitalist roaders" inside the party. This ignored Deng's earlier instructions that, as long as the provincial-level party leaders observed the Four Cardinal Principles, it was unnecessary to require strict adherence to them by lower-level cadre. He maintained that the party was in control, and that a certain amount of "bourgeois liberalism" was preferable to the chaos of a purification campaign.

Deng Liqun, however, utilizing the major organs of the propaganda department, *Renmin Ribao* and *Guangming Ribao*, proclaimed that the Cultural Revolution had been correct, that bourgeois tendencies had to be eradicated to ensure the integrity of the dictatorship of the proletariat. He reportedly stated that with regard to intellectuals, who were the conduits of bourgeois ideas, "it is necessary to pin them down, and suffocate and demoralize them." He also said that "we should strengthen ideological transformation rather than increase their (intellectuals) remuneration. We cannot spend money to buy an opposition party."[72] The attack against intellectuals was carried out by Chen Yeping, the former deputy head of the Organization Department, who wrote in *Renmin Ribao* that the intellectuals, though only a handful, had no intention of purifying their thinking. According to him, they were unrecalcitrant in the face of ideological education, and were most likely to become lackeys of hostile Western forces in their campaign to implement the "peaceful evolution" strategy against China. Chen Yeping, like Gao Di, editor of *Renmin Ribao*, and his fellow "leftists," Deng Liqun and Hu Qiaomu, was apparently trying to subvert Deng Xiaoping's May decision to stress ideological education within the higher levels of the party only.

By extension, the "leftists" were also openly challenging Deng's criteria for selecting and evaluating cadre for the Fourteenth Congress. His criteria, established in 1978, emphasized "productive forces," that is, the ability to contribute to the modernization effort. In a September 1991 article in *Renmin Ribao*, Chen Yeping criticized Deng's criteria in favor of those advocated by Chen Yun in a speech he made in 1940 as head of the Organization Department.[73] Chen Yun had stressed the need for cadre to have both political integrity and capability, a position advocated by Mao in 1938. Not coincidentally, Chen Yeping's 1991 article, "Having Both Political Integrity and Capability, With Stress on Former," was the title of Chen Yun's 1940 speech. Deng's criteria—more revolutionary, younger in average age, better educated, and professionally competent—were caricatured in the article. More revolutionary was called an "empty slogan," a soft target; younger in age was referred to as "young people"; better educated meant "diploma holders"; and professionally competent was rendered as "being experts."

By resurrecting Chen Yun's speech and linking it to Mao, the "leftists" were emphasizing the legitimacy of Chen Yun's criteria over Deng's. It was the old argument of "red" over "expert," with the Maoists—Gao Di, Deng Liqun, Hu Qiaomu and Chen Yeping—picking up where the Cultural Revolution had left off. Clearly, Deng was being challenged, and his policies of economic reform and opening to the world were about to be reversed. The red flag of revolution had been raised.

In response to these attacks, Deng reissued his twenty-four-character slogan, to which he added the following opinions: (1) The Soviet coup was an internal affair and no comments should be rendered; (2) To repay Gorbachev for his silence about the "4 June" incident, no satisfaction should be expressed over his downfall; (3) There should be no overt support for the coup; (4) If the coup succeeded, the Soviet Union would have been plunged into greater chaos. If Gorbachev had won, the economy was un-likely to improve; if Yeltsin succeeded, the economy might take a turn for the better, but would encounter opposition from the Communists. There-fore, there should not be too much speculation about any of these scenar-ios. He asked the Politburo to present him with a proposal with which to respond to Soviet events. That proposal was merely a restatement of Deng's twenty-four-character position.[74]

Jiang Zemin, Deng's handpicked successor to Zhao, was not supportive of Deng's low-keyed response. In Deng's absence from the political scene, he had seen the advantage of siding with the "leftists." However, by late September, when Deng launched his counterattack, Jiang acquiesced to Deng's demand that he revise his speech of 1 July.[75] But by then the "left-ists," led by Song Ping, Gao Di, Deng Liqun, and Hu Qiaomu, had estab-lished an "Anti-Peaceful Evolution Leading Group" under the Central Committee and mobilized the press for what looked like another "cultural revolution." During the fall, they openly attacked Li Ruihuan, Deng Xiao-ping's choice to handle propaganda on the Politburo. They criticized his effectiveness and called on Jiang to dismiss him. Jiang rejected their de-mands, reaffirming Li's responsibility for propaganda and ideology.[76] Deng also sought to bolster Li:

> In the Standing Committee of the Politburo, you are the one
> who is responsible for ideological work. The central authorities
> have not made any decision for others to assume the job. I know
> that there are some people who are not obedient, but even they
> must be told and be made to submit themselves to the interests
> of the party and state and of the people. On reform and open-
> ing up, our media has but one single objective and this is to
> publicize and support the reform and opening up forcefully.
> Do not be afraid of reproaches from other people. There is
> nothing to it. Let them go ahead and make reproaches. The
> truth is in your hands, so say what should be said and do what
> should be done."[77]

However, as Deng was not in a position to protect him, he recom-mended that Li leave Beijing for a while and visit the south, particularly Shanghai. There, in October, prior to the party plenum, Li held discus-sions with local officials, including the city party boss, Wu Bangguo, and

Mayor Huang Ju. Li told them "Comrade Xiaoping places great hope in Shanghai. Greater strides should be taken. Commentaries in *Liberation Daily* comply with the ideas of Comrade Xiaoping. Support the reform, publicize the reform, and seize on the central task of economic construction—that is the most elementary responsibility of every news media worker."[78]

Deng Counterattacks

Although Deng Xiaoping had retired, he still exercised informal power as a respected revolutionary-era elder. His traditional base rested with the military, going back to his pre-1949 days as a party commissar with the Second Field Army under Commander Liu Bocheng. He had also built a constituency among provincial party leaders, many of whom he had appointed in the years since 1949. He had in fact been brought back to power in 1978 through their combined efforts, and he intended to use them again. Qiao Shi, head of the Party's security apparatus, also came out in support of Deng's programs.[79] A protégé of Peng Zhen, himself no friend of Deng, Qiao had apparently convinced his mentor that Deng's program held the possibility of true economic modernization, and that any political education campaign would simply lead to disaster the way the 1962 Socialist Education Campaign turned into the Cultural Revolution.

Thus, when Deng summoned Jiang Zemin, Yang Shangkun, Qiao Shi, Li Ruihuan, and presumably the rest of the Standing Committee to his residence in late September to lay out his counterattack against the "leftists," he could not be ignored. He had the support of the PLA and the party security apparatus. In fact, when Jiang offered to resign, citing his failure to counter the growing ideological campaign against reform, Yang, at the behest of Deng, placed the PLA under Jiang's command in the presence of his brother, Yang Baibing, and Liu Huaqing. Effectively, Yang was giving up operational control of the army and re-subordinating it to the Standing Committee. At Deng's insistence, Jiang withdrew his resignation offer. With Jiang clearly Deng's choice as the "core," it was also made clear to everyone in attendance that it was the PLA that was guaranteeing Deng's program and his candidates.[80] While committee members Li Peng, Yao Yilin and Song Ping were clearly in Chen Yun's camp, they apparently decided it would not be wise to directly confront Deng. They could ignore him once they left.

At a subsequent work conference in Beijing on 25 September Deng, through Jiang and Yang, charged *Renmin Ribao* with using language associated with the Cultural Revolution. He asked rhetorically if they intended to criticize his line in "an all around way, " a reference to the language used during the Cultural Revolution during "education sessions."[81] He then proceeded to make the following points:

> (1) The Party's basic line, with economic construction as the center and with science and technology as the first productive force, had yet to be implemented; (2) world war will not break out and so long as it does not, then economic construction is the center of all efforts. All other activity must be subordinated to economic construction, the center. (3) The fact that China has a position in the new international environment is directly related to the successful policy of reform and opening up, which has enabled the people to obtain material benefit. Reform and opening up must continue, as well as adherence to the four cardinal principles. There may be risks, but we can bear such risks. There is absolutely no way out if we stop and go backwards. (4) Adhering to the socialist road is both a process of struggle and persuasion and education. If we are successful, we can convince those who have no faith in socialism. (5) Some people only pay lip service to Marxism-Leninism. They shout that they adhere to it, while criticizing others for pursuing non-Marxist policies. They suggest we study Mao's talks at Yenan on rectification. (6) It is imperative to be vigilant against peaceful evolution. It is important that the high-ranking leading cadres at and above the provincial level be alert and the key lies in the leadership groups. So long as the leadership groups adhere to Marxism and the party's basic line, we do not fear peaceful evolution. We must talk less about it to the lower levels, workers, peasants, and soldiers. (7) Internationally, we must learn how to be more circumspect. We must not strike a head-on blow and

say tough words, nor must we say them every day. It is no use. (8) The Soviet Union's peaceful evolution is successful. In the future, we shall not take ideology as the main aspect and carry on public debate, but carry on state-to-state relations.[82]

Deng was aware of the decision by the CPSU to disestablish the Soviet Union on 25 December, which would result in a vacuum in Southeast Asia. Coupled with the ongoing pullback by the United States from the western Pacific, Deng saw the opportunity to realize his long-held goal of establishing Chinese military and economic hegemony throughout Southeast Asia. Chinese strategists, as early as 1985, had recognized that the world was becoming multipolar. Deng saw China as one of the new poles, and tasked the PLA to change doctrine to reflect this. This led to a reduction in manning, development of a blue-water navy, a modern air force, and modernized weapons and organization.[83] Deng's success in swaying the Party, however, was limited at this point since he did not control the propaganda apparatus. He would again address the need to move into Southeast Asia during debates over the Baker visit in November 1991, but again to no avail. Only the Yangs and Liu Huoqing, of the PLA, Qiao Shi, Li Ruihuan and sometimes Jiang spoke out on his behalf.[84]

Yang, however, was successfully recruiting PLA support for Deng by stressing the benefits derived from reform policies over the previous ten years, and cautioning them to pay less attention to the issue of "peaceful evolution."[85] He called a high-level meeting of senior military leaders immediately following Deng's 25 September meeting. He directed the PLA to go on the offensive and support reform and opening and counter the Party media blitz that was attacking reform and opening as the cause of current problems.[86] Yang also warned the PLA that modernization was expensive, and that Deng had the only solution for long-term, consistent financing.

Deng's thoughts had been aired in the Huangfu Ping articles in Shanghai in the spring of 1991, in which he had expressed the opinion that at earlier times in China's history, such as prior to the Cultural Revolution, China had had the opportunity to go forward with economic development, but had instead diverted to political campaigns that wasted time, energy, and lives. Now, in 1991, with the collapse of the Soviet Union, China was at another turning point. If it again turned inward, stressing self-reliance, China would once again miss the opportunity to reform the economy and catch up with the West. Deng was determined that this would not happen. However, the power at the center was rallying around the call for ideological purity. Deng was on a collision course. His man on the State Council, Zhu Rongji, was outvoted by the presence of Yao Yilin, Li Peng, and Song Ping, who actually controlled economic policy from the Politburo Standing Committee, and Chen's protégé Zou Jiahua. The provincial leaders thus still had no weight in Beijing to counter the conservatives. All they could do was resist, and that threatened to break up China. Deng was clearly in a difficult position in the fall of 1991 prior to the Plenum, where he hoped to use his personal prestige to get his policies back on track.

Efforts to launch an ideological campaign along the lines of the Cultural Revolution were not sidetracked by Deng Xiaoping's intervention. Li Peng continued to advocate a Socialist Education Movement in the rural areas as part of his agenda for the Eighth Plenum to be held in November. Over the summer, he had authorized an in-depth study of internal conditions in China. Entitled "An Itemized Report and Analysis on the General Political, Economic, Social and Cultural Situation of 30 Provinces, Autonomous Regions, and Municipalities Across China," the report, drafted by the "leftist" faction in the State Council Policy Research Office, concluded that fourteen provinces—60 percent of China—should be classified as politically and socially unstable areas. As a preemptive measure, Li Peng had developed his plan to pacify those areas with "ideological" cadre.[87] The Organization Department, under the guidance of the "Anti-Peaceful Evolution Leading Group," was readying plans to send over 500,000 cadres into the countryside after the new year (February–March 1992) to carry out a Socialist Education Campaign.

The fall of 1991 was thus a time of increasing anxiety for Chinese peasants, with the prospect of another Cultural Revolution, with land reform, elimination of capitalism, struggle meetings, people's communes, and re-collectivization in the offing. There were reports of peasants killing their animals and hiding their money in anticipation of turmoil.[88] In fact, internal conditions had deteriorated to such an extent that even the "leftists" were concerned about events getting out of hand. It would seem that the more educated, privileged class of senior officials who wanted to limit reform also wanted to protect their positions. Another Cultural Revolution could turn out like the last one, with innocent victims caught up in the maelstrom that the center could not direct, much less control.

These fears were addressed in the September article written by Chen Yun's son. While critical of Deng's reforms, Chen Yuan wrote that "in the recently begun rural socialist education campaign, policy must be strictly controlled to prevent ideological trends that negate 10 years of rural reform. Reportedly, such trends are fairly universal among rural cadres, and their vigor is very great. Unless brought under control, they may result in new instability."[89] An initial campaign had been launched in 1990 with the approval of the Politburo and the Standing Committee, partly as a result of the incident in Tiananmen in 1989. It amounted to a full-scale assault on the local party structures similar to the one Mao initiated in the early 1960s, when he assigned PLA work teams to local party units to take over party certification and to review and purge members not supportive of his position. Only this program was to be carried out over two to three years in order to remake the local parties that would select delegates to the Fourteenth Party Congress.

The campaign would focus on "occupying the rural areas with socialist ideology and educating the peasants in basic socialist theories in a forthright and cogent manner in order to boost patriotism and train a new generation of four have's (ideals, morality, culture and discipline); comprehensively and correctly carrying out and implementing various policies and principles; integrating incentives for peasants' household operations with collective operations, boosting the economic power of collectives, and guiding peasants toward a path of common wealth; and strengthening the building of rural grass roots organizations that take party branches as the core, and raising the quality of party members; strengthening the party's fighting power, cohesiveness and appeal; where weak and disorganized grass roots party organizations are concerned, we must conscientiously carry out an organizational overhaul on the basis of ideological education."[90] Even though Jiang reported to the Politburo, in a meeting prior to the Eighth Plenum in late 1991, that the "peasants are generally afraid of the work teams or were antagonistic, and the obstacles were very big and the CCP's demands were not met, Li Peng obtained approval to dispatch an army of 500,000 party faithful to the rural front in the spring of 1992 to carry out a "socialist education campaign."[91] This would have wiped out all of Deng's efforts at transforming the party and the economy since 1978. While it was doubtful that the collectives could have been reestablished, the threat of ideological and political damage was real to Deng, and he was taking no chances. He put a stop to the movement when he moved against the conservatives in December.

The Baker Visit

If the 19 August coup in the Soviet Union had caused a crisis in the Chinese leadership, the impending visit of U.S. Secretary of State James Baker III was no less traumatic. America was regarded as the primary source of the "peaceful evolution" that was endangering the Chinese socialist system. Baker's visit, coming in the midst of preparations for the Plenum, further complicated the ongoing rivalry within the party. Chen was in no mood to compromise with the source of peaceful evolution; Deng's modernization demanded a compromise.

As a background for the fall discussions over the economy, the collapse of the Soviet Union, and the upcoming American visit, the first since such high-level visits had been suspended in the aftermath of Tiananmen in June 1989, the party distributed the record of an informal meeting held among the party elders on the eve of National Day (1 October). That meeting, called by Deng, included those first generation elders still alive, including Deng Yingchao and Nie Rongzhen and most of the Central Advisory Commission.[92] This largely honorary body consisted of party elders who had been forced to resign by Deng over the years since 1978. However, it still exercised considerable power, like the genro in nineteenth-century Japan, since its leader Chen Yun and several others sat in on Politburo discussions. At this meeting, Deng tried again to convince the elders of the seriousness of the situation in China and to secure their understanding and support for his economic reforms. Though mostly out of office, many had protégés who could further his cause. Deng told them that "so far, some comrades still do not agree with, or do not understand, or even oppose, the central decision of taking economic construction and modernization as the central task."[93] He reminded them of their responsibilities to the people to fulfill the promises they had made, which, according to Deng, involved developing the economy and solving the issues of productive forces better than the old system had.

To this end, he said "if the economy cannot be boosted over a long time, it will lose the people's support at home and will be oppressed and bullied by other nations of the world. The continuation of this situation will lead to the collapse of the Communist Party."[94] He went on to warn them against giving only lip service to their commitments to reform and opening: "We always say that we need to grasp the two basic points (the Four Cardinal Principles and the policy for reform and opening up), and the key lies in the proper handling of the relationship between the two basic points. We must not use politics to constrain economic construction or hamper the pace of reform and opening up. In peaceful circumstances, everything should serve economic construction, which is the central task of the whole party and nation and is the matter of prime importance."[95] Deng acknowledged the need to adhere to Marxism, but he warned his audience that, as they all knew, over the long term they, collectively, had not always understood and applied Marxism correctly. Despite all their past failures though, the party had managed to provide the majority of the people with a subsistence living, even allowing some to live comparatively well. This was no small accomplishment, and one of which they could all be proud. But Deng drew a line in the sand over the current trend to emphasize ideology over economic development: "We must continue to firmly and steadily develop productive forces, and take the development of productive forces as our first priority task. This orientation is completely correct, and there is no other option for us."[96] Deng had made it clear to the elders where he stood, but it was doubtful that they were listening to him. They had ignored his effort in the spring of the year in Shanghai to reignite the economy through his articles in *Liberation Daily*, and there was no reason to assume he could have persuaded them in the immediate aftermath of the collapse of the Communist Party of the Soviet Union. Deng was apparently powerless to stop what he believed was a slow slide into class warfare.

Other international issues were pressing down on the leadership. A series of informal meetings were initiated in early November in an effort to reach a consensus about how to handle Baker's visit, as well as set the agenda for the Plenum, which would include the issues of "peaceful evolution," cadre selection for the Fourteenth Congress, and economic policy.[97] On one side were Deng Xiaoping and his supporters, who argued for a "relaxed" response to the United States and "peaceful evolution"; and on the other were Chen Yun and his supporters—the Soviet faction—who advocated centralized planning and party reform to prevent a capitalist restoration like the one occurring in Russia. They advocated a tough response to America's "provocations."[98]

The meetings began on 9 November at Zhongnanhai, and were attended by the ten seniors of the Party: Deng Xiaoping, Chen Yun, Yang Shangkun, Jiang Zemin, Li Peng, Peng Zhen, Wan Li, Bo Yibo, Qiao Shi, and Song Ping. Only Yang, Jiang, and Qiao Shi could be expected to support Deng; the others were clearly in Chen Yun's camp. Background documents prepared for this meeting included one jointly authored by the Ministry of Foreign Affairs and the Propaganda Department, entitled "Propaganda and Education Arrangements Regarding the Current Basic Principles and Policies Toward the United States." It set forth five principles for state-to-state relations: First, no matter what drastic changes occurred in the international situation, China would strive to improve, adjust, and develop Sino-American relations according to the joint statements signed by the two governments, and China would settle and discuss issues based on the five principles of peaceful coexistence. Second, China would oppose U.S. interference in its internal affairs under the pretext of human rights. China would also resist the import of U.S.-style ideology through economic, technical, scientific and cultural exchanges, and it would openly expose "peaceful evolution" activities as necessary. Third, exchanges would continue in spite of ideological differences and respective internal conditions. Problems of trade would be settled according to international law and the norms of state-to-state relations. Fourth, various government departments and civil organizations would be permitted to take the initiative in expanding intercourse with the American people and those organizations that promote friendship and mutual understanding. Fifth, China would comprehensively examine and adjust its criteria for developing foreign economic relations and trade, scientific and technological cooperation, and educational exchanges where lopsided priority was given to the United States.[99]

It was also time to open to Europe and Japan across the board and to expand cooperation and exchanges with Southeast Asia, thus offsetting U.S.

threats and pressure about extending Most Favored Nation (MFN) trade status to China. The domestic portion of the report, likewise, included five parts: First, leaders at all levels were to understand the U.S. social system fully, that the nature of its ruling class was to seek world hegemony, arbitrarily interfere in other nations, and subvert the political, economic, and social systems of other countries. Second, it was necessary to study the white paper "China's Human Rights Situation" issued by the State Council, which reviewed the last one hundred years of Western imperialism and revealed the true purposes of anti-Chinese politicians who waved the human rights banner. Third, party members and cadres were to become more conscientious in overcoming the mentality of blindly admiring the United States and more conscientious in criticizing those advocating wholesale Westernization. However, U.S. advanced industry was to be separated from the nature of the ruling class. Fourth, patriotic and socialist ideological education should be strengthened to instruct the people about how the United States interferes in China by imposing economic sanctions and embargoes, and it should encourage the people to dedicate themselves to the motherland's four modernizations. Fifth, it was necessary to expose and attack the domestic "bourgeois liberalization" elements, which conspired with hostile forces to subvert and destabilize the social system through "peaceful evolution."[100]

Jiang Zemin reportedly approved the issuance of this document on the eve of Baker's visit.[101] It represented a compromise of the positions taken by Deng and Chen, although it still included an ideological campaign. Chen was challenging Deng directly for control of economic and foreign policy, in which, previously, Deng had been preeminent.

In the debate surrounding Baker's visit, the participants divided into two camps. On the one hand, Deng argued that Baker should not be allowed to go home empty-handed. He called for the concessions that China could make; however, on issues involving sovereignty and internal affairs, he stated that China would simply listen and clarify its stand. Above all, Deng wanted a successful conclusion to the talks as part of his efforts to take the initiative in foreign policy. In light of the collapse of the Soviet Union and the resulting demise of his "Middle Kingdom" strategy, he did not consider it politically astute to openly challenge the remaining superpower, one that was fresh from its overwhelming economic victory over communism, as well as its victory in the Middle East.

Chen Yun, on the other hand, argued that to give in to America would only result in a never-ending stream of Chinese concessions. At the 11 November meeting Bo Yibo, a CAC member arguing Chen's position, demanded that China make no concessions for the sake of MFN and better bank loans. He argued that the U.S., following the drastic changes in the Soviet Union, had now focused its efforts on China in an attempt to throttle the socialist cause. China, therefore, had to expose this tactic to the world and struggle against it. On 12 November, Chen Yun reiterated his warning: "if we make too many concessions, we will end up being led by others. The Soviet Union is a good example."[102]

However, it was on 13 November that the issue was resolved, when Deng gave his instructions to Yang and Li Peng. "We should be a little more flexible in pursuing the U.S. policy. We must stick to and show our general principles. Questions affecting the interests of both sides, such as the unfavorable balance of trade and intellectual property rights, should be solved according to international practice. We should clarify and demonstrate our position on the question of arms exports and nuclear proliferation, and on the human rights question, we should give our explanation. If no progress is made at one meeting, we can continue discussion at another. We must not oppose them or avoid the questions. We must be pragmatic." Deng monitored the talks with Baker, reportedly calling Jiang and Yang on 16 and 17 November and ordering them to show progress and to warn the foreign minister to be very careful in stating China's criteria, that is, do not upset the Americans with talk of "peaceful evolution."[103]

Deng had only been able to win a partial victory in this round. He had had sufficient clout to convince the seniors to avoid a break with the U.S. over trade issues and to force through the agreement on nonproliferation.[104] However, he was unable to change the text of the compromise document that pressed for continued confrontation over "peaceful evolution," and his call for less use of the charge against the U.S. was ineffective since he did not control the Party Propaganda Department. Deng had again lost on a major issue that could sabotage his economic reforms.

Once the issue of Baker's visit had been resolved, attention turned to the problem of "peaceful evolution." Once again, the participants were divided. As already noted, Chen Yun was extremely concerned about its impact. He declared that "peaceful evolution" waged by the West had already manifested itself in some parts of China. As a result, the party had lost prestige and the people's support. Only the state machine was capable of operation. Foreign ideologies, ideas, and cultures had occupied the Chinese marketplace. Chen used studies to prove that "peaceful evolution" had entered Zhejiang, Guangdong, Fujian, and Hainan provinces. He furthered argued that Western ideologies were spreading to the interior, and if the trend was not reversed, there would be more local rebellions similar to the one of June 1989.

Deng's spokesman—Yang Shangkun this time rather than Jiang, who apparently lacked the stature to antagonize Chen Yun—laid out the arguments for ignoring "peaceful evolution" and concentrating on reform and opening. According to him, if capitalist ideas had found markets in some special economic zones, it was only the result of the party's closed-door policy, and if the people had lost confidence in socialism, it would only be regained when the government improved the livelihood of the people. Yang also refuted Chen's statistics about the pervasiveness of capitalism in the special economic zones. He reiterated Deng's contention that if the party leadership were dedicated to socialist principles, it did not matter whether "peaceful evolution" was infiltrating certain areas, because the party would remain in charge.[105] No clear winner emerged in this debate; resolution had to await the Plenum.

The meeting then turned to the issue of cadre selection for the Fourteenth Party Congress. Deng laid out the criteria for selection of new members: they had to have strong party spirit; they had to resolutely support and implement the basic spirit of the Third Plenary session of the Eleventh CCP Central Committee; and they had to have made outstanding contributions since the Fourth Plenary Session of the Thirteenth CCP Central Committee. Those not qualified, according to Deng, were those who were negative and skeptical about the line and policies formulated since the Third Plenary Session of the Eleventh CCP and about reform and opening up, regardless of how strong ("red") their party spirit may be.

In this debate, however, it was clear that Deng had failed to counter the growing political weight of the old guard on the CAC. It was becoming apparent that Chen and the "leftists" were using the CAC to challenge Deng for leadership of the party and control of the selection process for the Fourteenth Congress. In CAC meetings held on 12 and 13 November, outside the venue of the meeting of the ten elders, Chen laid out his own

political agenda. First, the Eighth Plenary Session had to discuss and analyze the problem of direction in reform and opening up. Second, it had to
analyze experiences in the special economic zones—Hainan, Shenzhen,
Zhuhai, Xiamen, and Shantou—and correct the guiding direction and
strengthen party leadership. (To that end, he had dispatched Li Peng to
the SEZ to conduct an inspection campaign, and as Yao Yilin had in Shanghai, Li gathered ammunition to refute Yang's efforts to continue Deng's
reform program.) Third, additions to the leadership group had to be made
according to merit and character. Therefore, it would be necessary to carry
out thorough examinations and to extensively solicit opinions. (Li Peng was
going to use the socialist education campaign to force out party members
supportive of Deng; several senior leaders loyal to Chen had conducted
inspection tours throughout the provinces and "picked" likely successors
to the current incumbents.) Fourth, it was necessary to formulate measures
to deal with U.S. moves to use Western ideologies and values to change the
country's socialist system.

Thus, Chen Yun had thrown down the gauntlet; there would be no
compromise on the issues. All Deng's efforts at friendly persuasion had
come to nothing; he was totally ignored by the party elders. This was confirmed a few days later when, on 20 November, Deng Liqun stated at a
Central Propaganda Department forum "nothing is more important than
combating bourgeois liberalization; and struggle against the trend of bourgeois thought cannot cease at any moment. I have made up my mind to
carry on the struggle to the end. Liberalization now unremittingly emerges
in the party, newspapers, journals and even enjoys the support of leading
comrades inside the party and this is very dangerous."[106] Chen Yun was
apparently willing to associate himself with the radical views of Deng
Liqun, and in the process risk another mass campaign on the scale of the
Cultural Revolution.

Thus, we can see that Deng was slow to react, apparently unconcerned
at the pace of events in early 1991. It was not until the failed coup in
Moscow in August and the subsequent reaction of the conservatives that
Deng was spurred to act. And then he discovered that he was not only
ignored, but also politically limited in his choice of responses.

◆ ◆ ◆

Deng Is Ignored at the
Eighth Plenum

To understand the nadir of Deng's political life, one must examine the events surrounding the Eighth Plenum in the fall of 1991. If it was not enough humiliation to be ignored by the party elders on issues of international importance, the fact that the Plenum instituted policies that were clearly aimed at reversing the de-collectivization of agriculture and launching a new socialist education campaign in the countryside could only be interpreted as the total negation of Deng's personal and institutional authority. On the heels of the collapse of the Soviet Union and the end of his triangular foreign policy, the failure of the Plenum to adopt the only plan that could save China, that is, rapid growth, led Deng to the conclusion that he, like Mao years earlier in 1959, was being ignored and that he must act. He had to find a way to rally party support and challenge Chen Yun.

At the late September Work Conference on "The Current Economic Situation and the Issue of Further Improving State-Owned Large and Medium-Sized Enterprises," Li Peng confidently challenged Deng's entire reform program.[107] He had even made a trip to Shenzhen, one of the first SEZ, to make his point that while he would not abolish the SEZ, he would seriously rein in their freewheeling capitalism. Speaking for the Politburo, Li announced his program to give priority access to funds to the state enterprises. This would starve the local enterprises of cash and force many to close. He also announced that the target of 6 percent growth in the GDP would be slightly exceeded. After presenting a favorable picture of the economy following the Seventh Plenum, Li announced plans for 1992: the overall growth rate would not be too high, while industry grew at a slower rate and agriculture at a faster rate; reasonable credit practices would be enforced, limiting currency growth and credit; commodity prices would remain stable; the industrial structure would be readjusted; investment would be made in infrastructure; wages would be readjusted; the deficit would be reduced; and reform continued.[108]

He turned next to his solution to the problems of large and medium-sized state enterprises. His major recommendations included increased investment in technological transformation; reduced mandatory planning; increased depreciation write-off rates; increased set-aside funds for developing new products; lowered interest rates; continued guarantees of necessary funds and resources; reduced income tax rates; increased party participation in management; and greater efforts to move the enterprises towards market regulation.[109]

While Li was upbeat about general economic conditions, he had obviously made the southern governors angry with his attention to state enterprises. Since the tightening up after Tiananmen in 1989, such emphasis had been at the expense of the freewheeling southern provinces, which were plugged into the world economy with their emphasis on exports. Once again Li's economic plan, while sounding reasonable, would mean limits on the double-digit growth rates for the non-state sectors of the economy.

During Li's visit to Shenzhen in early October he had both praised the SEZ, in deference to Deng Xiaoping's authority, and warned them that all growth had to be incorporated into the state plan. Li publicly supported reform and opening to the outside world as "totally correct and very successful. . . . Shenzhen, as a showplace, demonstrated the superiority of socialism to the outside world."[110] However, he urged them to move beyond tourism and processing into high-technology areas. He further advocated developing the tertiary industries of finance and services, including stock markets, information, trade, and finance. However, he noted that such development could not happen overnight, implying that Shenzhen was moving too fast for Beijing. Further, he placed Shenzhen's activity within a framework: all investment, including foreign participation, had to be in accord with the national industrial policy, and greater vigilance had to be exercised over foreign-funded enterprises to avoid tax evasion and speculation.[111] He also proclaimed that there should be greater state control of the SEZ budgets so that they were in line with national investment plans, and that institutional consumption should be controlled while eliminating waste and corruption.[112] Seen in this light, the Work Conference, coupled with the results of the Eighth Plenum, significantly undermined Deng's reform and opening up. It was, in fact, an attempt to recentralize controls, contrary to efforts under way since 1978.

The most revealing document to come out of the Eighth Plenum was the "CCP Central Committee Decision Concerning the Several Issues of

Improving Agriculture and Rural Work." This document reviewed the progress in agriculture, beginning in 1978 with Deng's rural reforms, and laid out a course for the 1990s. It was a finely-crafted document that, on the one hand, sang the praises of the individual household responsibility system, while on the other stressed the need to reemphasize the collective economy. It also pointed to the necessity for conducting an in-depth social-ist ideological education campaign that stressed patriotism, collectivism, and socialism to achieve its goals. This movement aimed to resolve problems in the rural areas and cause the peasants to work harder to create a new generation of ethical, educated, and disciplined citizens.[113] The document addressed ten issues: (1) The achievements of agriculture and the work in the rural areas in the 1980s and the main tasks for the 1990s; (2) stabilizing and improving the party's basic policies for the rural areas and continuing to deepen the rural reforms; (3) continuing to readjust the rural production structure to promote all-round growth of the rural economy; (4) stepping up the implementation of the development strategy of advancing agricul-ture through the application of science and technology and promotion of education; (5) speeding up the comprehensive control of large rivers and lakes and carrying on extensive construction of farmland irrigation facili-ties; (6) increasing agricultural investment by a big margin and speeding up the development of the industries serving agriculture; (7) doing a good job of helping the poor areas and coordinating regional development for common prosperity; (8) making earnest efforts to strengthen the building of grass roots organizations in the rural areas; (9) continuing to carry on the education in socialist ideology to promote healthy social ethics, democ-racy, and the legal system in the rural areas; and (10) enhancing the party's leadership over the rural work.[114]

A communiqué issued by the Plenum reiterated Deng's point that while rural reforms had enabled the majority of the people to have sufficient food and clothing, the challenge was to improve the backward conditions of agricultural production. For without any improvement in the lives of the majority of the Chinese—the peasants—there could be no stability and all-around progress. The needs of agriculture had been set out in the Eighth Five-Year Plan and the Ten-Year Plan, but it could not be slighted during the strategic plan of the 1990s to reform the state industries. While reconfirming the party's commitment to the household responsibility

system, the hallmark of Deng's rural reforms, the way was paved for rein-
troduction of cooperatives in some form. The communiqué stressed that
while the responsibility system had worked, it had to be improved. In
some instances it did not help resolve certain rural problems, and thus the
"strength of the collective economy (must be) gradually expanded, in an
effort to guide the peasants onto the road of common prosperity."[115] The
state would also provide more investment in major agricultural structures,
such as lakes and river control. This was, of course, a subtle way for Li
Peng to mobilize support for his grandiose plans to dam up the Yangtze
River and collect taxes from the provinces that were holding back.

While Deng did not disagree with the necessity to continue rural reforms, he differed with the priority of placing all the emphasis on the rural
front at the expense of the industrial sector. Because of the continuing differences between Deng and Li, the Plenum failed to resolve the industrial
issues. Instead, the press noted that the two issues were related and hinted
that decisions made at the central committee meeting on industry in September, immediately following the events in the Soviet Union, would be
policy. The Plenum also endorsed Li Peng's decision to go forward with a
socialist education campaign in the rural areas. It was deemed necessary, as
part of the improvement in agriculture, to "make real efforts to promote
the building of socialist spiritual civilization which was linked to improvement in the material civilization."[116]

By the end of the Plenum on 29 November 1991, it was apparent that
Deng had been frozen out of the policy debate. He had been ignored on
industrial policy, as the party voted to continue on the path set at the
Seventh Plenum in the fall of 1990; he was ignored on agricultural policy,
as the Plenum voted to conduct a socialist education campaign to regain
control at the expense of local government; and he was ignored as the
party endorsed a plan that would make loyalty to Li Peng's retrenchment of reform and opening and countering "peaceful evolution" the
litmus test for local party members and delegates to the upcoming Fourteenth Party Congress. For Deng, the failure of the Soviet coup in August
had altered the geopolitical landscape forever, but he could not mobilize
the party. They saw the coup as a warning to reassert control; Deng saw it
as an opportunity to go all out for rapid growth. There was no apparent
compromise.

The Eighth Plenum had also decided that the Fourteenth Congress would be held in the fall of 1992. Thus, the party had to begin organizational work if the congress was to be held on time. As part of the preparations for the congress Lu Feng, director of the Organization Department of the Central Committee, called a national meeting of all provincial and municipal organization department directors. He outlined their task for the year leading up to the congress: "We should focus the organization work for the next year on making thorough organizational preparations for the 14th National Party Congress and, bearing in mind the central task of economic construction, administer the party strictly and energetically intensify the construction of leading bodies at all levels, grass-roots party organizations, and the rank-and-file party members and cadres."[117] Lu also reported that since the beginning of the year, the Organization Department had been relentlessly implementing the basic task of building up the party organizations. Touching on the real issues, control of the agenda for the Fourteenth Congress and control of delegate selection, Lu tried to prepare his directors for opposition from the entrenched reformers in the provincial structures: "We will be facing an enormous task of evaluating cadres and reshuffling leading bodies next year. We must comply with the following principles: It is necessary to promote people with both ability and political integrity, with the emphasis on the latter; attach importance to cadres' practical training and performance at critical moments; pay attention to set up rationally structured leading bodies; replenish and re-shuffle members of leading bodies in conjunction with the exchange and on-the-job rotational training of cadres; and select and promote competent people to fill the principal posts of leading bodies."[118] Lu went on to instruct the attendees on how the campaign would be run. In order to carry out a rebuilding of the party successfully, part of the evaluation and reshuffling process would be done on the basis of ideology, which meant support of socialist ideology at the expense of "peaceful evolution" and bourgeois influence.

Lu addressed the issue of cadre training in general, and noted that they would continue to send recent graduates to the countryside to receive training at the grass roots. Their training, as well as the ideological training of all cadre, according to Lu, had to respond to the three major challenges facing the party: governing the country; engaging in reform and opening to the outside world and developing a commodity economy; and opposing peaceful evolution. The Organization Department's task was to strengthen the party's faith in socialism and communism, so as to build a great wall of steel against peaceful evolution and provide a reliable guarantee for implementing the party's basic line. The ongoing socialist education campaign in the rural areas was a means to achieve this end. He urged his group to pay close attention to grass roots party building.

The significance of Lu's instructions was that they were contrary to Deng's instructions to put reform and opening at the top of the agenda. Those same instructions also included a discussion of the criteria for cadre selection, as well as delegate selection to the Fourteenth Congress. Lu Feng would make support of the "anti-peaceful evolution" campaign, support of the crackdown of 4 June 1989, and support of Li Peng's economic retrenchment the basis for selection. Clearly, Deng Xiaoping was being challenged for control of the congress, the last one he could hope to influence.

During this period the "leftists," under the direction of Wang Renzhi with the assistance of He Jingzhi, Gao Di, and Li Ximeng, undertook to effectively neutralize Li Ruihuan, Deng's man in charge of propaganda. At several propaganda conferences in October and November, Li Ruihuan was invited to speak as an authority on Marxism-Leninism, along with academic experts such as Hu Qiaomu, Zhu Muzhi and He Jingzhi. The point was to belittle Li's credentials, since he was just a carpenter, and to question his qualifications to guide the party's ideological campaigns. As He Jingzhi said at one such conference in November on "The Situation in the Summer of 1957," "Marxism-Leninism is a science. If one lacks the most basic knowledge of the science, how can one give guidance? What knowledge and capability does this person have to lead others? And how can he do a good job in the professional realm?"[119]

They gathered the signatures of several senior members of the Central Advisory Commission, as well as senior party and government officials including Chen Yun and Yao Yilin, on a petition requesting that the party strengthen control over propaganda, ideology, culture, and education. This petition specifically stated that "Comrade Li Ruihuan has lost the initiative and leadership expected of him, which explains why the correct ideological guidance has so far not gained the status of main currents in cultural and artistic fields and the comeback of non-Marxist intellectual thinking and bourgeois liberalization in a variety of forms."[120] Jiang, however, dismissed the petition and told its authors to respect Li, as he had the confidence of the Central Committee and State Council.

The conservatives and "leftists" then tried another approach. The major players, which included Wang Zhen, Song Renqiong, Chen Yun, Yao Yilin, Deng Liqun, Li Ximing, and Wang Renzhi, tried to approach the Central Committee directly. They drafted an "Emergency Report to the CCP Central Committee" in which they proposed calling a special work conference of the Central Committee to discuss the direction of China's revolution. The report set out their areas of concern: (1) The CCP should carry the banner of Marxism and struggle for the eventual realization of communism for mankind; (2) There is an anti-Marxist-Leninist ideological trend and force in the CCP, and the struggle between two roads is going on; and (3) Should China follow the socialist road or the reformist road, which is actually the road of capitalism? The group planned to have Wang Zhen approach Deng Xiaoping with the idea for the conference, backed up by the signatures of senior party members and veteran soldiers, and to have Li Ximing bring it up at a Politburo meeting. The whole affair backfired, though, when word of it leaked prematurely. Qiao Shi, along with Song Ping, Wen Jiabao, and Bo Yibo, confronted Wang Zhen with the details and ended his plot. Song Ping, apparently exercising discretion in light of Qiao Shi's role in denouncing the conspiracy, criticized Li Ximing. Bo Yibo perhaps felt that even Chen Yun and the advisors from the CAC had gone too far. Deng had been out of the capital on a trip to Shanghai, and when briefed on the affair, remarked that "General Wang loves to fight in the vanguard. But now no war has broken out, so what is there to fight?"[121] Thus, the "leftists" failed in their attempt to force Li Ruihuan off the Politburo Standing Committee. But their call for a cultural campaign, a Cultural Revolution to oust the reformers, was clearly discussed.

While in Shanghai in December, Deng had met with Mayor Huang Ju, party boss Wu Bangguo, and Li Xiannian to discuss the need to boost reform. That Li Xiannian was meeting with Deng and ignoring Chen Yun, who was in town at the same time, apparently to offer Shanghai's leaders more capital investment for their state enterprises in exchange for support of his conservative agenda, could be seen as an indication that some of the elders on the CAC were beginning to accept Deng's argument that reform needed to be speeded up in light of the changing world situation.[122]

The plan by Wang Zhen and others, including Chen Yun's signature on the petition, made it clear that Deng had only two bases of real support to rely upon: the PLA and the provincial leadership. He had helped most provincial leaders get their jobs, and his reform and opening policies had made them wealthy. Deng had been the architect of the PLA's modernization since his return in 1977, and while the army was last on the modernization priority list, Deng nevertheless treated it as his favorite toy, ensuring it a steady flow of funds from the treasury and by permitting it to sell its hardware overseas. He also maintained tight control of the PLA by placing it under the direct command of his longtime ally, Yang Shangkun.

3 | Striking Back

◇ Mobilizing the PLA

Deng had placed his faith in his ability to persuade the party elders of the wisdom of his policies, and he had failed. The only course of action left was direct action, or allow his efforts since 1978 to be submerged in a new political movement—a move inward, away from opening to the world. Deng had only two groups to approach for support: the PLA and the regional officials. He chose the PLA.

Deng moved against the party to regain political control as a result of the collapse and disintegration of the Soviet Union and the drastic response of the Chinese Communist Party to the situation. The agreement on 8 December to disband the Soviet Union was clearly foremost in Deng's mind when he called together the leaders of the PLA. As would become apparent throughout the following year, Deng and his supporters saw events in the USSR as an opportunity. The breakup of the Soviet Union eased military tensions to the north and permitted all-out concentration on economic development. It was during the one hundred days between the failed Soviet coup on 19

August and the disbanding of the Soviet Union on 8 December that Deng
devised and drafted his plan and mobilized his supporters to seize the
initiative and launch China on what he perceived to be an all-or-nothing
struggle. China would either achieve its economic goal or fail; failure would
forever seal China's fate as a third-rate nation, subject to bullying by foreign
imperialists.

Immediately following the Eighth Plenum, as Lu Feng was working
with the "leftists" to oust Li Ruihuan and get the jump on Deng's restructuring efforts, Deng was implementing his plan for seizing the initiative
from Chen and Li. He called an expanded meeting of the CMC during
the first week of December, with all the regional commanders and their
deputies, the senior commanders of the General Staff and the service
arms, and some Central Committee members in attendance. Most likely
Qiao Shi was there too, since he was part of the agreement that emerged.

While we do not know the exact agenda, we can speculate based on
subsequent events and press reports.[1] Post-Tiananmen personnel shuffles
among regional and General Staff Department (GSD) organizations were
discussed, as was the necessity of maintaining discipline within the PLA.
An education campaign to combat peaceful evolution among the rank and
file soldiers was not deemed necessary, as that was considered to be an issue
of concern only at the command level. Jiang Zemin and Yang Shangkun
did, however, affirm that it was necessary to ensure party control over the
military. To that end, commanders were to be on guard to prevent the
appearance of multiparty systems, political pluralism, or organizations like
Solidarity (the Polish labor party).[2]

Also discussed was the need for advanced technology and an expanded
military budget, particularly in light of the Gulf War. Indeed, the PLA,
which was the last priority under the Four Modernizations, had been slow
to modernize. It had even turned to selling its own weapons on the international market to pay for new technology.[3] Yang Shangkun was reported
to have said that it was necessary "to make money. . . . One can speak
louder only when one has wealth. In the final analysis, money represents
strength. Without economic strength, one will just be in a position of
being attacked."[4] It was agreed by the participants of the meeting that the
answer to the problem lay in an expanding economy. It was, therefore,
decided that the PLA would undertake to promote Deng's reform and
opening. They would go so far as to use their influence to persuade local

party leaders throughout China to support him, to the extent that they would ignore directives from Li Peng's State Council that were contradictory. The PLA was also prepared to guarantee party and state unity in exchange for an increased share of the budget pie. The difficulty with this, however, was that the central government could not afford to support increased spending on the PLA, much less modernization. The problem was that the provincial leaders had been reluctant to remit excess revenues to the central government, since they felt that they could invest it more wisely than Beijing, which in their view wasted funds on the inefficient state enterprises. Thus, the center was chronically short of funds for capital investment. Deng's solution was a compromise that would guarantee provincial leaders a role in central economic decision-making, in exchange for a negotiated rate of return to the national government.

The PLA would ensure that both sides abided by the agreement, in conjunction with internal security—represented by Qiao Shi—which in turn would police the PLA. For the party, the impetus to accept the compromise was the fear that the wealthy southern provinces might secede to form another "little dragon," thereby alleviating themselves of the burden of carrying the less well-off interior provinces. Thus, the PLA pledge to ensure the cohesion of the state was bound to be approved by the party elders. With the guarantee from the wealthy provinces that taxes or excess profits would be remitted to the national treasury, the center could continue to control a major portion of the national economy, although under the direction of provincial-trained economic reformers like Zhu Rongji.

In this way, Deng used the PLA and, later, the regional leaders and the elders to seize control of economic policy from Li and Chen. The PLA, however, was the key to success. Therefore, the military modernization process had to be continued, perhaps even accelerated. This entailed a major restructuring of the organization and staffing of the PLA, such as replacement of senior commanders, reduction and elimination of military regions that corresponded to regional economic units, and an institutionalization of a vertical chain of command from the CMC to the soldier in the field. The vertical integration was also applied to the PLA industrial sector as well. All of this was approved at the secret meeting in December and finalized later in Zhuhai in January, when Deng reconvened the CMC with Qiao Shi, Zhu Rongji, Bo Yibo, and the regional party leaders in attendance.

Immediately following the December CMC meeting, senior military officers, including Chief of the General Staff Chi Haotian, went from region to region to brief local commanders on the agreement so that there would be no misunderstanding. In mid-December, in Wuhan, Chi announced the results of the CMC meeting and discussed the changing world situation, especially in light of the Gulf War and the Soviet coup. He was quoted as saying that "the people of the whole country presently have full faith in the CCP Central Committee with Comrade Jiang Zemin at the core, and pin earnest hope on our socialist country. We must try to manage domestic affairs and the army well despite any changes abroad. We must build a quality Army in accordance with our purpose of serving the people heart and soul, to maintain the Army's unity and the country's prosperity and stability."[5]

He also highlighted the parts of the agreement hammered out at the CMC meeting: unity of the army, party, and nation (no regionalism, federalism, multipartyism, mountaintopism); strong army (increased budget financed by provincial remissions, restructuring and consolidating industries for efficiency); prosperous society (reform and opening to the world, not 6 percent growth); and stability (PLA and People's Armed Police [PAP] would ensure that local outbursts did not get out of hand). Chi also called for modernization of the PLA so that it would be ready for war at any time.[6] *Liberation Army Daily* also quoted Chi as demanding that his men have both "combat spirit" and modern arms and equipment. He said that to be ready for war, the army needed to improve its quality during 1992— that is, it had to have "a perfect mastery of high-level military training, including scientific training, to be ready to face any kind of situation." Finally, he called on the army to remain loyal to the ideological principles of the Communist Party.[7]

Deng Xiaoping, in turn, expressed his full support of the PLA through the *Liberation Army Daily*. Deng called for maintaining powerful armed and police forces in the face of the continued presence of imperialism. "It is inconceivable for the standing army, public security organs, courts and prisons to wither away under a condition in which classes and imperialism and hegemonism exist."[8] To accomplish this, "we must build a powerful, revolutionary army that is modernized and standardized."[9]

Deng also undertook a provincial tour to spread the word and drum up support. At Tianjin, a city receptive to Deng's message, he called for an alliance of all working people and patriots with socialism as the political foundation, an attempt to appeal to the people over the heads of the party leadership.[10] In Tanggu, in the company of Navy Commander Zhang Liaozhong, he inspected naval vessels, including missile destroyers and nuclear submarines. He was quoted as saying: "Our country is so big and our coastline is so long. Hegemonism still exists and the motherland has not been reunified. We must spend some money on building some advanced and sophisticated warships. Otherwise, we may be bullied and cannot be tough enough."[11]

Deng next ventured into the heart of the mammoth but inefficient state enterprises: Shenyang. There, on 24 December, accompanied by Bo Yibo and Li Desheng, Deng challenged Chen Yun's position that the state had to control the means of production. Deng stated that in order to fully develop the foundation industries—the heavy industries and chemical industries in northeast China—it was necessary to open fully to the outside world. This meant allowing foreign capital, technology, and management in. Deng told the managers not to worry about being criticized as capitalists. "Modernization will not happen to us naturally"—that is, it was permissible to copy the industrialization of the West.[12] While in Shenyang and later Dalian, Deng also praised South Korea's economic development experience.[13] He told the people to go ahead and copy the Korean example—throwing the issue in Chen Yun's face.

Deng next showed up in Jinan on 2 January 1992, accompanied by CMC members Liu Huaqing and Qin Jiwei, a sign that the military was supportive of his program and had openly sided with Deng against the legitimate party leadership in Beijing. It also made clear that Deng was in charge of the PLA. Deng next went to Shanghai on 15 January. On this visit he was accompanied by party chief Jiang Zemin, Bo Yibo, and another faithful military elder, Yu Qiuli.

As mentioned earlier, Deng visited the military and political leaders in northeast and central China prior to going to Shanghai in early January to give them the details of his December deal with the PLA. As part of that effort, he simultaneously dispatched his lieutenants to various other military commands to relay the message. Thus, Jiang Zemin showed up in Nanjing. He was already using the line Deng had formulated in Beijing. Jiang reviewed the world situation for his subordinates in the military region, stressing the point that the Army was subordinate to the party. He discussed the current party line of one center and two basic points as being the main focus of effort. He then went on to voice the new understanding between party and Army. He pointed out that "economic construction is the center; only by raising economic construction will it be possible for defense building to have a solid material base. In the final analysis, the relation between economic construction and defense building is one of dialectical unity."[14]

Yang Shangkun was dispatched to Xinjiang along with Liu Huaqing, CMC vice-chairman; Qin Jiwei, defense minister; Xu Xin, deputy chief of the General Staff; and Wang Chengbin, commander of the Beijing Military Region.[15] Officially, they were there to observe firsthand the effects of Russian disintegration on China's minorities in the border areas. Following their visit to the Lanzhou Military Region, which lasted seventeen days, Yang and the senior PLA and CMC officers next toured the Beijing Military Region, discussing with its various commanders and troops the world situation in general and Russian and Taiwanese affairs in particular.[16] However, as reports indicated that Deng's other lieutenants were traveling around the country briefing officials about the agreement that had been reached at the December CMC meeting, it is probable that Yang too discussed these matters with the regional commanders of Lanzhou and Beijing. Thus, Yang, Deng, and Jiang had visited all the military regions—Shenyang, Jinan, Lanzhou, Chengdu, and Nanjing—before ending up in Guangzhou for the enlarged CMC meeting in January 1992.[17]

Deng's support for an expanded presence and greater voice for the PLA was further reflected as part of an analysis of the world by the Army paper *Liberation Army Daily*, which refuted the theory put forward by the West that the importance of a strong army was decreasing as military conflict gave way to economic and diplomatic competition. The article noted that, while diplomatic struggle was an option, without a strong military nothing could be gained. The analysis concluded that if China wanted to protect its independence, sovereignty, and security, not only did it need an army, but also the army's scale and quality must conform to international standards and the demands of the state's interests and rights. To reinforce this analysis, Jiang Zemin was quoted as saying: "The building of socialist modernization requires a stable environment, so it is necessary to maintain a powerful army and consolidate national defense."[18] Deng had obviously agreed to an expanded role for the PLA in society.

At the same time as Deng and Chi were extolling the necessity of a strong and powerful army, *Liberation Army Daily* printed a review and justification of how the PLA had become involved in economic activities. According to the article, the PLA had experienced a funding shortage since the early 1980s. From 1950 to 1980, the state's budget for defense had averaged 17.2 percent annually. However, by the early 1980s, it had dropped to 12 percent, and after 1985 it had been further reduced, resulting in a serious, negative impact on the building and development of the Army.[19] The article compared per capita spending rates between China, Japan, and the United States, noting that while China had an army that accounted for 11 percent of all servicemen in the world, its spending accounted for only 0.6 percent of the world's total. China's spending compared with the United States was 1:58; with Japan it was 1:58.9.

The article concluded that, because China was in the initial stage of socialism, the army could not rely on the state for all its needs. Therefore, the army had undertaken various enterprises designed to provide better living standards for its troops by employing spouses and funding of projects beneficial to their priorities. Clearly, the Army could not give up these activities; however, it could eliminate waste. To that end, the Director of the General Staff Logistics Department and a member of the CMC, Zhao Nanqi, was quoted as saying that the CMC had concluded that all army enterprises would be brought under unified management.[20] Thus, the PLA was becoming a vertically integrated economic ministry. Deng had decided to create a state within a state, a powerful military complex allied with key central ministries that could well afford to support his comeback. In the future, Chinese rulers could rely on this sector to maintain production and order in the event of local outbreaks or disturbances. It was clearly a good deal from Deng's and the elders' point of view.

While Gao Di and the "leftists" were publicizing the ideological campaign of socialist education under way within the PLA, *Liberation Army Daily* ran an article in November on reform and opening that tied the fate of the army to the fate of the SEZ—clearly a declaration of the watershed agreement that had been reached at the CMC meeting on 3 December.[21] The PLA mouthpiece made the case for Deng's assault on Party "leftists": "Reform and opening up represent the road to building a powerful and wealthy country and give a strong impetus to Army building. This has been fully proved by practice in the past 10 years and more. Our troops stationed in the special economic zones and the open areas have experienced deeper feelings about this and have more and more clearly realized the correctness of the party's reform and opening-up policy."[22] The report—the obvious result of discussions about the need to mobilize the PLA to secure Deng's policies—was published on the eve of the historic CMC meeting in December, and clearly demonstrated the strength of his ties to the military and the support of the Yangs.

As it laid out the path the PLA would take to ensure Deng's reform and opening, the article merits a closer review. It was broken into five major headings: (1) Rapid Economic Development in Open Areas Fully Displays Superiority of Socialist System; Correctness of Party's Line, Principles, and Policies; Also Provides Rich Teaching Materials for Socialist Education for Troops; (2) People's New Mentality, Ethos in SEZ, Open Areas Have Inspired Troops, Added New Dynamism to Army Building, Reform; (3) High Intensity of Educated Personnel, Advanced Technology in SEZ, Open Areas Help Troops Study Scientific, General Knowledge, Mastering Both Military, Civilian Skill; (4) Vigorous Development of Commodity Economy in SEZ, Open Areas Have Provided Favorable Conditions for Troops to Develop Their Own Production, Arranging Job Placement for Officers' Spouses, Children; and (5) Two-Civilization Construction in SEZ, Open Areas Have Promoted In-Depth Development of "Double Support," "Joint Construction," Promoting Army-Government, Army-People Unity.

Under the first broad topic of rapid economic development in the SEZ and Open Areas, it was noted that, over the preceding ten years, officers and cadre from the military regions had investigated cases of economic development. The statistics for economic growth for Guangdong province between 1978 and 1990 showed that overall growth for the period multiplied 4.16 times, for an average annual growth rate of 14.6 percent. This was, according to the article, greater than that of the Western developed nations and greater than that of Singapore, Taiwan, Hong Kong, and South Korea during their economic takeoff periods. The article proudly noted that the province was referred to as the "fifth little dragon" in the Asia-Pacific area. Overall, consumption levels had increased by 140 percent, as compared with pre-reform and opening. Such facts, it concluded, proved the superiority of the socialist system, but they also demonstrated that reform and opening were the keys to building China into a powerful and wealthy nation.

Section Two was an attempt to equate capitalism's ethics with those of the PLA's hero, Lei Feng.[23] In this case, Lei was seen as the ideologically pure and ideal soldier and hero. He was the personification of the worker in the SEZ or Open Area, who respected knowledge and education and had acquired a sense of reform, competition, efficiency, and information—an individual who paid close attention to time, science, speed, and efficiency. "Time is money and efficiency is life" was his motto. The article praised the original pioneering spirit of the SEZ and Open Area residents, who had had to struggle when the areas were first allowed to implement the reform and opening policy. Shortages of labor, funds, material, and ideas had not deterred them. It encouraged the soldiers to learn from the SEZ and Open Areas that a military unit needs a high degree of centralization and unity and a strong sense of time, accuracy and efficiency, and a realistic attitude. With such an example, PLA units were to cultivate a new work style characterized by telling the truth, reporting to superiors the facts, doing solid work, and striving for solid results. Habits of telling lies, covering up problems, indulging in window-dressing, and making false reports were to be checked. The subtle message was that capitalism had its applications in a socialist army.

Section Three was a bow to the technical expert at the expense of the "red" expert. People in the SEZ and Open Areas, according to the report, realized that science and technology constituted the primary factor in productive forces. The people of these areas respected knowledge and people with talent and ability. This had led to a great flowering of educational institutions and a major increase in the numbers of educated people in the province, which included PLA members. Most cadres, according to the report, after spending time in Guangdong, had completed their primary education, and many discharged military persons, who had received advanced education, were able to obtain posts in civilian enterprises. As a result of the stress on education and knowledge, scientific and technical education was highly prized.

Section Four was a description of the successful venture into the local commodity production system by local PLA units. Starved for funds to increase troop pay, improve living accommodations, and provide cultural benefits while maintaining war readiness, the PLA had imitated the civilian sector and developed productive enterprises of its own. Such enterprises provided jobs for the spouses of military personnel and provided funds for local improvement in housing, all of which served to improve morale. Additionally, the profits from PLA enterprises went back to the center in the form of taxes. Thus, while the state could not spare funds for the army, the PLA could supplement the state.

Finally, the fifth section spelled out the political line that the PLA had agreed to: "Reform and opening up represent the common interests of the whole party, the whole Army, and the entire people of the whole country. The troops and the people all sincerely support the party's basic line of 'one center, two basic points.'" The article continued: "Reform and opening up constitutes a solid ideological foundation for the unity between the Army and the government and between troops and civilians." Finally, the key to the "Grand Compromise": the people in the SEZ and Open Areas promised that they "would not forget national defense in the course of reform and opening up" and "would not forget the people's guardians when living peacefully and working happily." The article reported that, over the years, the provinces had provided funds to supplement the PLA budget to care for the troops and provide improvements in living standards and to care for families of martyrs,' and because of a positive attitude, they had procured an oversupply of inductees each year. Therefore, the Army had many good reasons to support the SEZ. "Officers and servicemen are all glad to see the SEZ develop and feel honored to see the wealth of the local people. The troops have been extensively carrying out the activities of 'loving the SEZ, loving the local communities where the troops are stationed, and loving the people.'" In addition, several joint enterprises financed by the PLA and the local communities had been undertaken; in addition to everything else, this had led to an effective unity between the people and the Army. Moreover, it had led to social stability. In conclusion, the article laid down the task for the PLA: "Follow the principle of laying stress on both economic development and spiritual civilization, resolutely carry out the party's basic line of 'one center, two basic points' and the principles of Army building in the new period, and keep up with the pace of reform and opening up. In that way the PLA will be able to fulfill its tasks." Clearly, the PLA was embracing Deng's policies and warning the center. They were a new voice in economic policy.

The "leftists," however, were also busy on the propaganda front. Their articles stressed the PLA's involvement in the socialist education campaign.[24] A 4 December *Xinhua* report on the history and progress of the socialist campaign in the PLA was timed to counter the effects of the decision at the CMC meeting to drop ideology and forcefully push reform and opening. Since Gao Di did not permit any reporting on the meeting in the local party papers, it was easy to continue with the line that the army was actively involved in the ideological movement. The article noted that the socialist education campaign in the PLA had begun in the fall of 1989, the result of a General Political Department (GPD) work conference to address ideological problems arising out of the Tiananmen Incident. The GPD had decided at that time to make socialist education its focus. Over the next two years, cadre from all levels were rotated through courses that included works on Marxism, Mao, and Deng. Such courses explained the differences between scientific socialism and capitalism. (This, of course, flew in the face of Deng's efforts to halt the debate over socialism and capitalism.) They also included lectures on patriotism and stressed the idea that, without the Communist Party, there would be no China. All soldiers were then instilled with the line of absolute party control over the army. Since the education campaign had begun, the GPD had published numerous articles and held conventions to further the development of faith in the socialist system. *Xinhua* concluded its report with praise for Lei Feng and the renewal of his spirit within the army. It noted that the campaign had clarified for the soldiers major issues of right and wrong; it had convinced them of the correctness of the principles of not privatizing the economy, not practicing a political multiparty system, not having pluralistic ideological guidelines, and not having a "non-party, non-political" PLA.[25] Clearly, the "leftists" were trying to line up PLA support, in spite of the fact that Yang Baibing, in charge of propaganda in the PLA, had apparently decided, along with his brother, that their future lay with Deng's policies.

It is evident that the ideologues recognized that they could not control the PLA. They had to rely on propaganda to undercut its resolve to participate in the political fray—a ploy that had little chance of success. In the end, Deng was able to mobilize the PLA by giving it a major stake in his modernization program, and in a stable and unified China.

◆ ◆ ◆

Rallying the
Regional Officials

Once Deng had mobilized the PLA, he still had a major chore to undertake: he had to convince the regional leaders that it was in their best interests to agree to a fixed rate of return to Beijing, one that would support the central government yet not starve regional efforts to help themselves. And, most importantly, he had to convince them that no province or region would be allowed to go it alone—to separate itself from China. It was in this environment that Deng undertook his historic tour of south China over the New Year's period of January 1992. He had sealed his deal with the PLA; now he had to deliver the regional rebates and secure their agreement to the new pact.

Chen Yun had traveled to Shanghai to warn industrialists that, if the city wanted central funds, it had better back the conservative plan.[26] Nevertheless, Deng had reason to expect support from the southern governors, who had gained enormous financial clout as a result of his policies. Deng was also assisted in his plan by the machinations of unwitting conservatives, who thought that Deng was no longer playing an active role in politics. The southern governors were already upset by the economic hardships caused by Li Peng's efforts to restrict bank funds and foreign trade initiatives at the local level to pay for his massive new plan to reenergize the deficit-producing central economy, as well as by his plans for a new system of taxation that would directly challenge local controls. These policies had the effect of throwing millions out of work. The southern governors and party leaders were greatly concerned about the possibility of open revolt, especially if the planned socialist education campaign went forward. Thus, Deng found it easy to mobilize southern dislike of Li Peng's policies as a force against the center.

Deng went to Shenzhen on 19 January 1992 with a mission to save the SEZ and his policies of reform and opening. At the first of the year, several members of the CAC had sent a letter to the Politburo calling for the abolishment of the SEZ.[27] Their letter accused the SEZ of promoting capitalism, being capitalist in nature, and being hotbeds of peaceful evolution. Clearly expressing the charges often made by Chen Yun, it was highly likely that he had sanctioned the effort, even though he had not signed the letter. Deng needed to make clear to the party, government, and people that there was no question as to his determination to preserve his policies. Indeed, he unequivocally stated, "Reform and opening is necessary and I would use the Army as a guarantee for it."[28]

During the previous year the party had ignored him on economic issues and prevented his message from reaching the people; this time Deng was going to have his way. Once in Shenzhen, a city not under the thumb of the "leftist" media controlled from Beijing, Deng lost no time in getting his message out. He played to the foreign reporters, tourists, and local government press, praising Shenzhen's, Zhuhai's, and Guangdong's achievements. He said that Guangdong was the leading force for the economic development of all China. It was necessary, he said, "to carry on economic construction as the leading factor; no matter how the international situation is going to change, we must stick to the principle of stability overriding everything; to keep stability, we must boost the economy; and Guangdong should set a good example in this regard."[29] Deng elaborated on his thoughts about the economic miracle under way in the SEZ: "Some people say that stock transactions are a capitalist practice. We have carried out experiments in Shanghai and Shenzhen and they proved to be successful. It seems that some capitalist practices can also be applied under the socialist system. It does not matter if mistakes are made in application. There is no 100 percent perfection in the world. In reform and opening, it is necessary to be bolder and to open on a larger scale; without carrying out reform, China will not have a bright future. Reform and opening up is China's only option. If China does not carry out reform, it will just move into a blind alley. Whoever is opposed to reform must leave office."[30] Clearly, Deng was in no mood to compromise.

Deng also stated that China should build several Hong Kongs, of which Shenzhen would be one. His idea was to turn the Pearl River delta region of southern China into the "fifth dragon" of Asia, like the economic powers of Hong Kong, Taiwan, South Korea, and Singapore. Deng's message, echoed by his ally Yang Shangkun, was that reform and opening had to be accelerated and the scope of experimentation broadened, while the areas opened had to be expanded even more.

Deng also aired the internal party debate over his SEZ. His major critic, Chen Yun, sided with the authors of the December letter to the Politburo on the issue of creeping capitalism and the need for an ideological education campaign. Deng succinctly stated his position: "There will be no campaigns which lead to instability; there will be no reversing economic policies in the face of Soviet collapse; the SEZ will be allowed to develop in their own manner; and the economy is the measure of stability."[31] Deng was quite categorical for one who had retired. He was allowing no misunderstanding of his message. He was confident with the PLA backing his play.

Deng toured many sites while he was in Guangdong, but the message was the same everywhere, and Yang Shangkun echoed Deng as he spoke up for the SEZ, stating "the Special Economic Zone should not be too conservative but should constantly seek progress in its construction."[32] Yang also made clear to the Beijing leadership that "I will support all the policies and measures that are favorable to reform, opening up, and development. Some previously favorable policies (on hold since retrenchment after Tiananmen) should be restored and more flexible policies should be adopted according to the new situation in reform and opening up. That is, the scale of opening up should be further expanded. In the course of its development, the special economic zone should continue to break new ground and should not be too conservative."[33]

Based on pledges of those two distinguished visitors, the local SEZ officials were confident that the policies on hold since 1988 would be reinstated. Yang, speaking both as President of China and head of the PLA, was quite explicit: "It is time to revive those special policies and preferential treatments shelved due to the economic retrenchment, as we have wound up the austerity program."[34] Yang clearly was signaling to Beijing that he and Deng were setting out to reverse the Plenum. To accentuate his point, he stated that, without special treatment, the SEZ would be no different than other parts of China. Without the SEZ, there were no preferential policies. Yang, as well as Deng, urged the SEZ to develop faster.[35]

Before going to Shenzhen, Deng had already completed a tour that included visits to major cities in northern, central and southern China, during which he undoubtedly lined up support for his move against Beijing's policymakers. Meanwhile, his supporters had also spread out over China to convey to local leaders the content of the December CMC meeting and Deng's plan to seize the initiative. His less-than-inspiring lieutenant, Jiang Zemin, visited Shanghai and Nanjing, accompanied by local party and

PLA officers, including those in command of the military region as well as retired PLA colleagues Yang Dezhong, Ye Qing, Liu Mingpu, Ma Zhongchen, and Hui Liangyu.[36] While ostensibly there to inspect state enterprises, he took the opportunity to tell local cadre that party policy and direction had been determined, and that it was their responsibility to carry it out. They were told to rectify their work styles and get closer to the masses. In short, he warned them that the party had to clean up its act if it was to retain the confidence of the people.

Among those who helped spread the word was Tian Jiyun, a Politburo member, vice-premier, and longtime supporter of Deng. He visited Hainan province, where he praised local efforts to develop it as a SEZ. He encouraged them to pursue the policy of opening with greater courage and faster steps. He acknowledged that reform and opening entailed risks, but he cautioned that there was no other course for China. He assured officials that the central authorities would back them in their efforts—a major statement in view of Beijing's official policies.[37] Meanwhile, Li Ruihuan, the propaganda czar, toured the Northeast, spreading the word to those provinces that Deng had missed.

Jiang eventually ended up in Shenzhen, along with Zhu Rongji, Bo Yibo, Yang Shangkun; members of the CMC, including Chief of Staff Chi Haotian; and several CAC members, including Li Desheng and Yu Taizhong. Although Deng had no formal party or government position, they came in testimony to his continued informal, personal power and his obvious support from the military. Publicly, the high-level officials and elders were there to voice support for Deng's accelerated reform and opening. Privately, they were there to help Deng force a policy change in Beijing.

Bo Yibo publicly stated that he was there because Deng had asked the elders to see the SEZ for themselves. Bo was amazed at the success of Shenzhen in transferring almost 97 percent of commodities from a planned price system to one based on market forces. He termed the price reforms a miracle and exclaimed, "We have gained experience in our successful experiments with reform in the zones in the first stage in the past decade. What we should do in the next step is to deepen these experiments and search how to expand it to the other places in the country."[38]

Qiao Shi, as head of the party's Political and Legal Commission, was simultaneously in Zhuhai and Shenzhen for a public security meeting. He endorsed Deng's reform and opening: "in 1991, cadres and police in charge of judicial and procuratorial work earnestly implemented the party's basic line and various principles and policies and made positive contributions to serving reform, opening, and the socialist modernization drive and in maintaining political and social stability."[39] He stated that the 1990s were crucial to China's development. "We must have a strong sense of mission and urgency and grasp the rare historic opportunity to carry out economic construction with high concentration and determination." Of course, none of this was possible without social stability. "Social stability is the most basic prerequisite to promote economic construction."[40] Qiao Shi represented the party internal security forces as well as the interests of the party rank and file. His patron was Peng Zhen, so it was obvious that Deng and Peng had come to an agreement that pleased the elders, which accounted for Bo Yibo's outspoken praise of Deng's SEZ. Bo was number two man on the CAC, and thus was clearly speaking for a faction that had aligned with Deng. Thus, Deng had agreement from the PLA, the regional officials, the public security forces, state security forces, and the elders—a formidable hand to take back to Beijing.

While in Guangdong, Deng also convened a meeting of what can be called an expanded CMC. Held at a local military base, Huizhou, it included all the players: Jiang Zemin, Yang Shangkun, Yang Baibing, Liu Huaqing, and Chi Haotian from the CMC, the senior commanders from PLA headquarters and the specialized arms, as well as the regional commanders from the seven military regions.[41] This meeting picked up where the December CMC meeting had ended, with the PLA telling Deng that to modernize they needed money. Deng laid out his plans and the role agreed to by the various armed forces of China, that is, to ensure stability for reform and opening in exchange for the means to modernize.

During this meeting, the participants also discussed the theory and strategy for coping with the realities of modern warfare in the aftermath of the Gulf War. First, the Army would have to produce better troops and simplify administration to cope with the new international and domestic situation. Second, military leaders would have to have a uniform level of training, with an emphasis on younger and more professionally trained officers.[42] While we only get a glimpse of what was discussed, we can piece it together from the reported results of a full CMC meeting held in Beijing in April, after Deng returned from his southern tour and his "thoughts" became policy by directive of the Politburo.

Thus, we know that two other events were discussed and authorized at Huizhou in January, though only later would evidence of such emerge when, at the March 1992 NPC meeting, Yang Baibing announced that the PLA would start an official campaign, headed by the GPD, to "escort reform and opening."[43] Referring to "a recent Central Military Commission (CMC) meeting," Yang was quoted as saying "the PLA will serve as 'an escort' for China's reform and opening to the outside world as well as its economic development."[44] Yang called on the PLA to support Deng's reform and opening—the "one center and two basic points"—as the highest summation of experience in economic development since the founding of New China. He also called on the PLA to subordinate its work to the state's needs, and to support the current policy with concrete action. As part of his campaign to "escort" reform and opening, Yang called on the PLA to be patient, thrifty in its own economic construction, and to exercise efficiency. He affirmed that the PLA fully understood that it was in the interests of the state and the PLA to let certain localities and individuals gain wealth, since it contributed to the national wealth, which in turn meant more funds for the PLA. He ordered all senior commanders to make the pilgrimage to Shenzhen and the other SEZ to view the success of Deng's policies personally. The army was also ordered to assist the localities in major construction projects in their areas—obviously, an attempt to reestablish the bond between the army and the people, badly tarnished by Tiananmen.[45] This effort also further solidified the role of the PLA in the local economy.

Deng left Shenzhen for Shanghai, where he "ordered" the Politburo and vice-premiers to come to the city for general discussions that were held over two days, 3 and 5 February. By forcing the leadership to come to him, he was signaling that he was in charge. The fact that the PLA was visibly backing Deng was not lost on those who responded. Those attending included Jiang, Song Ping, Li Ruihuan, Qiao Shi, Wan Li, Bo Yibo, Deng Yingchao—and Chen Yun, already in Shanghai for his annual New Year's visit.

By the time Deng had arrived in Shanghai, he had already contrived with Jiang to take delegate selection for the upcoming congress from Song Ping, ending the conservatives' efforts to control the new congress by dispatching thousands of supporters throughout the countryside to remake the local party committees, just as Mao had done prior to the Cultural

Revolution. Following the Eighth Plenum in November, the party had begun the selection process for delegates to the Fourteenth Party Congress. The task had fallen by right to the Organization Department, then under the control of Song Ping's protégé Lu Feng, as discussed earlier. In alliance with Chen Yun's "Soviet Faction," the "leftists" had adopted his criteria for determining qualification, as laid out by his son Chen Yuan in September. Delegates had to be morally correct, as well as politically qualified, had to endorse the crackdown on the students at Tiananmen, and had to believe that party ideology should be stressed. The latter qualification was especially aimed at Deng, who demanded that selectees support his modernization and opening first and foremost.

To thwart Chen, Deng had ordered Jiang Zemin to take over responsibility for the planning and agenda of the Fourteenth Party Congress. That task had in turn fallen to Jiang's office director, Zeng Qinhong, who also served as the deputy director of the General Office of the Central Committee.[46] From these two offices—the latter responsible for reviewing all party work—Zeng, and thus Jiang and Deng, controlled all aspects relating to the upcoming party congress. They effectively neutralized the Organization Department's control over the selection process, which had been under way for over a year, as the Department had set about recertifying local party members under criteria supported by the leftists. In Shanghai, for example, the Organization Department was allowed to select three delegates, while local officials selected the vast majority, 90 percent of Shanghai's eighty delegates. In this manner, Deng was preparing to stack the congress with local delegates, answerable to local officials. He was seizing power from the ground up, just as Mao had done. Thus, the Fourteenth Congress would be elected by delegates taking directions from the provincial party leadership, not the central party apparatus in Beijing. This was a reversal of previous years, when Deng had controlled everything from Beijing, but desperate times had forced desperate measures.

While still in Zhuhai, on 25 January Deng had also laid out his criteria for holding government office. "Both the central authorities and localities must resolutely take action. You cannot keep waiting but must sack, as soon as possible, those who hesitate to move and who are indifferent to, or even try to boycott, reform. If these people are allowed to stay in office, they will turn out to be tremendous obstacles to the reform, and thorough implementation of the reform policies will be impossible. It will be abnormal for leading party cadres to keep their posts without implementing the party's policies."[47] Deng was determined to remake the party and government and to nullify Chen's influence.

At meetings in Shanghai on 3 and 5 February, Deng further expanded on his criteria for holding office. He developed the Eight Shoulds: "one should emancipate one's mind, more boldly blaze new trails, carry on the reform in depth, expand the opening up process, be brave in introducing foreign capital and technology, speed up the pace of reform, broaden one's field of vision, and work in a down-to-earth manner."[48] This meant that those who supported reform in public but privately obstructed it, those who failed to understand the policies and thus failed to take appropriate actions, and those who were indifferent to reform and did not promote it were all candidates for removal from office. Deng called on the party to take resolute action against those failing to support his polices, without concern for upsetting elites. He obliquely criticized Chen and Li when he remarked that incumbent leaders had attempted to thwart his efforts at getting rid of those not supportive of his plans, that is, Gao Di, Deng Liqun, and He Jingzhi.[49] Deng went on to praise the efforts of the people and leaders of Shanghai in economic construction, and instructed all present to go all out to build a large socialist metropolis with Chinese characteristics: "Give full play to the Shanghai spirit."[50]

Chen Yun met with Deng on 2 and 6 February in an attempt to reach a compromise. Prior to the meetings, Chen Yun's supporters in the Propaganda Department had been circulating a document that preached against all that Deng had been building since 1978. That document leveled charges that the party was again riddled with "right opportunists" (the same charge Mao had leveled against the party years earlier, on the eve of the Cultural Revolution) who, though a minority, were misleading the masses by advocating bourgeois liberalization. The party, it declared, had to reform the leadership and purge it of this bourgeois element. That leading members of the party would level such charges, and against Deng, quite clearly had to have had a chilling effect on Deng's supporters. Deng had to take resolute action to counter this trend toward equating his SEZ, reform, and opening with "peaceful evolution" and "rightist opportunism."[51]

The talks with Chen dealt with three major topics: the party's central task, how to cope with capitalism, and the SEZ. Chen advocated the importance of ideology in confronting the serious problems of corruption and bourgeois liberalization. He warned that the reason the Soviet Union had collapsed was not because of poor economic construction, but because of changes in the leadership and a betrayal of socialism. Chen warned that if China did not reevaluate the results of reform and opening and eliminate the corruption and bourgeois liberalization, the face of Chinese socialism would change. China would turn into a capitalist country via peaceful evolution, led by the Chinese Communist Party.[52]

Chen then addressed corruption in Deng's SEZ and the spreading influence of capitalism. If the party did not address these issues, he declared, the negative phenomenon introduced by the opening to the world would become malignant, and the party would pay a dear price to cut them out at a later date. Chen was not afraid that the party would lose out to democratic forces; he was merely calculating the expense of purging the bad elements from society. It was cheaper, he advocated, to do it sooner rather than later.

Finally, he turned to his real charge against Deng: creeping bourgeois liberalism. It had to be openly criticized and curbed. He was unhappy with the failure to act. As Chen told his New Year's audience, "they had to wage a tit-for-tat struggle against the 'peaceful evolution' plot of Western countries, headed by the United States, which are carrying out a policy of intervention, subversion, sabotage, and infiltration against our country."[53]

In response, Deng told Chen that the party elders supported him. They agreed with his prognosis that, in the long run, if the party did a good job of economic construction it would maintain its leadership position. If it failed, it would not survive, and socialism would not survive.[54] Deng supposedly told Chen "one can only speak loudly when one has much money."[55] This harkens back to the discussions Deng held with the PLA leadership at the December CMC meeting, when the PLA concluded that only with modernization could China grow to be wealthy and powerful and support a strong army. According to participants, Deng also shouted, "Any leader who cannot boost the economy should leave office."[56] As for the issue of dealing with capitalism, Deng still advocated taking on its good points—his black cat/white cat position. As he had stated in Shanghai, reform and opening up "includes taking over the useful things of capitalism. We should absorb more foreign capital and more foreign advanced experiences and technologies, and set up more foreign-invested enterprises. Do not fear when others say we are practicing capitalism. Capitalism is nothing fearsome."[57] Finally, on the issue of the SEZ, Deng refused to get sidetracked by "tributaries," a reference to corruption, prostitution, and other illegal activities. Deng had already stressed the need to run the SEZ properly. He would not let other leaders deny the "great, proven achievements of the SEZ."[58]

Deng's Shanghai visit had mixed results. He had not gotten any concessions from Chen, who failed to return for the Politburo meetings in February where Deng's new policies were discussed. However, on a more positive note, local Shanghai papers immediately began publishing editorials supportive of Deng's new policy of going all-out for reform and opening, and Jiang returned to Beijing to spread Deng's message to the party.

At an emergency Politburo meeting on 8 February, while Deng and Chen were still in Shanghai, Jiang announced Deng's new policies and relayed the content of the Deng–Chen discussions. On February 12, an expanded Central Committee meeting was held at which provincial leaders, state officials, PLA officials, and most Central Committee members, as well as Politburo members, were in attendance. Thus, Deng was able to get his views past the propaganda and media censors and to the masses, especially the party members outside of Beijing. The Chen-controlled press had ignored his comments for over a year and had ignored his tour. It was now clear to all that the regional party apparatus was backing Deng, as was the PLA. At an expanded Central Committee meeting, Chen's supporters like Song Ping and the astute politician Li Peng jumped on board, while Bo Yibo, Wan Li, and other elders stood up for Deng, fracturing the CAC, Chen Yun's bastion of support against Deng's economic reform efforts.[59] Finally, on 9 and 10 March, a Politburo Plenum formally proclaimed that Deng's thoughts were to be implemented as the collective wisdom of the party, and were to be laid out as Central Document Number 2 of 1992. Its content had been disseminated to all levels of the party for discussion and implementation on 28 February, nine days prior to the Plenum. Deng would have been justified in proclaiming success over the Li Peng–Chen Yun faction, but that would have been premature; the battle was still being waged.

Deng had gone to Shenzhen by way of Shanghai, the Northeast, and central China, stopping in the major cities—Shenyang, Tianjin, Shanghai, Wuhan, and finally Guangzhou. His lieutenants had visited or would visit other major military political centers in the aftermath of the agreements forged in Shenzhen. Qiao Shi, Wan Li, Tian Jiyun, Zhu Rongji, Yang Shangkun, and Jiang Zemin—all with appropriate military and party escorts—had visited Hainan, Guangzhou, Zhejiang, Shenyang, Nanjing, Wulumuqi, and Guangxi, as well as Beijing. In this way, all the military regions had been brought on board between 3 December and 12 February.[60] Thus, Deng had mobilized the core elements of his compromise: the PLA, the elders, the public security forces, and the regional party bureaucracies.[61]

However, Chen was not about to abandon his view that he knew what was best for China. In that respect, he was not unlike Deng. Chen returned to Beijing from his vacation in Shanghai and meetings with Deng to rally a counterattack against what he perceived—correctly, as it turned out—an all-out campaign by Deng to seize the initiative over policy formulation. Chen was not yet powerless; he still controlled votes on the Standing Committee, and the CAC was his vehicle to influence the elders. He could still influence policy.

Policy Showdown

Deng had formed a coalition and seized effective control over policy, but Chen Yun still had considerable support and resources to mobilize against him. This time he would not back down. The only option for Deng, once he realized Chen and the ideologues would not see it his way, was to restructure the policy bodies, giving him effective control. But first, he would try compromise.

Chen Yun retreated to Beijing following his showdown with Deng in Shanghai. He did not attend the 12 February Expanded Politburo meeting, as he was aware that his policies had already been reversed by Deng. Instead, he rallied his forces for a counterattack. He invited several CAC members to his residence on 17 February, including advisors to key ministries and central committees. His charges against Deng were presented in a paper entitled "Several Opinions on Current Problems." Chen aired his

complaints against Deng and attacked Deng's famous Four Modernizations: "We are promoting the building of socialist modernization, we
must take Marxist-Leninist theory as our guide. If we deviate from this
theory, we cannot even begin to talk about building the four modernizations with a socialist nature."[62]

Chen told his audience that the most important task, as opposed to
reform and opening, was to build up the party with Marxist-Leninist
theory and cultivate a large number of cadre and successors who had a
firm faith in Marxism-Leninism.[63] The CCP was a Marxist party, he said,
and only Marxist theory could guide it. Any other thought or ideology
amounted to deviation from Marxism. He stated that, in upholding socialism, one had to differentiate clearly between real socialism and revisionism,
or the democratic socialist road. Chen explicitly equated Deng's liberalism
with democratic socialism. Such deviation, according to him, would only
lead to setbacks and failure for China's revolution. Chen's proposed solution was to sum up experiences and guard against destruction, such as that
caused by the ultraleftism of the Mao era and that caused by the rightist deviations of the previous ten years—which could only mean Deng's
policies.[64]

Chen next turned his attention to the SEZ and the spreading influence
of capitalism. He expressed concern over the spreading corruption and
bad practices, which he blamed on opening to the world, as he had told
Deng in Shanghai. If the party did not address these problems, the negative phenomenon introduced by opening and the abuse of privilege by
party members would become malignant tumors, and the party would pay
a dear price to cut them out at a later date. Finally, he repeated his most
damning charge against Deng's policies, that of facilitating creeping bourgeois liberalism. Chen demanded that the trend be openly criticized and
curbed.

According to Chen's paper, the party's task was to pursue the realization
and perfection of socialism. The party had determined the course, and no
one was entitled to change it without thorough debate, discussion, research,
and vote, since it involved the party's organization and principles. But that
is precisely what Deng had done. He stated that the current planned and
proportionate development of the economy, with 70 percent controlled by
the plan and 30 percent controlled by the market, was still the most suitable

for China's conditions. He expressed concern that the SEZ had not had a long enough history to be recorded as successful, not to mention the disturbing, abnormal, and unhealthy factors associated with them.

Chen next launched an assault on Deng's program of "one center, two branches." Whereas Deng had been advocating the primary line of development of the economy, Chen raised the importance of the party's organization and ideology in the light of the rapidly changing international environment. According to Chen, if the party did not grasp ideology and propaganda as outlined by the Four Cardinal Principles, then socialist construction would deviate and fail. The only way to prevent a collapse like that in the Soviet Union was to strengthen party organization and ideological education. As Chen saw it, "we must guard against the leftist tendency in economics and the rightist tendency in politics."

Chen then stepped back and allowed his sycophant Deng Liqun to enumerate the most serious charges against Deng Xiaoping and the reformers. In his speech, entitled "Where Does China Go in Revolution and Construction?" Deng Liqun charged that a new class had emerged within the party, a class that had castrated the principles of Marxism-Leninism and had adopted a set of principles that were contrary to it. Clearly, this charge resonated with Mao's charge in the early 1960s that capitalist roaders had emerged in the party. It would appear that Deng Liqun was calling for another assault on the party apparatus, another Cultural Revolution. Indeed, his statement talked about the duty of Communists to protect Marxism, even to the extent that they give their lives to protect it. Deng was clearly demanding action, a battle between good and evil. In fact, he called on the CAC to present a proposal to the CCP Central Committee to convene a special work conference to solve the problem of the line and direction of revolution and construction in China.

Clearly, Chen was headed down a road that he and Deng Xiaoping had agreed was a disaster—the Great Proletarian Cultural Revolution. The CAC, with Chen as its chairman, had submitted such a proposal to the Central Committee, though the effect was watered down somewhat since only 50 percent of the members were in attendance. Key members, such as Song Renqiong and Bo Yibo, were absent, perhaps in an attempt to put some distance between themselves and Chen. In any event, the proposal was a serious challenge to party stability in general, and Deng Xiaoping in particular.

Deng Xiaoping, however, had already seized the initiative from Chen, since his remarks from his southern tour had already been distributed throughout the party as documents from the 12 February Expanded Central Committee meeting. Thus, in February 1992 there were effectively two camps within the CCP: one loyal to Mao and Marxism, and one loyal to Deng and the "market" economics—whether capitalist or socialist was unimportant. Thirty years earlier, a division within the party had led to a civil war that had left deep scars which had not yet healed. It was not likely that Deng could let the charge go unanswered.

Indeed, Deng Xiaoping did not sit idly by while the "leftists" attempted to launch another Cultural Revolution. On 2 March, Deng called a meeting at his home in Zhongnanhai. Those attending included Wang Ping, Li Desheng, Wu Xiuquan, Yang Dezhi, Xiao Ke, Yu Qiuli, Qiao Shi, Zhang Jingfu, Geng Biao, Huang Hua, and Chen Xilian—all close comrades-in-arms. Deng did not mince words. He was aware of the charges and of whom his enemies were: "not all were old comrades, some were on the Politburo and within the government."[65] According to Deng, some people in the government said they supported reform and opening, but did not. It was good that they had shown their hands. Deng, like Mao, was not above using internal discussions to single out enemies for future reference. Deng also stated that he was willing to allow his views to be subjected to a reality check, unlike some comrades within the party.

As authority for his trip to the south and the publicizing of his views within the party, he cited the resolution of the Fifth Plenum of November 1989, which asked for his continued hand at the helm. Thus, it appears that Deng retained a measure of control via his tie to Yang Shangkun. Deng also pointed out that the party and the CAC had agreed to the "one center, two basic points" policy. In 1992, however, people were adding leftist ideas to the debate and charging that his policies of construction and productive forces were capitalist. These same people, he charged, were calling for class warfare within the party, when it had been agreed that class struggle had subsided. He also complained that these same people had seized on the Four Cardinal Principles, which were only part of the "one center, two basic points," and held them up as the central focus of party efforts. This had given rise to the "two centers" controversy within the party: One center economic construction, and the other ideological and organizational reform.

Deng countered Chen Yun's charge that he had arbitrarily changed party policy with the charge that the Politburo was being ignored with the connivance of the CAC. He held up to his audience a letter signed by thirty-five senior CAC members, including Chen Yun, Li Xiannian, Wang Zhen, Wang Renzhong, Deng Liqun, Hu Qiaomu, and He Jingzhi.[66] That letter made six proposals: (1) uphold the Marxist-Leninist party's founding line; (2) correct promptly the direction of development that had deviated from the socialist path; (3) conduct rectification movements of communist ideology, ideas, and ethics; (4) conduct propaganda and education in socialist ideology, morality, and spirit in enterprises, units, schools, and neighborhoods across the country; (5) launch a struggle against the infiltration and inculcation of Western ideologies and corrosive peaceful evolution; and (6) launch reforms, opening up and self-perfection that are socialist in nature.[67] Deng was obviously stung by the charges coming from Chen that were clearly splitting the party. As Deng charged, even if certain elders did not like what he, Deng, had to say, so be it. Everyone had a responsibility to obey the Politburo. If Deng was wrong, he still had the right to have his views aired.

Deng repeated, for his audience, what he had included in his earlier "views." He charged people to be bold, to try new things, and not worry about criticism. Whether the party was socialist or capitalist was not based on book worship, he reiterated. It was based on whether it could develop social productive forces and improve the people's standard of living. Deng suggested that the party and government publicize the party's line of economic construction, and let the people help supervise and evaluate the results.[68] Deng then made his final charge: "In summing up experiences in 42 years since the nation's founding, and in the decade of reform and opening up, danger comes mainly from 'leftism.' This is manifested by the fact that Marxism-Leninism is taken in the form of dogmatism and book worship to formulate policies and principles."[69]

The Politburo held a Plenary Session on 9 and 10 March 1992, at which it gave its stamp of approval to Deng's views. Released to the party faithful as Central Document Number 2, it contained the pronouncements Deng made during his New Year's tour of the south in January and February 1992. The Politburo also made some pronouncements. Echoing Deng's statements as directives to the party, the Politburo charged that the major political danger facing the country was from the left wing of the party, not those calling for bolder reform. Therefore, while remaining vigilant against rightist deviation, the main force of attention would be on guarding against "leftist" deviation.[70] However, as would become apparent, it was difficult to translate the rhetoric of the Politburo Decision and Central Document Number 2 into concrete policies, since Deng still lacked any effective control over the administrative apparatus of the party and government. Nevertheless, the Politburo committed China to reform and opening for one hundred years. Economic development was the country's number one priority: "It is imperative to unswervingly adhere to taking economic construction as the central task, and stick to the Four Cardinal Principles and to reform and opening to the outside world." According to the press, the resolutions also stated "as long as the country upholds the reform policies and will not waver even for 100 years, the country will be able to maintain long-term stability and will be hopeful."

The Politburo also called for reform and opening to the world to be carried out in a bolder way, with more innovation and experimentation. In a final resolution of the yearlong debate over whether a thing was socialist or capitalist, the Politburo declared that "to judge whether a move is 'socialist' or 'capitalist' will depend mainly on whether it will benefit the development of the productive forces under socialism, the enhancement of the comprehensive national strength of our socialist country and the promotion of the living standard of the people." As for Li Peng's call for self-reliance and an avoidance of foreign capital, the Politburo stated that "the party and country should be bold in absorbing and learning from all the achievement of the civilization of mankind, and in absorbing and learning from the advanced management methods of other countries of the contemporary world, including the developed countries in the West."

However, Deng was in agreement with the "leftists" and Chen Yun on one account, which was also a resolution of the Politburo: "the Party must increase military strength and consolidate its power through the means of dictatorship."[71] The resolution acknowledged that it would be necessary to combat bourgeois liberalization and peaceful evolution for twenty years or more. Thus, the Politburo agreed to all that Deng had requested.

At this point, it would be useful to review Central Document Number 2, as it spelled out Deng's political philosophy and provided a guide by which his "compromise" would be implemented.

The document was distributed down to the county and regimental level

on 28 February, prior to its discussion at the Plenary session of the Politburo on 9 March, but after the internal discussions in Shanghai and Beijing in early February and the Expanded Central Committee discussions of
12 February, and after Chen and the CAC had attempted to derail it with
their appeal to the Central Committee. Thus, the party was made aware of
Deng's position vis-à-vis Chen and the conservatives. The introduction to
"Central Document Number 2, Chinese Communist Party Central Committee Circular on Transmitting and Studying Comrade Deng Xiaoping's
Important Remarks" pointed out its significance and its historical setting:
"At a crucial moment for the socialist modernization program of China,
Comrade Deng Xiaoping made these extremely important remarks to air
his views on a series of major issues, namely, steadfastly implementing the
party's basic line of 'one center, two basic points,' upholding the road to
socialism with Chinese characteristics, and, in particular, the necessity of
seizing the present favorable opportunity to speed up the pace of reform
and opening up and to concentrate energy on economic construction."[72]

The Politburo instructed all party members to understand and implement Deng's instructions, of which the main point was to seize the
moment:

> In the past, we only mentioned developing productive forces
> under socialist conditions, but we did not mention how reform
> and opening would emancipate productive forces. In fact,
> reform and opening up mean to follow the party's basic line
> and to carry out the principles, policies, and line since the
> Third Plenary Session of the 11th CCP Central Committee.
> The key lies in persistently upholding the "one center and two
> basic points." The basic line should be valid for 100 years, and
> must not be shaken. Only by keeping this line can we be
> trusted and supported by the people. If we do not carry out
> reform and opening up, do not develop the economy, and do
> not improve the people's living standards, we will then only be
> on the road to ruin. The common people will not allow any-
> one to change the principles and policies of the basic line, and
> those who do may be overthrown at any time. I mentioned this
> point several times. That is, only by adhering to the basic line
> can we have a way out.

I can only say that if there had been no achievements from
reform and opening, we might not have been able to pass the
test of the 4 June incident, and if we had failed to pass that
test, there would have been a chaotic situation that could have
led to a civil war. That was the case during the "Cultural Revolution." The reason our country could continue to be stable
after the 4 June incident was that reform and opening up had
promoted economic development and improved the people's
living standards, and that the armed forces and the government
also supported this road, this system, and these policies.[73]

In his "Remarks," Deng also took on the conservatives in the party who
had argued that his reforms in the SEZ had amounted to capitalism. He
stated that reform and opening required big leaps forward and courageous
experimentation. It should not proceed like "a bound-footed woman."
While it was impossible to avoid mistakes, the emphasis would be on
identifying problems, solving them, and moving forward. When considering reforms, the issue was not whether they were capitalist or socialist, but
whether the people's living standards were improved. In one short phrase,
Deng reduced Marxism and socialism to mere efficacy: if it worked, it
must be socialist. The old white cat/black cat saying had finally become
official policy. He was clearly arguing to maintain the party's dictatorship,
but it was no longer based on any tome or economic theory found in the
hallowed halls of Marxist libraries. It was based on simple efficiency: if a
policy made the people's livelihood better, it was "socialist." This interpretation is fundamental to understanding Deng's maneuvering throughout
1992 and thereafter.

Thus, Deng declared, "leftism is the greater handicap, as compared to
"rightism." He called for an end to name-calling and arguing over socialism and capitalism. Instead, he called for more, greater, faster, and bolder
reform and opening:

Now that the peripheral countries and areas have the lead on
us in economic development, if we fail to catch up with them
or if we advance at a slow pace, the public may have grievances
when they make a comparison. Therefore, if an idea can help
speed up development, we must not stop it but should try to

make development still faster. In any case, we must set store on efficiency and quality. We must seize every opportunity to make the country develop quickly. We have a good opportunity now; if we fail to seize it, it will be gone very soon. Slow development simply means to halt. We must strive really hard to upgrade the economy to a new level every few years. Never try to launch any unrealistic reform.

In addition, we must pay attention to coordination. If Guangdong plans to catch up with the four little dragons of Asia within 20 years and wants to speed up its development, it will have to quicken its pace further. Shanghai definitely can go faster. By quickening the pace of development, the situation in the four special economic zones, in the Yangtze Delta, and in China as a whole, will be quite different from what it is at present. From now on, we must speed up reform and development. Now, when I review my work in retrospect, I think one of the great mistakes I committed is that I did not make Shanghai one of the special economic zones at the time when the four existing special economic zones were founded."[74]

His "Remarks" addressed the fear that foreign corporations were taking over in the SEZ. Deng responded that the state was still the predominant owner in the SEZ. Further, the state was able to gain revenues from taxing the foreign firms, which also provided jobs for local inhabitants. Moreover, the state benefited from exposure to and importation of technology and management skills. In Deng's opinion, the benefits outweighed the disadvantages. In his mind, "the demarcation between planning and the market is not the substantive difference between socialism and capitalism, and this does not have any inherent link with the choice between socialism and capitalism. The planned economy is not the same as socialism because capitalism also involves planning. On the other hand, the market economy is not equal to capitalism either because socialism also has a market. Both planning and the market are economic means."

Deng also countered the conservative criticism that the wealthy coastal cities and regions were leaving the poorer interior regions behind in the race for profits, thus undermining the basic principles of the party. He acknowledged, "some areas would be allowed to get wealthy, if conditions permitted. Those areas less well favored would be pulled along, as wealth was transferred from the rich to the poor, to achieve common prosperity. The mechanism would be a tax (which Zhu would implement in 1993)."

Deng's "Remarks" also took on Chen Yun's major criticism of the SEZ, the growth of crime and corruption. Chen and his faction felt that the negative aspects outweighed the positive. Deng thought otherwise. "We must uphold the principle of paying attention to both aspects, promoting reform and opening on the one hand, and fighting all kinds of criminal activities on the other. Both aspects are very important. We must not show any mercy when dealing blows to all kinds of criminal activities and eliminating all ugly phenomena. To catch up with the four little dragons of Asia within 20 years, Guangdong Province not only must straighten out its social order and cultivate a fine general social mood. Both issues must be handled properly; that is the essence of socialism with Chinese characteristics. Since opening up, some ugly phenomena have arisen in some parts of China. We must never take a laissez-faire attitude toward such evil things as drug addiction, prostitution, and economic crimes, but must deal with them."

Lest anyone fear that Deng had a liberal thought along the lines of democracy, he disabused everyone. He stated: "Historical experience shows that to consolidate a political regime one must use the means of dictatorship. Democracy is to be applied to the people, and dictatorship to the enemy; that is what the people's democratic dictatorship means. Under the people's democratic dictatorship, consolidating the people's political regime is a just act, and there is no room for hesitation. In the whole process of reform and opening to the outside world, from beginning to end, it is necessary to uphold the four cardinal principles. At the Sixth Plenary Session of the 12th CCP Central Committee, I suggested opposing bourgeois liberalization for 20 years. It seems today that the struggle should be carried out for even more than 20 years. If bourgeois liberalization is allowed to spread unchecked, the consequences will be extremely serious. We have spent 10 years or so building the special zones to be as they are now. To make them collapse would be a matter of only one night, just as the case of the Soviet Union."

Finally, Deng got to the crux of his mission: how to perpetuate the party and the state. Here we have the full understanding of Deng's final campaign. "In a sense, the key as to whether or not Chinese affairs could be handled well, whether or not socialism with Chinese characteristics could be adhered to, whether or not the economy could be developed more quickly, and whether or not the state could maintain long-term political stability lies in 'man.' In pursuing 'peaceful evolution,' hostile forces pin their hope on the people of several generations following us. People of Comrade Jiang Zemin's generation can be considered the third generation, and there are people of the fourth and fifth generations to follow. When we people in the older generation are still around [the elders] and have weight [sit on Politburo discussions], hostile forces are aware that no change can be effected. However, when we old people are dead and gone, who will escort the emperor? Efforts should be made to manage our Army well and to educate the people and youth well." Here, in effect, Deng acknowledged the existence of an elders' advisory body, similar to the genro in Japan's history. In addition, he stated that the PLA would be the guarantor of the state and party, when the elders were gone.

Deng continued: "If something wrong occurs in China, it will come from within the Communist Party. We should be sober about this matter and should stress the training of successors to the revolution. Leaders should be selected according to the four requirements of being revolutionary, more knowledgeable, more professional, and younger in average age. People who have both ability and political integrity should be chosen to leading bodies." Deng was also not about to be second-guessed on his earlier selection of successors, Zhao and Hu. He acknowledged "two people I selected in the past ended in failure. They suffered a setback on the issues of adherence to the socialist road and opposition to bourgeois liberalization, and not on the issue of economic work."

Deng was also concerned with the old party members who refused to change with the times. He accused them of formalism, relying on book knowledge. He urged them to "put the essence of Marxism on applicability." For those afraid that Marxism would become irrelevant, he argued that to the contrary, "it would prosper as it showed the way to economic development, as was happening in China." In the coming battle between China's socialism and capitalism, Deng was confident: "Capitalism has developed for several hundred years. Socialism in our country has developed just for a period of time, and moreover, we ourselves have delayed it for 20 years. If we spend 100 more years building our country into a developed one, that will be amazing. From now on to the middle of the next century, our responsibility is very immense and our burdens very heavy."[75]

Li Peng was quick to recognize that Deng had seized the initiative. Once Deng's policies were proclaimed at the expanded Politburo meeting in February, he announced that the government would comply. However, since there was no indication that he made a self-criticism at the 9 March meeting, it was probable that he was feigning compliance, while actually working against reform and opening. At the Plenary Session, Song Ping, Yao Yilin, and even Jiang Zemin had made self-criticisms to gain Deng's confidence and keep their jobs.

In his address to the Thirteenth Plenary Session of the State Council in Beijing, Li adopted the rhetoric from Central Document Number 2. However, he also patted himself on the back by proclaiming that, under his tenure, the three-year retrenchment program had put the national economy back on the right track. He failed to mention the Zhao years, when economic development had been greater. He called upon all government departments and sectors to accelerate the pace of reforms and opening to the outside world, and for reform of the state enterprises to make them more responsive to market forces. He also called for the streamlining of the administrative organs of government.[76]

Li Peng's speech at the Fifth Session of the Seventh National People's Congress was likewise self-congratulatory, and made it clear that he and Chen Yun were not about to back off their policy of measured, steady growth despite all the go-fast rhetoric. He indicated that while the economy grew at a 7 percent rate in 1991, he was only forecasting a growth rate of 6 percent for 1992. This was the same rate that had been set at the Plenum in November 1991 and which had so upset Deng. Li again proclaimed that the three-year retrenchment program had been a success, without referring to the high growth rates of the previous years. He lumped those years into the ten-year period of reform and opening. He warned the NPC that while the three-year period had just ended on a successful note, caution was still in order; destabilizing factors remained, and emphasis should be placed on resolving such structural abnormalities.

Li's speech called for the people to rally around Jiang and the core leadership, and to uphold the "one center, two basic points" policy. He also called for reform and opening up, but qualified it with a need to uphold the Four Cardinal Principles and to maintain social and political stability. Li stated, "at present, favorable conditions are available both at home and abroad. In addition, we are ready to give full play to this country's resources to run any big project. Therefore, in the long modernization process to come, we need and can launch a series of programs stage by stage, which are designed to achieve a pretty high growth rate and good economic returns. Opportunity knocks but once. We must seize this good opportunity, concentrate our resources, and further speed up economic development. The focus of economic work in 1992 is to step up structural readjustment and operations to improve economic returns. In particular, we must strive for greater success in boosting agriculture and invigorating large and medium state-owned enterprises."

Next, while affirming the contract responsibility system for agriculture on a household basis, with remuneration linked to output, he called for improved management from both the unified and individual perspective. He also called for an expansion of the collective sector of the economy, as well as the allocation of more technology to that sector.

On the industrial front, Li called for structural adjustment to improve the large and medium state enterprises. He declared that measures instituted in 1991, which included speeded-up capital turnover, reduced production costs, greater profits, and more sound management, were to continue throughout 1992.

Overall, Li praised his efforts over the previous few years: "Fundamentally speaking, reform is aimed at changing the economic structure which restricts the development of the productive forces, setting up a socialist economic structure full of vitality and vigor, and promoting the development of the planned commodity economy. In the last few years, China's society and politics have remained stable, its economy has seen sustained development, and the work of improving the economic environment and rectifying the economic order has been smoothly completed. All these have created favorable conditions for deepening reform and expanding the scope of opening up. We should continue to emancipate the mind, be bold in blazing new trails, and make bigger strides in reform and opening up." Referring more specifically to the SEZ, he noted that after more than ten years of hard work, "our country has implemented opening up on a comprehensive scale. We must further expand the scope of opening up, increase efficiency, and raise opening up to the outside world to a new level." What this really meant was that "we must continue to successfully manage the SEZ and various other economic and technological development zones, open cities and open areas in order to bring about faster economic growth and more rapid urban construction in those areas and enable them to play a better role as windows and radiators for the cause of reform and opening up, thus expediting the development of an export-oriented economy."

Not to be outdone by Deng, Li also called for the creation of a better social and political environment. During 1992, the government was to work to embody overall modernization building more fully while consolidating and developing a stable political environment that promoted economic development. That meant streamlining government organizations, and separating administration from management. He continued his call, picked up by the "leftists," for ideological work. He was concerned that under "the situation of deepened reform and opening wider to the outside world, many new states of affairs and problems have appeared on the ideological and theoretical fronts as well as on the educational and cultural fronts. Therefore, we should carry out in-depth, protracted education in adherence to the four Cardinal Principles among the broad masses of the people, particularly youth, at different levels and different means. Leaders at all levels must persistently follow the principle of paying equal attention to material progress and cultural and ideological progress, and increase the faith of each consecutive generation of Chinese people in taking the road of building socialism with Chinese characteristics." Clearly, Li could not give up on the plan to launch another socialist education campaign in order to capture the necessary party seats and votes for the Fourteenth Congress.

Li also included the PLA in his economic report to the NPC. According to him, the "PLA, the armed police, and the public security police constitute a solid pillar for safeguarding the motherland. . . . They have invariably appeared where there were difficulties and danger and made important contributions to safeguarding state property and the people's lives and security. The Army should further improve its quality and develop itself in the Chinese way. It should strive to be politically reliable, militarily capable, highly disciplined, and have a fine work style. It should provide a powerful guarantee and enhance its fighting capacity comprehensively to make new achievements in safeguarding state sovereignty and modernization construction."

Finally, Li turned his attention to the international scene. After making a pitch for reunification with Taiwan, he noted "drastic changes that had taken place: the Gulf War, the civil war in Yugoslavia, and in particular, the disintegration of the Soviet Union." While the old world order had collapsed, a new order had yet to emerge, according to Li. He characterized the international situation as moving towards multipolarity. Within that environment, he declared China would pursue its policy of not seeking hegemony and pursuing an independent foreign policy of peace.[77]

With that, Li had thrown down the gauntlet. He was mouthing Deng's new policies, but in effect sticking to the ideas that he and Chen had been espousing since they regained control of the economic levers in 1989. While Deng had forced the party to adopt his call for faster, bolder, and greater reform, he had not replaced those who actually controlled the power. Li's policies of 6 percent growth, reform of state enterprises, efficiency in resource allocation, and structural reform in the SEZ could still cripple Deng's programs. Clearly, the two camps had failed to resolve their conflicts, but Deng was still marshaling his forces.

Deng had mobilized the military. He had rallied the powerful regional party and governmental officials, who controlled revenue and delegate selection to the Fourteenth Congress, to his cause. He had seized control of party personnel affairs by first giving Jiang Zemin's office oversight authority over the Organization Department, and then by naming Bo Yibo to the working group that supervised appointments to the Fourteenth Central Committee.[78] Though Bo would share this task with Song Ping and Lu Feng, Bo had the added clout of his "elder" status, his alliance with Deng Xiaoping, and the additional support of Jiang's personal secretary, who was also deputy director of the Central Committee General Office.

One other element was crucial to guaranteeing that Deng's policies would be perpetuated, and that the party would remain in power. That was the voice of Qiao Shi. His mentor was Peng Zhen, so it must be assumed that Peng, like Bo Yibo, had come to the conclusion that Deng was right—that the moment was now, and might never come again. China had to seize the initiative while Russia was down and foreign money was available. Qiao Shi planted the state security forces firmly in Deng's camp when he stated, on 25 March, that the Chinese people should "sense the urgency" and grasp Deng's thought on socialist construction.[79] According to Qiao, "the people should have the sense of urgency and should lose no time since there is not much time left until the end of this century, and it is no easy job to realize the second-step objective of quadrupling China's 1980 gross national product and making the people live a comfortable life by 2000."[80] Qiao Shi, of course, had been invited to sit in on CMC meetings and was considered, it seems, a de facto member. As director of all public security forces, he was crucial to any efforts to maintain social stability.

At the same meeting on 25 March, Zhu Rongji was named to head the upgraded State Production Office, which clipped the wings of the State Planning Commission, Chen Yun's instrument for controlling the economy.[81] Thus, Deng had maneuvered Zhu into a position to challenge Chen and Li in the economic arena.[82] The Office had been set up as a committee in 1989, following Tiananmen, to tackle economic problems, with Chen and Li in charge. Thus, Zhu now held economic power, though he still lacked support throughout the government bureaucracy. That would have to wait until the Fourteenth Congress.

It is interesting to note that Deng's pronouncements indicated an evolution in his own thinking. He was advocating a form of state capitalism. Whatever worked to increase wealth and the standard of living was "socialist" in nature. He was also advocating a type of stewardship; if the public approved, the Party retained its mandate to rule. Asian societies, like South Korea and Singapore, were examples to him of how Confucian societies could modernize without liberalizing. Deng was remaking the party with emphasis on technical expertise, and the military was being professionalized. Society, under the guidance of an elders' council, would work out a power-sharing scheme, similar to those in Japan, Singapore, and South Korea, in which the state maintained the dominant role in the economy. In some respects, Deng's evolution reflected the final years of the Manchu Dynasty. Gone was the rationale for governing, the "mandate": the result was warlordism. When a new ideology was found with sufficient appeal to overcome localism, a new China emerged. Now that communism had failed, Deng and others strove to avoid a similar breakup. Instead, Deng and his reformers were calling for a new ideology, one all could understand: stability and economic growth. That practical philosophy would maintain them in power as long as the major participants continued to prosper.

The conservatives had been temporarily overwhelmed by Deng and the PLA. But Li Peng, with Chen Yun's backing, was still able to stall the implementation of Deng's plans through his control of the economic levers. Deng had not succeeded in changing policy, even with the backing of the PLA.

4 | More, Better, Faster

◇ Opening China

Deng had succeeded in seizing control over economic policy in the spring of 1992, but he had not ousted or converted his opponents. What would happen if he died before Chen Yun? Would his policies survive him? It is important to note what his policies were, and how they were used to solidify control over the party.

Deng returned to Beijing in February, in time to learn of Jiang's self-criticism at the Politburo meetings in February. Among his shortcomings, Jiang confessed to saying on several occasions: "through economic rectification and improvement, we should make the individual households lose all their family fortunes; Party spirit should be placed above loyalty to the people; bourgeois liberalization is a force within the country to coordinate with the peaceful evolution scheme of the imperialists."[1] Jiang also admitted that since the previous summer, he had been following the dictates of Chen Yun and Li Peng.

Bo Yibo, another "elder," who sat on the economics control board with Chen and Li, had come out in full support of

Deng's policies. He had drafted an internal document for senior party members, which defended the liberals' position, even though he had been in Chen's camp.[2] Thus, it would seem that without Deng at the helm of Chinese politics, there had been a great deal of fluidity between the two major factions. Deng's mission was to end the uncertainty.

At the Plenum in March, Deng had finally convinced the party elders to endorse his programs for accelerating reform and opening up to the world. The gloved fist of the PLA was no doubt helpful in convincing those who had vacillated, including Jiang and Bo. At the meeting, Deng's views were collected into a document and released to all party and government officials for study and implementation as Central Document Number 2. However, there was continued resistance to actually implementing the changes.[3] Deng, nevertheless, was insistent that China be set on a path towards market socialism, with little possibility for his successors to reverse that course. As he had made institutional changes within the PLA to ensure its allegiance to his policies, he pursued institutional changes in the economic arena.

In late April, Deng tasked Jiang and Zhu Rongji with implementing his reform and opening. Just as he had relied on Yang Shangkun to handle institutional reform of the PLA, the onus was on Zhu Rongji to carry out economic reform. Zhu was to take the place of the deposed Zhao Ziyang as Deng's bright and shining economic czar. Jiang was to have no actual voice in economics; his weakness over the previous years had cost Deng enormously in terms of credibility.

Jiang, however, was still Deng's chosen leader and in control of the party machine, so in that capacity it was he who wrote a letter to the Politburo Standing Committee in May, asking the party to follow up on Central Document Number 2. This would require the issuance of a new document that would spell out in detail what the party meant by accelerating reform and opening. This new document was discussed at high-level meetings and resulted in a comprehensive program, under the guidance of the State Council, to "change the superstructure and the central policy."[4] Document Number 4, entitled "The CCP Central Committee's Opinions on Expediting Reform, Opening Wider to the Outside World, and Working To Raise the Economy to a New Level in a Better and Quicker Way," was intended to be the Magna Carta of economic reform for the next one hundred years.

The significance of Document Number 4 cannot be overstated. It upgraded the State Council Production Office to the Economic and Trade

Office (ETO), headed by Zhu Rongji, with responsibility for macro-economic control and coordination of the economy.[5] Zhu had been in nominal charge of the economy since his elevation to vice-premier a year earlier, but with Li still effectively controlling economic policy along with Chen Yun, he had been ineffective. This new organization, coupled with the policies inaugurated by Document Number 4, effectively gave Zhu administrative authority to set and control macroeconomic policy. Specifically, Document Number 4 addressed further opening to the outside world; strengthening macroeconomic regulation and control; transforming enterprise operational mechanisms; and restructuring the government.

As to further opening to the outside world, the document enfranchised most of the provinces of China, correcting an error Deng acknowledged when he stated that he should have included Shanghai on the original list of SEZ. Deng realized that the first attempt at opening was too limited to ensure nationwide support. It had the effect of driving a wedge between the richer coastal areas and the poorer interior provinces, thereby playing into the hands of Chen Yun and the leftists. Now Shanghai would be the head of a long dragon, which would extend inland along the Yangtze River to include Wuhu, Jiujiang, Wuhan, Yueyang, and Chongqing.

In addition to the interior, border areas were given SEZ status in an effort to take advantage of special situations. This was clearly a move to take advantage of the breakup of the Soviet Union, whose former republics on the border with China had closer trading ties with their neighbors than with Moscow. It also gave China increased political as well as economic leverage with its minorities and their relatives across the border. These newly opened areas included Pingxiang and Dongxing in Guangxi; Hekou, Wanding, and Ruili counties in Yunnan; Yili, Tachen and Bole in Xinjiang; and Erenhot in Inner Mongolia. To entice entire provinces, many of which were economically backward and jealous of the special benefits bestowed on the coastal SEZ by virtue of location, Deng made the leading cities in these border areas equal to SEZ: Harbin, Huhhot, Urumqi, Kunming, and Nanning. Under the new measures, all the areas and cities were to pursue foreign funds and foreign technology aggressively. Each SEZ along the coast and each province involved was to select a port city to open as a bonded export zone.

Deng offered to open all of China to the status of a SEZ. Preferential measures for certain regions and industries were to be extended as part of opening up to the world. New areas for investment were identified; and efforts were to be made to tap the foreign capital in Hong Kong, Macao, and Taiwan. According to the document, all major projects and new technological projects which had been approved by the state and which were in conformity with industrial policy, irrespective of locality, would enjoy the preferential policies for developmental zones. The spheres for using foreign funds would be extended to include finance, trade, commerce, communications, tourism, and the tertiary industries. Foreign-funded banks could be established in certain cities, as well as foreign-invested retail firms. While a form of economic federalism, the economic arrangements were part of Deng's overall desire to recentralize the unitary state.

Once Document Number 4 was implemented, all that remained to recentralize power was to alter the institutional makeup of the Politburo. Deng would have to wait, though, until the party congress in the fall to engineer that. He could remake the PLA, but the Politburo was more difficult, which explained his emphasis on controlling the agenda for the party congress. Unless he could engineer a new central committee that reflected the balance of power he had constructed to ensure reform and opening, and install a similar balance on the Politburo, all his efforts could be rolled back. Naturally, the Politburo could reverse course at any time to concentrate on inflation or to recentralize economic powers recently transferred to the provinces, but with a balance in Beijing that reflected the compromise it would be very difficult to ignore provincial demands, which were ultimately backed by the PLA. The kingmaker—the PLA—was not interested in who was king, only that his policies did not hamper its modernization efforts.

On the international scene, Deng had struggled since 1973 to keep China from painting itself into political isolation. He had deflected Mao's attempt to form an alliance with the United States against the Soviet Union in the early 1970s. He had been forced to tilt towards the United States in the 1980s only when Moscow proved recalcitrant. In the late 1980s, he had been able to reopen relations with Moscow because of Gorbachev's rise to power and his policy of perestroika. In 1989, he had broken with the "American faction," because they had wanted to plant China in the American camp. By 1992, though, he had at long last placed China's foreign policy on a new plateau, reflecting his lifelong goal of an independent course.

Deng had opened all of China with Document Number 4 and given the provincial leaders an economic interest to ensure that the central planners around Li Peng and Chen Yun would not close China off to the technological revolution then under way, in their fear for survival following the collapse of the Soviet Union. If Deng had made one thing clear since his return to politics in 1992, it was that this time China would not close in on itself, as it had done so many times in the past. This was the point of the Huangfu Ping articles, in which Deng explained that in the past, at critical moments, China had turned inward or limited its international options, to the detriment of its economy. He would tolerate bourgeois liberalization and peaceful evolution; the leaders could handle that. But he would not permit a return to Mao's policy of self-reliance of the 1960s, or to an emphasis on strengthening party control to combat peaceful evolution.

While in a broad sense Document Number 4 fostered greater reform and opening and implemented a structural change in the political power equation in Beijing, it also put forth a series of concrete measures to reform the way state enterprises operated. Deng had long been concerned with the economic drain inefficient state enterprises had on the central government. He also could not ignore the capital investment in and size of that sector of the economy. He found his answer through Zhu Rongji. Zhu had developed a plan for Shanghai's state enterprises which did not necessarily mean shutting down the factories and laying off massive numbers of workers— something no one would willingly do in the extremely unsettled Chinese industrial environment, characterized by a floating work force of over 100 million people. The trick was to develop a scheme to turn the inefficient into the efficient, subject to market forces. This Zhu had done, and Deng had made it into national policy. Regulations were written giving enterprises decision-making authority to include responsibility for profits and losses and capital appreciation. They were thus free to make personnel decisions, set wage and price policy, decide on investment strategies, and determine import and export policy. Inefficient enterprises would be shut down, but over time the efficient ones would be placed under a contract system. They would be permitted to form corporations and conduct international trading and institute a share-holding system.[6]

As part of the reform, the SPC's powers were curtailed. From this office, Chen and Li had attempted to roll back Deng's reforms. With his return to power in the spring of 1992, Deng had transferred power over the economy to Zhu and the ETO. However, this in no way meant that the personal power and influence of Chen had been diminished. Li and Chen would continue to be a thorn in Deng's side until he could rearrange the Politburo. Of course, once that was achieved, it would not really matter to him what organization was in charge—the old SPC, or something super-imposed like the ETO—since the economy would have been restructured to his specifications. He and Zhao Ziyang had used similar methods to undercut central planners in the early 1980s, then under Chen Yun's con-trol too. While the SPC's role had been downgraded, it still had a role to play in economic policy. Under changes mandated by Document Number 4, the SPC's main function and tasks were to properly formulate the over-all strategy; control gross supply and demand; guide reform; work out general programs; make overall arrangements; adjust ratios; keep a compre-hensive balance; exercise overall control; arrange key construction projects; and formulate annual plans.[7]

Reforming Enterprises

While Document Number 4 was being drafted, Deng had decided he needed an example to illustrate what he and Zhu had in store for the ailing state enterprises. Thus, just as he had taken a southern tour to announce his plans to transform the non-state sector of the economy, he took a northern tour to announce his plans to reform the state-controlled enter-prises. In May, while the finishing touches were being applied to Docu-ment Number 4, he and Zhu visited the Capital Iron and Steel Corporation (Shoudu) in Beijing to announce his new reform policies for state enter-prises. Afterward, he would travel to the Northeast, China's major industrial area, to preach his gospel of industrial reform based on the Shoudu model.[8]

Deng went to Shoudu to praise the factory, and to declare that all state enterprises should similarly experiment in order to raise efficiency and profitability. Early in the reform effort, Shoudu had implemented the fac-tory responsibility system of delegating more power to the enterprise and the factory manager, at the expense of party and state regulatory interference. As a result, it had begun to return huge profits to the state treasury. Deng had argued that only by freeing the enterprises from needless outside regulatory interference—the SPC—could they succeed. If large state enterprises became successful, then others would benefit from the freed-up capital and from these experiences. Moreover, successful enterprises could absorb weaker ones and, through vertical integration, produce a strong, efficient, and profit-making enterprise.

At Shoudu, Deng preached the message he had delivered during his southern tour. Only this time, the audience was different—this time, his audience was the state employee. They had a right to be suspicious of Deng, since he had been campaigning constantly, since his return to power in 1978, to reform these money-losing enterprises. This time, however, Deng had a new message. He preached liberation of the mind in order to save the state enterprises. Deng told the workers and managers at Shoudu that "policy was set and now it was up to the people to take the necessary steps. Those that refused to change their minds would not be able to move fast enough to accomplish his goal." He wanted to prove his critics wrong when they said that the rapid development rate of Shoudu could not be imitated. Deng challenged the workers to "open their minds to change, without fear, since the policy was set." Deng pointed out "if the experiments like Shoudu were not imitated and successful, how could China prove the superiority of socialism."

In short, Deng was advocating capitalist principles for state industries. Recall that he had already granted the PLA independence to pursue vertical integration of its industrial sector. Only the strong would survive the competition. This was measured not by labels, but by economic statistics. Deng again stated that slow economic development meant a standstill, and standstill meant regression. Again and again, he denounced the 6 percent growth rate fixed in the Five- and Ten- Year Plans, charging that it retarded economic growth. "The National People's Congress set a growth rate of six percent. It seemed that whoever exceeded six percent would disrupt the harmonious development. That is incorrect. I think that if the growth rate of six percent is rigidly kept, there will be retrogression." Deng continued: "Being content with the growth rate of six percent will only lead to retrogression and the opportunity will be missed. Japan and Hong Kong first seized the opportune moment for their development." Deng repeatedly pointed out that the moment was now. If it were not seized, the opportunity would forever be gone.

To further stress his point, Deng pointed out the reversal of the roles of Shanghai and Hong Kong. "Today Hong Kong now leads Shanghai, where years ago the roles were reversed. Now, China had to mount a third stage, to attempt to double again gross national product. If China kept to the growth rate of six percent, it could not achieve its goal." Deng's national pride was evident in his policy: "A low growth rate will only please foreign powers." Some would think that Deng feared inflation, but he stated, "How can some people withstand the pressure and continue to raise their growth rates? Because they have lofty aspirations and firm determination. Shenzhen's growth rate was as high as 47 percent so it could develop into what it is today." Deng touched on his guiding philosophy for reform of the state enterprises: "The enthusiasm of the enterprises must not be dampened and the living conditions of the masses must not be affected."[9]

The key, in Deng's mind, to a successful policy would be found in economics, which would explain his promotion of Zhu Rongji and why he had placed so much responsibility and pressure on him. Zhu stressed that it was a matter of urgency to solve the problems plaguing state enterprises—over one-third were running at a loss, another one-third were bordering on a loss.[10] The only way to save the enterprises was to make them efficient, profitable, and yet able to support a surplus labor force. Vertical integration had to reach the economies of scale to support the 100 million workers in state enterprises. Those laid off could then be retrained in subsidiary enterprises and fill in as industry expanded to meet national and international markets. Deng was quick to praise Zhu. While at Shoudu, he admitted that he knew very little about economics, but he did know those who did. "Zhu Rongji is quite capable in this connection. I think one cannot be regarded as qualified if one does not understand economics, no matter how strong one may be in the political aspect."[11]

The direction of Deng's party building was becoming evident. He was deliberately restoring the old party icon, the red and expert, to a position of authority. Zhu was politically correct—a red. He was also technically competent—an expert. Whereas the edict under Mao and the radicals of the Cultural Revolution had been to put "reds" in charge, Deng had argued for both "red" and "expert" in one official. In Zhu and several others, he had established his "red" and "expert" team that would guide China

through the remaining years of the twentieth century.[12] Deng would manip-
ulate the membership of the upcoming congress to reflect his desires for the
future. He would not trust blind fate in the transfer from one generation
to the next.

It is apparent that Deng was seeking a balance. To challenge the central
planners, led by Li and Chen, he had to have someone who was better at
their game than they themselves were. The perfect candidate would be an
economist, or someone who understood economic statistics at least as well
as the leading Marxist economists advising Li and Chen. But Zhu was a
reformer who paid little attention to Marx and more attention to economics as a science. He could support a major state role in heavy industry, or
he could allow the state to step aside. The effect was the same: profits to
the central treasury, a strong state. With reformers in charge of long-term
economic planning, regional and national goals might continue to clash,
but it was a clash among people with a shared goal, which did not include
the dismantling of either the state structure or the destruction of each
other.

Thus, Deng had taken the steps prior to the congress to release the productive energies of all those willing to challenge the old thinking. Those
willing to throw off the yoke of past traditions could strive to be rich.
State enterprises no longer had to fear progress; they could also join in the
market economy.

The regulations for reform of state enterprises had been drafted for
presentation to the NPC in March, but the fact that Deng had to address
the issue specifically in Document Number 4, as he did in his visit to the
Capital Iron and Steel Corporation in May, would seem to indicate that he
was unhappy with the pace and direction Li Peng was guiding enterprise
reform.[13] Li had set out twenty measures for correcting the problems of
state enterprises in his "Outline" to the NPC in March 1992, but as he
had not recommended a basic change in the philosophy of operations nor
had he finalized regulations drafted in conjunction with the State Council
to implement the enterprise reform laws, it was left to Zhu to recommend
the principles for enterprise transformation. First, the guidelines should be
general in nature, allowing for variation in specific applications in specific
industries. Second, the rules would use legal language that clearly spelled
out the rights and obligations of ownership and operating rights. The factory director, for instance, had to guarantee the state that he would either

return a profit, or resign. Third, the manager had to have control over internal personnel and labor issues, as well as distribution.[14]

Zhu also offered advice on how to implement the new guidelines. Before giving the factory manager the right to hire and fire personnel, regulations would have to be in place to provide security for those laid off, that is, job training and career advice. Change had to be implemented in such a way as to ensure social stability. On the sensitive issue of responsibility for profit-and-loss and the role of state regulation and direction of production, Zhu advocated the reduction of regulatory bodies, while those remaining would offer only guidance, not direction. The manager would make his own decisions; however, after a year, some form of supervisory body, including the necessary state agencies, labor representatives, bankers, and entrepreneurs, would audit the enterprise to determine whether it had met its goals. Finally, he suggested that wage increases be tied to the overall productivity of the industry involved. Thus, if the major enterprises set wage increases for a fixed percentage, all other enterprises in that sector could only increase wages up to that amount. Further, wage increases would also take into account years when there were losses. The practice of giving all profits over to wage increases, with nothing held in reserve for a bad year, forced enterprises to borrow from banks. It was better to have a reserve fund established for such situations. Zhu concluded that unless his ideas were incorporated into the reform regulations for enterprises, the effort was bound to fail.[15]

When Deng visited the Capital Iron and Steel Corporation, he had authorized the state enterprises to implement these new mechanisms, establishing Zhu's program as national policy. They were formalized when the State Council made them law in August 1992, under the title "Regulations for Replacing State-Owned Industrial Enterprises' Operating Mechanisms."[16]

Deng's faction also released Document Number 5 during this period, which spelled out conditions for developing the tertiary or service industries. This area of the economy was to be allowed to develop a market economy at a faster pace than that of state industry, to complement the former and to provide urban and rural areas with the services of commerce, finance, agriculture, tourism, law, accountancy, auditing, real estate, and business consultancy.[17] It was hoped that this would also help absorb some of the labor surplus.

While the economy took off at a rapid pace during the second half of 1992 in reaction to Deng's new policies, the reform faction nonetheless felt compelled to justify Deng's policies to his supporters and detractors alike. A public campaign was launched to portray Deng's new economics as a theoretical development in line with socialism, and having Chinese characteristics. The latter point was important since, to many, Deng seemed to say that socialism and Marxism no longer mattered and that he was advocating nothing less than capitalism to speed up economic growth and development. The campaign was based on the philosophy of the "socialist market economy." Jiang Zemin introduced the concept in a speech to the Central Party School on 6 June. Subsequently, several articles were published that discussed the new term and provided justification from a Marxist point of view. It was also used to explain Deng's policies at the Fourteenth Party Congress.

The concept was an attempt by loyal supporters to put the best face on the fact that Deng had virtually rejected Marxism with his conclusion that a sound socialist policy was any economic policy that improved the people's standard of living. By that measure, capitalism, if it improved the standard of living, was no longer capitalism but socialism, though with Chinese characteristics. Their efforts necessitated the redefinition of terms. In the standard Marxist dictionary, "market economy" was synonymous with "capitalism." However, Deng had said during his southern tour that capitalism had planning and socialism had markets, and planning was not tantamount to socialism, and markets were not tantamount to capitalism. Thus, Deng had attempted to end the debate over what was in a name, socialist or capitalist. Even if his new policies looked like capitalist measures, they were also applicable to socialism. In the Marxist lexicon, the explanation had to be more specific: "the planned commodity economy is also a commodity economy, which after developing to a certain point becomes a market economy."[18] The key was that the market economy was not the commodity economy with a quantitative increase, but with a qualitative increase. In the commodity economy, the market mechanism did not play a role in distributing labor and resources. The market economy had turned all economic relations into markets and currencies.

The purpose of the new formulation was to take the government out of micromanagement of the economy. Document Number 4 reduced the role of the SPC and increased that of the markets. This new formulation made it quite clear that the pivotal role was that of the market mechanism that controlled all distribution. Central planning would continue in the new formulation, but the government would no longer interfere in enterprises through administrative orders. Instead, it would regulate and standardize enterprise operations through non-mandatory planning and the use of economic levers, such as taxation, interest rates, and industrial policy, much like the Japanese did through the Ministry of International Trade and Industry (MITI).

Whatever machinations were used to explain Deng's "socialist market economy," it could not be denied that Deng had completely cut Chinese development off from the tree of Marxism, though he would not agree with that interpretation. He rationalized using capitalism within socialism. He did not, however, see this as being an issue for the party, since its only interest was to stay in power. Again, Deng believed that the party survived Tiananmen only because, unlike the Soviet Union, the Chinese people valued economic growth more than political liberties. Indeed, he saw that this was the case with the other authoritarian regimes throughout Southeast Asia that had become economic powerhouses. The key to understanding Deng's policies was to realize that first, last, and always, Deng was dedicated to a unified state and maintaining the party in power.

Two things occurred on the eve of the Fourteenth Congress to complicate Deng's plans for reshaping the party and policy. First, his old critics, including Song Ping, Lu Feng, and Li Peng, and even Chen Yun to an extent, had begun to sing the praises of accelerated reform and opening. Second, the economy had taken off since his southern tour, reflecting Deng's arm-twisting in February and March to force the party to shift into high gear on economic reform.

The State of the Economy

Zou Jiahua, vice-premier of the State Council and minister in charge of the SPC, briefed the Standing Committee of the NPC on 1 September on the execution of the 1992 economic plan for the first seven months of that year.[19] According to Zou, inspired by Deng's important speeches during his southern tour and the decision of the Politburo, "the people had emancipated their minds, enhanced their vigor, and displayed a high spirit and strong will. As a result, the pace of reform and opening up to the outside world had quickened and economic activity had flourished, and the national economy had entered a new stage of rapid growth." Zou credited the accelerated economy to Deng's efforts. The net result, according to the State Statistical Bureau, was that the gross national product was up 12 percent from the same period the previous year; and primary, secondary, and tertiary industries had grown at a rate of 6.7 percent, 17.5 percent, and 6.7 percent, respectively.

Zou also described the economic conditions in the various sectors of the economy. In the rural sector, the weather had cooperated, and there was a bumper harvest of grain that summer, topping the previous record. Cotton, oil-bearing crops, and sugar had also registered modest gains. The secondary activities of animal husbandry and fisheries had likewise shown gains. Pork, beef, mutton, and aquatic products were up over 10 percent. Even village and town enterprises had continued to grow in spite of the three-year rectification policy instituted by Li in 1989, due, no doubt, to Deng's tour, which had forced a change in money and lending policies. Indeed, these industries had a spectacular growth rate, with total output of over 525 billion yuan for the first six months of 1992, up 38 percent from the previous year. The export economy increased at a phenomenal rate too, up 58.5 percent over the same period in 1992.

Overall industrial production was up by 19 percent over the same period from the previous year, a far cry from the planned 6 percent advocated by Li Peng and Chen Yun. Within this figure, though, the real leaders were the collectives, townships, and non-state enterprises, with rates as high as 27 percent. The state enterprises had come in with a growth rate of only 12.8 percent. While Zou gave several reasons for the rapid economic acceleration and growth, the most significant ones were (1) social demands had accelerated, resulting in increased investments in consumer production; (2) under Deng's urging, the social forces seized the initiative, and all enterprises did their best to take advantage of the new reform and opening policies; and (3) the acceleration of the export economy. In short, the economic miracle was the result of Deng's challenge to the conservative policies of Li Peng. It had succeeded in releasing pent-up demand and growth.

In other areas of his report, Zou pointed out that investments in fixed assets had also accelerated, although he failed to acknowledge that the funds invested in state enterprises, over 163 billion yuan, up 35 percent from 1991, still constituted throwing good money after bad. Nevertheless, other non-state enterprises also got investment funds, which had an overall positive effect on the private or market sector of the economy. While investments were up, responding to the three-year shortage of funding under Li, the economy was aided by the fact that there was an abundant supply of basic consumer goods, so prices remained stable. Market sales increased over 14 percent from the previous year, aided by an increase in the money supply. The bumper summer harvest had given the peasants more income, so the rural sector of the economy had accelerated growth also. Finally, the foreign trade sector also registered accelerated gains. The value of exports grew by 19 percent, while imports grew at a rate of 33 percent. Total foreign investment, something Li and Chen had been loathe to take for fear of infringing on national sovereignty, grew at an astounding rate of 43 percent, while direct investment grew by 102 percent. Tourism was up 12 percent, and foreign exchange earnings were up 30 percent.

Nevertheless, there were major problems that needed to be addressed. Zou listed eight major areas of the economy that merited continued monitoring and occasional adjustment. First, accelerating economic development had to be based on improving economic performance. Quantitative changes would not do; qualitative changes were needed. In addition, China had to optimize its basic infrastructure, improve technology, develop the export sector, and improve efficiency. Since these were long-term strategic goals, Zou urged concentration on the more current issue of transforming the enterprises' operating mechanisms, which would allow them to change their products in response to local and international markets. Failing enterprises would no longer be protected. Finally, steps would be taken to reduce losses and increase profits within the year.

Second, Zou emphasized the need to continue to make inputs in the agrarian sector of the economy. Two areas in particular were to be given close attention. First, the farmers' well-being was not to be tampered with. All steps were to be taken to see that farmers got a fair price for their crops, and that goods would not be paid for with worthless promissory notes. In addition, local enterprises were to be supported while actively pushing for efficiency. Secondly, the government was also to emphasize disaster prevention and development of major water conservation projects that were beyond the means of local enterprises and farmers.

Third, Zou addressed the need to control investment. He called for stricter control of investment funds by limiting the authority of local officials to approve investments, by thorough audits, and by new regulations that would effectively guide local and state investment into targeted sectors or projects. He also called for more flexibility and experimentation, to include share-holding and allowing enterprise managers total responsibility for investment profit and loss. He did, however, urge regulations for establishing new developmental zones, with a goal of instituting standard, uniform laws on property rights, land use, and taxation.

Fourth, in addition to supporting strong regulatory, or macroeconomic, control of investment plans, Zou called for a sound policy on regulating banking and currency circulation. In line with policy to accelerate interior development along the borders and major waterways, Zou called for regulation of bank funds to push them in the direction of export programs and market sectors.

Fifth was Zou's call for development of the tertiary economy across all sectors—local, regional, and national. The emphasis was on developing goods for a consumer market, and at the same time fostering a consumer market. Enterprises were to develop products for all sectors of the consuming public. They were also to enter into the service sectors of law, insurance, accounting, consulting, technology, and investment. In a key statement, he advocated: "State-run large and medium-sized industrial enterprises, while carrying out the transformation of their operating mechanisms, should gradually allow their logistics services to compete in society and divert their excessive manpower to tertiary trades." To that end, Zou announced that a national conference would be held, before the end of the year, to set up regulations to implement such a plan for the remainder of the 1990s.

Sixth, Zou touched on the driving force of economic modernization: foreign trade. Zou called for allowing many more private firms to become involved in foreign trade, and for greater emphasis on using foreign funds more effectively. According to Zou, the international situation favored China and its efforts to expand exports. Thus, China should seize the moment and push exports that favored its workers, consolidate the markets it had, and open new markets. Nevertheless, he cautioned that such expansion should be implemented in a balanced manner, so that structural readjustments could be carried out and foreign exchange receipts remained balanced. To that end, he also recommended strengthening industrial policy to control the rational utilization of foreign capital and direct its investment.

Seventh, Zou picked up on one of Deng's favorite topics: increased attention to science and technology. Echoing Deng, Zou called for increases to education to produce more scientists and technicians. He also called for a limited "cultural flowering" to support new thinking. Though not a call for another One Hundred Flowers campaign, he was advocating a flowering to support the new socialist society that would emerge.

Eighth, he touched on the decision to separate government administration and regulation from the daily running of state enterprises. He called for giving the enterprise managers the authority to manage, while the government took on the role of macroeconomic controller. He called for further acceleration of price reforms, planning, finance, banking, and foreign trade. He left nothing to guess: "When reforming the planning system, we are primarily going to further change the functions and methods of planned management in a bid to enable planning to correctly reflect the market, provide effective guidance for the market and give play to its role in providing overall guidance for and exercising macroeconomic control over economic development in a better way." That was the general line—market mechanisms would be tried. In addition, there would be an attempt to rationalize the relations between the central and local governments, one of the keys to Deng's institutional change to the power arrangements. The state distribution system that favored state enterprises would be revised to reflect a market economy; the budgeting process would be altered; taxation and financing changes would be adjusted to reflect market needs; and local areas would be given guidance on implementing foreign investment developments.[20]

Thus, on the eve of the Fourteenth Party Congress, in the economic sphere, at least, it would appear that Deng had achieved his goals. The economy had taken off. Deng had successfully forced Li and his central planners to loosen the economic reins—so much that even Zhu had begun to worry about overheating the economy. Speaking to a restricted audience in late August or early September, most likely at an informal expanded

Politburo meeting to include the ETO and State Council leadership, Zhu reviewed economic growth since the reforms and indicated that it was necessary to rein in certain activities.

What is significant is the approach Zhu took to resolving the problem. He spelled out the issues: "the striving for a faster growth rate mentioned in Deng Xiaoping's southern tour talks bears three attributes: good efficiency, high quality, and export orientation. Any blind high growth rate not in keeping with the aforementioned three conditions will lead to trouble."[21] Economic growth rates for the year were considerably in excess of the planned 6 percent advocated by Li Peng and Chen Yun. Indeed, overall growth had surpassed the planned rate by 10 to 20 percent, and had not produced any problems to date. Zhu was concerned with the trend in investments. Capital construction investments were up 40 percent over the previous year, most of which were beyond SPC control since local administrations had the authority to approve such projects. The influx of new capital had outpaced the ability of the economy to absorb it, which affected Deng's criteria for efficiency and exportability. Small breweries, cigarette makers, and other small consumer industries had sprung up, protected by local authorities, making it difficult to control investment. The overall trend was that the target investment goal of 400 billion yuan had been exceeded before the end of June. To "guide" investments to the proper channels, the State Council had to revise investment and loan regulations and attempt to coax the state enterprises into sound reinvestment schemes to build infrastructure. In line with the planned economic changes in enterprise management, the State Council implemented new price reforms, raising the price on primary and basic products, raising fees, raising the state purchasing price for agriculture products, and removing state controls on over 570 products, allowing manufacturers to set their own prices. The net result was that, on the eve of the Party Congress, the state controlled prices on a mere 89 products, whereas 80 percent of price fixing powers had been transferred to the enterprises.[22] Zhao had failed in 1988; Zhu had succeeded a mere four years later. In between, the world had shifted.

The overall situation in September 1992 was a mirror image in many respects of the conditions that existed in 1988, when an overheated economy had led to retrenchment. Bank loans had reached a record 20 percent for the year, while output increased by only 12 percent. Currency in circulation had reached a level second only to that of the historic high year of 1988. Compounding these problems, inflationary pressures had also risen; credit and loans had risen dramatically—twice as high as the planned rate, and twice as high as for the same period in 1991; currency circulation was being implemented ahead of the planned schedule, while currency withdrawal had slowed to the lowest level since 1982, excluding 1988; and bank deposits by enterprises were up, while consumer deposits were down by 3 percent from 1991.[23] The reason inflation had failed to manifest itself as a major issue was due to the relative balance between supply and demand in the consumer market, aided by a third year of bumper harvests that contributed to price stabilization. While consumer savings were low, they had grown over previous years. Overall, the general situation going into the party congress was a very heated economy, but a manageable one for perhaps 12 to 24 months. This was not a very optimistic forecast, but Deng had achieved his goal set in January: the economy had rallied. Deng was only interested in the grossest of economic figures. He had to force the people, the leadership and the bureaucracy to see the value in economic growth and to lure investments from the West. Once it had tied up large amounts of Western credit, China would be able to take off on an expansion similar to that in the other Asian dragons—Singapore, Hong Kong, Taiwan, and South Korea.

In spite of institutional changes and high growth rates, Deng made no effort to remove the state from its role as formulator of industrial policy, nor was there any effort to transfer control of those industrial assets to the provinces or private individuals. The state, including the PLA, maintained control of the key industries, such as steel, armaments, electronics, chemical, and natural resources. Instead, Deng gave power to those technocrats loyal to the party and the idea of state capitalism. These new entrepreneurs were not capitalists but Stalinists, ideologically closer to the views of Chen Yun but more practical. They recognized the value of the market economy in employing China's large rural labor force. They, like Chen, believed that China would be a powerful nation-state, with a powerful central government financed by a heavy industry controlled by the state. In fact, the PLA now constituted a state within a state in its ability to influence policy. When allied with the central civilian industries, the military-industrial complex would dwarf all other sectors of the economy.

Deng had set out to seize control of the policy-making levers that he had surrendered at the Fourth Plenum of the Thirteenth Party Congress in November of 1989. Once that was accomplished, he needed to ensure continuity of his policies. Thus, new economic policies and economic growth did not satisfy Deng's long-term strategy. He could not trust the likes of Li Peng and Zou Jiahua. He had to implement structural change of the party and government if his policies were to survive him.

5 | The PLA As "Protector and Escort"

◈ New Age, New Strategies

Before documenting the changes at the Fourteenth Congress, it is important to understand the new and increased role of the PLA in Chinese society. After all, the leadership had taken great efforts to get the PLA back to the barracks following the Tenth Congress in 1973. As a result of the chaos of the Cultural Revolution, Mao had turned to the PLA as the embodiment of his ideology and as the only organized force capable of restoring order and production in society. Deng subsequently had been called out of political exile to help dismantle the military hold on power. In large part, he had been successful. Clearly things had either changed, or Deng was desperate. In either case, one must understand some recent PLA history, in order to comprehend the significance of Yang Baibing's actions in early 1992, when he pledged that the PLA would support Deng's efforts to reignite economic modernization. Yang, basically, was placing the pistol of the PLA at the head of the Party Central. They blinked, and Deng emerged victorious. But the PLA now had a significant role in policy, as never before.

To understand the role of the PLA in Deng's scheme to seize power and to redirect economic policy, one must understand its recent history and Deng's role in its development. When Deng returned to power in 1978, he returned to take charge of the PLA. He was appointed Chief of the General Staff. However, his real power had nothing to do with the office; Deng was one of the "Long Marchers" and had power by virtue of his ties and revolutionary credentials. He was also given back a seat on the Politburo Standing Committee, as well as a position as State Council vice-chairman. He eventually ousted Hua Kuofeng from power, but instead of taking the job as secretary general, he gave it to his protégé, Hu Yaobang, while Deng retained a seat on the CMC and control over the PLA as de facto commander in chief, through a long history of association, as well as his nominal office on the General Staff. When Deng launched his Four Modernizations in the early 1980s, national defense was the last priority. Thus its budget was never sufficient to modernize the personnel-heavy peasant army of which Mao had been so proud.

Deng and his advisors reviewed the world situation in the early 1980s and concluded that the Soviet Union was a major threat. This meant moving slightly closer to the United States when normalization efforts with Moscow ran aground in the aftermath of Soviet support for Vietnam in the 1979 Sino-Vietnamese War and the subsequent Soviet invasion of Afghanistan. In 1980 and 1981 China's strategic analysts, in a reassessment of Soviet power, concluded Moscow had overextended itself, and was on an inexorable decline.[1] With that conclusion came the corollary that there was little likelihood of a major war between the superpowers. A period of peace could be expected. As a result, Chinese defense planners felt that less money needed to be diverted from the urgent task of modernizing the economy—industry and agriculture—for the army.

In order to ensure a minimal reinvestment, Deng and his advisors had allowed the PLA to enter the export market. Thus, in 1979 the PLA began to sell weapons on the international market. The timing proved fortuitous for the PLA, as the Iran-Iraq War had begun. However, it was more likely that the timing was designed to take advantage of Moscow's reluctance to supply Iraq, because of its efforts to shore up relations with the new Islamic Republic of Iran on its border. The situation gave China the opportunity to be a player in superpower politics. In any event, China rapidly became one of the five leading arms merchants in the world. Although its weapons were no match in quality to those offered by the West—the United States, Great Britain, France, and Germany—its weapons were cheap and easy to maintain. In the Third World, it was often not the quality as much as quantity that mattered. So, during the early years of his modernization campaign, Deng allowed the PLA to sell off its own weapons to obtain the funds to develop new ones. He also allowed the PLA to manufacture civilian products in its plants. Instead of manufacturing armaments, defense industries turned to making washing machines, cars, bicycles, and televisions. Money made from civilian economic enterprises was in turn used to develop new weapons systems.[2]

With the election of Ronald Reagan as president of the United States, the Chinese concluded that Soviet influence and power were on the decline, and especially so after Gorbachev came to power. Thus, Deng and his advisors began to revise military doctrine, away from a strategy of preparing to fight a general war with the Soviet Union to that of preparing to fight small-scale, localized, but intense wars around the periphery of China.[3] This reassessment, in 1985, meant that a large standing army was no longer necessary. Indeed, Mao's ideal of maintaining a large peasant army to fight a defensive war of attrition by luring the enemy deep into China's heartland was no longer valid. Instead, a smaller, technologically sophisticated force, equipped for speed and mobility and capable of bringing concentrated firepower to bear on specific targets, was needed. China's defense planners had come to the realization that modern military technology granted an aggressor the capability to seize the initiative in the opening battles of a war, and those first battles would be crucial in future wars. Mobilizing the entire country and the people was no longer an option.

Contemporary and future warfare required standing forces capable of quick and lethal responses. Therefore, it was determined that each military region would be tasked as a general theater of operation and trained to respond to local wars on its periphery. They would also participate in joint operations, and develop new units as necessary to meet new technologies or strategies. China also developed "fist" forces for rapid, hard-hitting deployment, much like the United States' Ranger forces. Along with its plans to strengthen the PLA, China prepared also to expand its navy, from coastal to blue-water.[4] Thus, a marine corps was formed and plans drawn up for an aircraft carrier. A CMC meeting was convened in 1985 to initiate this change in strategy.

Whereas during the middle 1980s the PLA was starved for state funding, all of that changed in 1989. The necessity of calling on the PLA to put down the students no doubt facilitated double-digit budget increases. However, two things occurred in 1991 that forced a renewed look at the role of the PLA in Chinese society. First was the United States' demonstration of overwhelming technological superiority over Iraq's combat forces, whose equipment was standard among communist forces. The United States' victory was essentially a victory over PRC weapons systems that were mere copies of the Soviet equipment in Iraq. China would obviously have to modernize its weapons systems if it was going to compete in the international arms market. Cheap had its value, but in the end the wealthier nations would buy quality. Second was the failed coup in the Soviet Union in August of 1991. The Soviet army had not obeyed the party. For China this was ominous, since units of the PLA had refused to march against the students in Tiananmen in 1989. Several senior field commanders had been disciplined and relieved of command. In the end, the PLA had moved in as ordered. Nevertheless, the dictum of the party controlling the gun had broken down along the edges.

Thus, when Deng called a CMC meeting in December 1991, he was already considering how to continue reform of the PLA and ensure loyalty to the party. He announced in *Liberation Army Daily:* "It is inconceivable for the standing army, public security organs, courts and prisons to wither away under a condition in which classes and imperialism and hegemonism exist. We must build a powerful, revolutionary army that is modernized and standardized."[5] At the early December CMC meeting, he cleared the way to fund the modernization effort, and undertook internal reforms to deal with army insubordination at Tiananmen. In a more significant move, he decreed that the PLA would retain control of its industrial enterprises for as long as his policies prevailed, that is, for one hundred years. This was reflected in Yang's instructions to the Army: "in order to perform our duty well, it is imperative for the Army to study the basic line of the Party, subordinate all of its work to the state economic development and support the country's reform and economic construction with concrete deeds. If we keep to this line unwaveringly for 100 years to come, there would be great hope for China."[6]

Immediately following the CMC meeting, Deng's supporters in the military, as well as those in government and the party, fanned out to spread his message and make arrangements for his assault on the party. Deng himself set a grueling schedule of going into the countryside to deliver the message that the PLA was supporting him. Deng showed up in Jinan on 2 January 1992, accompanied by CMC members Liu Huaqing and Qin Jiwei. It was clear to anyone watching—the PLA had openly sided with Deng against the legitimate party leadership in Beijing. Deng next went to Shanghai on 15 January, accompanied by Yu Qiuli, also a PLA veteran. Deng left his message with the party leadership in Shanghai and departed for Guangdong and Shenzhen on 18 January, arriving in Shenzhen on the 19th. In Shenzhen, he completed the arrangements of the "Grand Compromise" among the PLA, the regional officials, the public security forces, and the elders. He was thus ready to return to Beijing and Party Central after the New Year and make policy changes.

Thus, following Li Peng's Work Report to the NPC in March 1992, Yang Baibing was prepared, with Deng's backing, to announce publicly that the PLA would provide an "escort" for Deng's new call for greater, faster, bolder reform and opening.[7] Though he was not the first to proclaim PLA support for Deng's economic program, he did speak on the record for the CMC and the PLA: "the one center and two basic points line of the Party is the highest summation of the experience, both positive and negative, in economic development since the founding of New China." He further stated that Deng's policy reflected objective law and was a fundamental guarantee for making the country rich and strong (fu qiang). This latter statement reflected a mindset that had emerged within the leadership which saw China restored to its rightful place in the family of nations—a power equal to that of the Western nations, which had for so long dominated China and continued to haunt its psyche.

Commenting on Li Peng's NPC address, Yang called it a very good report: "It reflects Comrade Deng Xiaoping's judgment on building socialism with Chinese characteristics and clearly shows the principal theme of accelerating the pace of reform and economic development and opening wider to the outside world." Yang continued: "When speaking about 'safeguarding or protecting,' we are referring to safeguarding economic construction. We should not only have a clear-cut attitude toward this issue, but should also take realistic action. First, we should be conscientiously patient and build the army with diligence and thrift. We should understand the state's problems, refrain from asking for help, be more patient, apply careful calculation and strict budgeting, strive to conserve and reduce expenses, and increase the effectiveness of military expenditures. Second, it is necessary to teach cadres and soldiers to understand the principle that 'individual people's wealth leads to state wealth which will produce military strength' so that they will react positively to various policies and measures implemented in the course of accelerating the pace of reform. Recently, with the approval of the CMC, the PLA GPD organized two groups of military regional leaders to visit special economic zones, including those in Shenzhen and Zhuhai. The goals were to study and show our support for reform and opening. Third, the army should actively participate in major construction projects undertaken by both the state and various localities." Here, beyond all doubt, Yang was linking PLA industrial efforts to that of the civil sector.

Elements of the "Grand Compromise" echoed in these and other comments made for public consumption. According to Yang, "by maintaining constant vigilance and keeping good conditions, the army provides an effective guarantee to the country's safety and stability, and the most effective support to reform and opening. We should do well in reform in the military, political, logistics and scientific research fields in accordance with the tasks formulated by the CMC."

Yang Baibing was not the only senior PLA officer to speak out in favor of Deng's new policy, as articulated by Li Peng at the NPC session. Qin Jiwei, the Defense Minister and a CMC member, described Li's speech as "practical and inspiring." "We should implement the party's basic line of 'one central task and two basic points' with more conscientiousness." He called for the nation to seize the initiative to speed up reform and opening, to achieve faster economic development, echoing what Deng had identified as the crucial point—timeliness. However, to achieve this goal, he noted that the PLA would have to emancipate its mind and overcome formalism. He declared that the PLA would actively push ahead with its internal reforms as called for by the CMC, while it continued to implement the party's basic line.

Chi Haotian, the chief of the PLA General Staff and CMC member, added his praise, and further defined the PLA's new role in society as protector of internal stability as well as guarantor of national security. According to Chi, "the spirit of reform would penetrate into all the work of the army." He spelled out the fundamental task: "to ensure a secure and

stable environment for the country's economic construction and reform
and opening to the outside world." In order to perform its tasks of safeguarding national security, social stability, and supporting economic construction, he called on the Army to be bold and creative.[8] Thus the PLA
general staff, the CMC, and the Defense Minister all spoke in favor of
Deng's new policy of bolder, faster reform and economic development and
opening. There could be no misunderstanding as to where the PLA stood.

Deng lost no time in his effort to force the party to toe the PLA's line
of making money to pay for a strong country, strong army. He called
senior PLA officials to his residence almost immediately after the NPC
session, on the night of 28 March, to reassert his long-term goals. The
meeting—an informal, enlarged CMC meeting—included the commanders and political commissars from the military regions, the special services
and arms, and the various academies. The gathering also included, by name,
Jiang Zemin, Yang Shangkun, Qiao Shi, Ding Guangen, Wen Jiabao, Hong
Xuezhi, Liu Huaqing, Yang Baibing, Chi Haotian, Zhao Nanqi, Qin Jiwei,
and Li Desheng.[9] Deng took the opportunity to reaffirm the PLA's role:
"I think the people's Army work should be focused on the eight Chinese
characters meaning 'defend the motherland, build the motherland.' The
Army should do a good job in increasing its cultural level, obtaining more
military knowledge, and improving military skills, so that the three armed
services can always be on the alert and in a perfect state. This is itself a powerful deterrent force. Only thus can the Army provide the central work of
the whole party and whole nation with a realistic guarantee and support."[10]
It was clear that Deng was using the PLA to blackmail the party into sub-
mission, and he was clearly exhorting the PLA to engage in economic construction in the interests of modernization.

Deng went on to explain the importance of science and technology in
the new world, as clearly demonstrated in the Gulf War. He stated that
most countries of the world were busy carrying out reforms and accelerating development in these fields. Thus, it was vital that China do the same;
otherwise "we will surely lag behind for a long time and be unable to raise
our heads and will be bullied by others."[11]

He next addressed the critical issue of who controls the PLA. It had
always been axiomatic that the party controlled the gun, but Deng was not
taking chances. Deng restated the principle: "The Party commands the
gun. The gun should be absolutely subordinated to the Party's command

and should most firmly and rapidly carry out the Party's calls and orders. Thus it will provide a reliable guarantee for adhering to the Party's basic line for 100 years."[12] He had the PLA leadership at his residence for one purpose: to pledge personal loyalty to Jiang and the Party, as represented by the gathered elders.[13] He directed that the PLA subordinate itself to his designated successor, Jiang Zemin: "you are under the leadership of Jiang Zemin, the younger chairman of the Central Military Commission, and he will work with you to open up a new situation of the PLA and march toward the 21st century."[14]

In addition, Deng got a personal pledge of support for Jiang from the commanders, delivered by the Guangzhou Military Region commander Zhu Dunfa, who pledged, "The people's Army will absolutely carry out the party's line and obey Chairman Jiang's orders, whether in a peaceful environment . . . or even under the circumstances of violent storms."[15] Since economic construction was the pillar for national defense development, the generals also pledged, "under the new situation in which beloved Comrade Deng Xiaoping has called for speeding up reform and opening up, we, various large military regions, must take real action to support and defend reform and opening up. While carrying out the Army's central work, we must support the construction and work in various parts of our country and render our contributions gratuitously."[16] This was translated into a seat on the Politburo for a select group of generals.[17] It was also the go-ahead for economic endeavors.

While Deng was taking steps to solidify party control over the PLA with the assistance of the Yangs and Liu Huaqing, the political watchdog over the military—the General Political Department, headed by Yang Baibing—launched its own program to reinforce loyalty. In an article written after the failed Soviet coup, GPD propaganda asserted the party nature of the PLA.[18] The article pointed out that peaceful evolution had affected the Army. Bourgeois liberalization had seeped in, and the idea that the PLA should be depoliticized and de-particized had gained an audience with a small number of officers and soldiers. According to the article, "it is necessary to eliminate the influence of such fallacies that the army should be depoliticized and the party and the army should be separated and make it clear that our Army is the Army of the Party."[19] It also argued that the notion that the army was neutral and should not interfere in politics was a fallacy. "The Army is an armed group carrying out the party's political tasks and is a tool for political struggle."[20] Deng had placed the PLA back under the direct control of the leading group on the Standing Committee, and the elders.

For those who had any doubt about the Army's perceived role in domestic politics, the article was quite clear: "Internally, opposing subversion and protecting the people's peaceful labor also represents another important function of the Armed Forces. . . . the suppression of counterrevolution soon after the founding of the republic and the quelling of the counter-revolutionary rebellion in Beijing in the late spring and early summer of 1989 have fully proven that a powerful people's army is of decisive importance to stabilizing the situation. . . . The fundamental task for the PLA is to maintain stability as a basic precondition and important guarantee for advancing socialist modernization."[21]

The article went on to list a host of domestic situations that required constant monitoring. First, while the party had decreed that class struggle was a thing of the past, since the exploiting class had been wiped out, it was accepted that class struggle could still arise in certain areas and intensify at any time. Second, while the PLA had been successful in curbing the Tiananmen uprising in 1989, the clash between the Four Cardinal Principles and the forces of bourgeois liberalism would continue for years to come while China attempted to modernize, just as elements hostile to modernization would continue to go to any lengths to sabotage the program, and the economic impact of rectification could also spark violent outbursts. Third, the reform process itself would be subject to mistakes from time to time, which would provide hostile forces opportunities to sow discord. For all these reasons, the article concluded that it was important to discard any notion that the PLA was only for use against external enemies. Instead, it argued "the Armed Forces should consistently be loyal to the party, the people, and socialism, be ready at all times to deal with breaking situations to safeguard party leadership and the socialist system."[22]

While the GPD was stressing the need for political correctness and loyalty to the party, other articles published in the PLA paper *Liberation Army Daily* were spelling out the requirements for a modern army. China's military had been involved in armaments production over the years; however, as noted above, in the early 1980s, Deng had ordered the PLA to concentrate on civilian-oriented production as well as foreign arms sales. The PLA had initially objected, since this would slow the reequipping of its own forces. But with the collapse of the Soviet Union, Deng was able to convince the PLA leadership that it was easier, in some instances, to buy modern weapons and military technology than produce it. Of course, this required money, and the only way to get that was through economic modernization, as had been discussed at the December CMC meeting. Deng decided that the quickest and most efficient way to achieve this was to unite the leaders of industry—national and local—with the military leadership to forge the classic military-industrial complex.

The PLA would not be forced out of the industries it controlled in manufacturing, electronics, and weapons production, but it would increasingly share the field with more efficient state-owned or privatized industries. Xinxing, Norenco, and Poly Tech, to name a few PLA trading companies, would be modernized so that, through vertical integration and horizontal cooperation, they would be able to compete on the world market and absorb surplus labor—the plague of the economy, and currently plaguing the state enterprises. Future areas of cooperation would also be opened with their counterpart civilian state enterprises. The ultimate goal was to create mammoth *zaibatsu*-like combines, as in Japan and Korea. Under such arrangements, the state industries would not necessarily have to be as efficient as those in the West, but the degree of cooperation among management, labor, state, and army would be quite high.

Other articles published in *Liberation Army Daily* addressed modernization. According to one article, "modernization in the last 20 years had come to mean improvement in quality, not quantity. It was the margin of victory. An army ill equipped to match the superior quality of an opponent would be defeated, even if it had a force of 1 million troops. The PLA was facing a turbulent, unsettled world with intense competition. Hegemonism and power politics were present. To cope with the new international environment, it was necessary to improve the technological level of the PLA. Such an improvement, though, was not limited to arms only, but included a myriad of subjects, including politics, theory, structure and personnel."[23]

The article went on to review the recent changes in warfare, which was important since the PLA now realized that Mao's old theories of falling back and drawing the enemy in, followed by attacks of massive numbers of troops, would no longer work. Modern wars could be over in a number of days, without ground forces ever engaging each other. Clearly, the pride of the PLA—its large numbers—was no longer a blessing, but a burden. Senior PLA theorists had watched and analyzed the wars in the Falklands, the Middle East, Grenada, Libya, and Panama. They had come to the star-tling conclusion that warfare had changed. Now, the chief threat was from limited wars, fought with high-tech weapons. Future wars would be char-acterized by electronic warfare and unified theaters of operation using com-bined forces of air, sea, and land, as well as space. Command and control would be centralized, with wars fought from a distance, using such mod-ern weapons as cruise missiles, without hand-to-hand combat. The author issued a call for the military to change to meet the new conditions. The Gulf War of 1991 had been the testing ground for the new, high-tech arms: "Stealth bombers, cruise missiles, 'Mavericks,' 'Patriots,' a new generation of operational platforms, electronic-warfare equipment, remote-sensing equip-ment of superior quality, night-vision devices, advanced systems of com-mand, control, communications and intelligence." The net results of such qualitative improvements in warfare—high-speed, high-accuracy weapons with high-destruction levels, as well as high-survival rate of systems—had changed the nature of modern warfare, with the air force emerging as a dominant player. The Gulf War had revealed the nature of all the new technologies of modern warfare, and China had to pay attention.

The articles above spelled out the reason that the PLA had agreed to its pivotal role in Deng's "Grand Compromise." As the author stressed "The greatest interest for China's survival and development in the next two decades rests on realizing the strategic goal of economic renovation. The realization of this goal calls for domestic stability, security along the bor-ders with peripheral states, and a world order that falls in line with the common interest of the world's people. All of this requires us to further augment building military strength while attaching importance to politics, economic science, technology and diplomacy."

For the PLA, the beginning of its recognition of the revolutionary change in warfare had come when it adopted Deng's policies in the 1980s, which moved away from the belief that numerous troops equated to power. In 1985 Deng, as head of the CMC, had decided to reduce the PLA by one million men. "It was that momentous decision that broke the shackles which impeded our Army's modernization for a long time." Again, in late 1991, after turning to the PLA, Deng changed doctrine to reflect the need to fight short-duration, localized, standoff wars, or brush fires. His policy mirrored those of Western nations that had emerged strong, based on strong national economies. Their national economies had led military technology, and were dependent on trade and peace to advance.

Deng launched China on a Westernized economic transformation, with the military-industrial relationship paramount to success. Lest anyone doubt China's continuing feelings of inferiority as the spur to greater productivity, the article concluded on a ringing, patriotic note, guaranteed to send chills down the spines of its Asian neighbors: "Between now and the year 2000 is a crucial period in which our national and Army construction will be accelerated. It has a bearing on whether or not China will realize the strategic goal of making rather great economic developments by 2000, and whether or not our Army will fulfill its wish to become one of the most powerful armies in the world in the mid-21st century."[24] Only through linking national economic development with military modernization, would China become rich and powerful on the world scene. The military-industrial complex was cemented in Beijing, with an ominous warning to the world. There was no mention of separating the PLA from its economic enterprises. In fact, it was just the opposite; as noted, the chief of staff had called for greater vertical integration to increase efficiency.

An editorial in *Liberation Army Daily* on 1 January 1992, which addressed both issues—party loyalty and modernization of the army—called for improved control measures as part of a modernized army. It set out the Army's major tasks for the new year: to implement Deng's theories on Army building in the new period, stressing quality and the traditions of hard work and frugality, and to continue readjustment, reform, and improvement of the cadres' work style. The editorial called for "research in national defense science in order to ensure more effectively the party's absolute leadership over the Army and to boost fighting capability comprehensively."[25] In order to improve quality, troops and commanders had to possess high degrees of political awareness; advanced military education, to include scientific and technical training; modern, sophisticated weapons and equipment; and modern military formations combining men and arms. In addition, the army had to reorganize into elite units—flexible, rapid-reacting, with high firepower.[26]

The modernization of the PLA was one of Deng's major goals, and the core modernizers could be expected to be loyal to him. The losers, however, could be expected to present problems. In 1985 he had launched the

ten-year million-man, force reduction program, due for completion in
1995. An article in the July 1992 issue of *Liaowang* stated that the reform
effort was only in its seventh year.[27] Already, though, the change from an
infantry-based force was evident. Sixty percent of the PLA had been transformed into composite, or group army forces. Such forces were integrated
units of artillery, engineers, tank, communication, chemical, and electronic
countermeasures specialized forces, or corps.

Gone, according to the article, was the rustic soldier, replaced by a new,
more refined soldier. The Air Force and the Navy were now the favored
services. As for the officer corps, over 40 percent held college degrees. Since
the reforms had begun in 1985, a coherent education system, headed during
its formative years by Deng's stalwart supporter Zhang Zhen, was evolving
that would eventually replace the old field army loyalties as the common
bond among the PLA elite. Over 600,000 troops had passed through the
new education system. Naturally, the highest emphasis was still on political loyalty; indeed, the article pointed out that in recent years the PLA had
maintained a spotless reputation for placing loyalty to the party above all
else.

The net result of such education was an army that still regarded the West
as an enemy—not an adversary or sporting competitor, but an "enemy."
Jiang Zemin made the statement that "anyone who criticizes me for clink-
ing glasses with Western leaders, should know that this is only for tactical
reasons. I am aware of the fact that the West remains our chief enemy."[28]

On the eve of the Eight Plenum in October 1991, Deng held a Politburo Standing Committee meeting with the CAC, or at least several elders,
present. In addition to arguing for a renewed drive for reform and opening
to further cement the bonds of loyalty from a new generation of PLA
leaders, Deng took responsibility for the 4 June Incident, which meant that
the PLA—old and new—did not have to shoulder any blame other than
following orders. Deng had called for a pledge of personal loyalty by all to
his selected leader, Jiang Zemin. Yang Shangkun declared that Jiang would
henceforth decide CMC affairs. Yang, as secretary, could no longer move
troops or implement orders without Jiang's signature.[29] The presence of
both Liu Huaqing and Yang Baibing indicated that Deng was solidifying
power within the PLA, under the direction of a core of longtime supporters or PLA elders. In turn, CMC members and leading generals were
to sit in on Politburo discussions.[30] Thus, consensus would rule the chain

of command from the Politburo and the Standing Committee and CMC through the GSD to the field commanders, many of whom had sat in on policy discussions, ensuring the correct political line.

In a further move to consolidate the alliance of the PLA and the regional party officials—many his own appointees—Deng moved to recruit Ye Xuanping, the son of Marshal Ye Jianying, former governor of Guangdong and a leading reformer. Ye Xuanping was married to the sister of Zou Jiahua, who was regarded as a political conservative in Chen Yun's camp. Zou subsequently made a statement to the effect that the country could stand a growth rate of 20 percent, if it was based on efficiency.[31] The close relationship of Ye and Zou amounted to tacit endorsement of Deng's new policies, and a major defeat for Li Peng. With Zhu and Zou, both from the Shanghai stronghold of Jiang Zemin, allied with the forces of change in Guangdong, Deng was able to seize virtual control of economic policy. The military-industrial complex was forming across ideological lines. The leaders of key economic provinces were establishing close working relationships with powerful central government military and civilian leaders in an effort to allow the smooth, unhampered growth of the economy—local, regional, and national. The result of such relationships would boost total growth and propel the PLA's budget upward. Industry, both private and state-owned, would benefit.

In December, the Army's mouthpiece had printed editorials justifying the Army's role in production—something the PLA was not prepared to give up—pointing out that it benefited all Chinese, since the PLA ran its industries efficiently, and thus was not a burden to the state. As the article stated: "To be sure, the Army must never give up production and economic activities."[32] The Army's response was that, in the present circumstances, where little was available from the state for spending on the military, the army had engaged in production to be self-sufficient and a lesser burden on the state and people.

But the situation did present a dilemma for the Chinese leaders. "On the one hand, the Army is the state's military arm for carrying out special missions—the Army's duties mean that it is unsuitable for it to be involved in production and economic activities, but on the other hand, as China is now at the initial stage of socialism, the Army cannot possibly rely completely on the state for provisions in the near future, and therefore cannot give up production and economic activity."[33] The PLA had been attempting to separate economic and military activities and it had generally been unsuccessful; most units wanted to maintain the enterprises because they were big moneymakers. However, over the long term, the PLA command was committed to a unified administration of the enterprises.[34] In any case, Deng had agreed in December that the PLA would be guaranteed money to modernize, and for that reason allowed to keep its enterprises.[35]

April CMC Meeting

The April CMC meeting picked up where the January Zhuhai meeting had left off. It was an expanded meeting, attended by all senior commanders, military region commanders, and commissars. While not mentioned, Qiao Shi no doubt attended, since he was given overall control of the armed police forces (People's Armed Police) and special "secret service police" as a means to assure party control.[36] Thus, Deng, Peng Zhen, and Yang Shangkun sealed the "Grand Compromise." The meeting, according to Taiwanese sources, discussed policy for the remainder of Deng's tenure. A key issue was a decision to restructure the PLA and eliminate the seven military regions—a move that would place all PLA forces under the unified and direct control of the CMC.

As part of the deal to nudge the senior PLA leaders into retirement and to give up their powerful regional commands, Deng established an advisory commission to the CMC, whose members retained the privileges enjoyed while on active duty. As a result, hundreds of new field and command assignments opened up for younger, more-educated officers—technically competent and politically neutral or, more precisely, loyal to the party. In short, Deng was giving the younger officers a stake in the new order that would make China a first-rate military power. They, in exchange, would support the party, protect the unified state, and put down any threat to its livelihood, foreign or domestic. Thus, according to the Taiwanese source, reshuffling the military commanders and eliminating the commands would ensure central control.[37]

The decisions reached at the April enlarged CMC meeting were later disseminated as Central Committee General Office Document Number 26. It, along with Yang Baibing's Army Day speech, provided the details of the reform and optimization of the PLA, based on rationalization, readjustment, and retirements.[38] The seven regions were to be reduced to four—a movement away from geographical commands to functional, mobile commands in order to increase efficiency and institute a modernized, scientific command and control structure. Command prerogatives were also drastically reduced in favor of direct command by the General Staff and the CMC. The overall troop strength was to be cut by another one million men, as had been done in 1985. Further, the many schools and academies were to be closed to streamline education and provide for a more manageable, centralized education process controlled by the General Staff, thus further eroding field army ties. Surplus officers were to be transferred to the military districts, which now had the main function of cementing close economic ties with the people. This translated into joint economic construction projects.

The main emphasis of Document Number 26 was on centralization of the command structure in Beijing under the CMC and General Staff. As part of that effort, the specialized arms—artillery, chemical, armored, and engineering—were merged into one branch directly under the General Staff. With the emphasis on composite, or group armies, the chain of command now bypassed the military region. The group armies—the new rapid-reaction forces being trained for short-duration, lightning combat—would be under direct supervision of the General Staff and have a new corps of commanders who had graduated from a military schooling system that in recent years bore the stamp of Zhang Zhen and other modernizers—a new generation of "Whampoa-style" graduates. Deng was building a politically reliable force—not a force divorced from politics, but totally controlled by the leading group at the top, the CMC.[39] He was following in the steps of Sun Yat-sen and Chiang Kai-shek; each demanded personal loyalty. In Deng's case, loyalty was to the party and its current leadership.

The April meeting also discussed future personnel changes for the military regions, districts, and specialized arms, including Liu Huaqing's promotion to first vice-chairman of the CMC. However, the changes would not be made until after the party congress, to ensure that Deng had loyal forces available until Zhu and Deng's other lieutenants were in place and

Chen Yun was neutralized. At that time, the shift of power from his generation to that of Jiang's and Zhu's would be complete, with a few select elders, anointed by Deng and Peng Zhen, to sit in on Politburo discussions and provide guidance.[40]

Liu's elevation to first vice-chairman of the CMC was also further proof of Deng's rearrangement of the power relationship among the elders, the Politburo, and the CMC. By virtue of his membership on the Politburo Standing Committee as well, Liu's promotion restored Standing Committee supervision of the CMC. Yang Shangkun would be elevated out of the Politburo to the all-powerful elders advisory body, where all important issues would continue to be resolved, and Yang Baibing, whose office in the CMC was abolished, would continue to influence PLA issues as a member of the Politburo.

The April CMC meeting was not entirely without dissension, especially over the issues of streamlining and force reduction. Soldiers were concerned about loss of benefits—housing, food allotments, commissary privileges, salary, and medical care. The state lured many senior officers into retirement with promises of sinecure jobs in industry, which would provide a pension and a house and, for some of the most senior officers, membership on the boards of major companies and a car. Thus, for this group, they and their families suffered no loss of position or income. The vast patronage available in its economic enterprises provided a safety net for senior members of the PLA. For the vast majority—the foot soldiers—however, being mustered out meant returning to a home village that could not support them. Some were formed into local militia units, which provided some extra pay, but for the most part those affected by the military downsizing were cast into the labor pool at large and expected to fend for themselves.

The Army paper published a number of articles justifying downsizing or structured optimization, as it was called in 1992.[41] A May article argued that, while a modern military force depended on three major ingredients—modernized weapons and equipment, high-quality personnel, and a system to organically integrate the weapons and personnel—the focus in the PLA had been on improved weapons and personnel, with little attention to the scientific organization that provided for the organic integration of man and weapon. The article discussed foreign military strategists from the United States and the Soviet Union, who stressed the singular importance of structural organization. Whereas people could show a one-for-one improvement in military force with the addition of new weapons, improvements in organization had a multiplying effect in combat. The ability to respond to the change of battle in a timely manner was the determining factor in victory or defeat. The PLA was concerned that the Army was not optimally organized to fight a modern war. Organization and structural changes could improve efficiency and weed out the ineffective. These things required little time and did not demand major investments. Thus, the crux of the issue: China did not have the funds available to invest in weapons, equipment, and personnel. Devoting all its efforts to economic improvement, the state had no extra money for the PLA. According to the author, it was unrealistic to expect improvements in men and weapons in the short term, whereas structural improvements could be achieved. Thus, officers and soldiers should not fear the ongoing optimization of the PLA; it was for the good of the Army and the people. "If the concept of quantitative superiority is not changed to the concept of qualitative superiority, it is difficult to rationally reduce armed forces personnel; if the concept of waging war according to the status of the armed forces is not changed to the concept of building the armed forces according to future war requirements, it is difficult to determine the pattern for structural optimization."[42]

As part of Deng's efforts to retain the loyalty of the senior military until they could be retired, at the January meeting in Guangdong he and the CMC authorized Yang Baibing to organize the senior commanders and commissars from the seven military regions and the specialized arms into a series of inspection visits to Shenzhen and Zhuhai to see how successful Deng's reform and opening up had been. The commanders reportedly returned from these visits vowing to support and carry out reform and opening. Deng had lulled them into a false sense of security about their commands.[43]

Following the April CMC meeting, Deng developed his modernization program even further. Central to his efforts under way since 1985, but especially so since 1989 and Tiananmen and the failed Soviet countercoup in 1991, was Deng's obsession with establishing a mechanism to ensure total party control of the military. Thus, it was no surprise that Deng was implementing a unified command structure, similar to those in the West, or that he proposed abolishing the seven military regions, which he had already reduced from eleven to seven a few years earlier.[44]

Over the summer, following the CMC meeting, the GPD under Yang Baibing's control swung into action, putting out numerous articles attesting to the loyalty of the PLA, its desire to participate in local economic reform and construction, and its praise of Deng's policies of reform and opening. By Army Day—I August—the PLA rank and file were well aware that massive structural and personnel changes were imminent, especially following the Fourteenth Party Congress. Propaganda units were in high gear. Documents, such as those released after Deng's resignation from the CMC in 1989, were recirculated. They stressed the role of the party cell within the PLA, which promoted loyalty to the party. These documents traced their origin to the early days of the Red Army, when the battered forces failed to collapse under Kuomintang (KMT) attack because of the presence within the Army of the party cell.[45]

In addition to the "Minutes" of the 1989 CMC political work meeting, there were other documents published to provide guidance for proper training in loyalty. Three others formed the core texts that spoke to the fear the party had over loyalty of the Army, in light of its slow response to the events in Tiananmen in the summer of 1989. They were: (I) "Outline on Army Building at the Grassroots Level; (2) the "PLA Political Work Regulations," and; (3) "Rules on Routine Ideological Army Work."[46] The basic principle throughout was the unquestioned maintenance and strengthening of absolute party leadership over the Army. The documents stressed the party's history and the role of education. The emphasis was on upholding Marxist theory on Army building, preserving Army quality and aims, correctly performing the Army's role in the new period, and building a modernized, regularized, and revolutionary army with Chinese characteristics.

Party leaders were to emphasize study, unity, clean administration, and pragmatism, as well as concern themselves with the minute details of the lower-level party cell—the nerve ending, or forward position—the grassroots party branch. Reportedly, tens of thousands of these cells had been studying and focusing on party leadership. The climate was perceived as the best in recent history to realize its control. "The party is most proud of the systems and principles it has established since Red Army days to ensure absolute party leadership. These principles include: 'Under no circumstances must one seek insubordination or contend with the party for military power; all actions must remain under party command and no one is allowed to transfer or command armed forces units without authorization; it is absolutely impermissible for other political parties or groups to set up their organizations or carry out activities in the Army; all activities must be subordinated to and serve the party's program and line; and the leader work division responsibility system and democratic central- ism must be adhered to under collective leadership."[47]

What emerges is a consistent theme: the party controls the gun. Deng was aware, however, that "he who controls the gun controls the party," which was the threat he brought to the table in Beijing in the spring of 1992 to get his message across. It was a case of the Army playing the role as guarantor for whoever won the internal party battle and paid their fee. As the PLA paper stated on Army Day, "The extraordinary road from 1927 to 1992 shows this basic conclusion: China cannot not do without the People's Army; and the Army would not have developed, grown, or ful- filled its mission without absolute party leadership." This was the army that had pledged to escort and protect Deng's policies into the next century.

As part of the PLA's task of guaranteeing the economic policies of reform and opening, Deng had initiated reform and change within the PLA. Thus, in taking up its historic mission of protecting Deng's reforms for one hundred years, the PLA was also placing a demand on itself to streamline and centralize at a rapid enough pace to keep itself abreast of a rapidly changing world, where technological breakthroughs could overwhelm an opponent that did not keep pace with change. Reflecting Deng's thoughts, but published under Yang Baibing's signature as director of ideology and in charge of the *Liberation Army Daily,* Yang explained the new PLA role: "The basic line should be in force for 100 years and must not be shaken. The Army and the state power should safeguard this road, this system, and this policy. This set forth a new and glorious historical task for the Army. To perform the escort task, on the one hand the Army is required to main- tain a high degree of stability; on the other hand, the Army is also required to take concrete action to quicken the pace of reform, to increase the in- tensity of reform, to seek its development through self-reform, to effect a high degree of centralization and unity through positive development, to increase its cohesive force, and thus fully raise its ability to escort reform, opening, and economic development."[48]

What emerges in all the internal documents, including, of course, the September 1991 and February 1992 documents in which Deng discussed the world situation, was the one constant: "the situation is ripe with meaning: If we do not seize this opportunity to reform, the world political environment might never again be so favorable to China."[49] With a weak Russia to the north, an American withdrawal from the western Pacific, and the willingness and availability of foreign capital to invest in China, Deng argued that it was now or never. Reform and opening must be pushed to the limit. The just-completed Gulf War showed the futility of the Maoist military concept of drawing invaders in and countering with massive numbers of soldiers. In the future, one might never see an enemy soldier. Instead, cruise missiles could penetrate deep inside one's territory, and without proper defensive systems the battle would be lost in a number of days or hours.

Deng was clearly trying to get his point across, with the help of the Yangs: "In the contemporary world, which is full of competition, in order to grip a favorable and leading position, the key lies in 'seizing the opportunity to develop oneself.' This is not only applicable to the economic field, but is also applicable to the military field. A new driving force should be gathered through studying Comrade Deng Xiaoping's important talks; an opportunity for the in-depth reform of the Army has come and conditions have become ripe. Whether we can seize this opportunity to conduct the Army's reform in depth will decide this Army's future destiny. If one misses the opportunities given by the times, one may incur unforgivable losses. We must have a strong sense of urgency and mission in this regard."[50]

Yang Baibing's
August Address

Perhaps the truest expression of Deng's thinking was presented in Yang Baibing's August I editorial in the party's massive circulation general newspaper, *People's Daily*.[51] It should be compared to what Deng said through Huangfu Ping and Tian Jiyun to find his ideological perspective. Yang placed the current situation in context: "The world trend is toward multipolarity. Peace and development are two issues facing the Chinese people. Deng has seen the moment and called for a renewed effort at reform and opening. The PLA, which is safeguarding the motherland, is determined to protect the people's interests and will protect and escort the reform and construction called for by Deng."

Given the past history of the party, Yang admitted that mistakes were made along the way. These were corrected "only after the Third Plenary Session of the 11th CCP Central Committee, represented by Deng, having adhered to seeking truth from facts, and combined the basic principles of Marxism with the concrete reality of Chinese conditions, put forth the theory of building socialism with Chinese characteristics, and established the basic line of one center and two basic points and guided China's modernization effort on the correct road. Deng had advocated the strategic three steps to modernization that would lead to a China as an intermediate-level developed country in 100 years from the founding of the state."

Yang also grasped the fleeting moment, as had Deng. "Propelled by the rapid development of science and technology and sharp international economic competition, mankind will face a new period of development in the last few years of this century and the beginning of the next. This is a golden opportunity for China's reform and construction. If we do not accept what heaven provides for us, we may otherwise be blamed; if we do not meet the time, we may otherwise be punished. We must make full use of the current favorable conditions both at home and abroad to push our economic construction onto a new stage and lay a solid foundation for rapid development in the next century. If we say that from the mid-1800s to the mid-1900s, the Chinese nation finally stood up through more than 100 years of heroic struggles, in which one stepped into the breach as another fell, then from the mid-1900s to the mid-2000s, through another 100 years of struggle, our country will completely shake off poverty and truly stride along toward becoming a developed and prosperous country as a giant in the East."

Deng's simple program of doubling the GNP, doubling it again, and then once more by the mid-2000s had already achieved success. According to Yang, "the GNP has already doubled. The problem of food and clothing has been solved, and by the end of the century the GNP will be doubled again. In a critical period of international and domestic affairs, Deng has now stepped forward with a renewed call for accelerating the pace of reform and opening up and promoting economic construction faster and better. *It is under these circumstances that Deng, the party central and the CMC has requested that the PLA undertake to carry out a mission of protecting and escorting the reform and economic construction."*

The PLA was also instructed on where its position was in the economic equation. The party and the CMC had instructed the PLA to serve the reform and economic construction mission, a task that was to endure for one hundred years, the length of time Deng had called for adherence to reform and opening. This is in line with Deng's agreement in December 1991 to guarantee the PLA a stable source of income for as long as it supported reform and opening, that is, one hundred years. Again, Yang pointed out how the party had gone astray over the years. It had missed several opportunities to take advantage of science and technology to catch up with the developed world. Thus, the gap between China and the developed countries had widened.

By the time Deng finally was able to turn policy towards economic construction in 1978, the world was already entering a period of heightened economic and technological competition. The real question was whether or not China would be able to promote economic construction rapidly enough to catch up with and maintain a position among the advanced nations. Again, it was in this context that China had missed other opportunities, when the world situation was different; if it missed the current, limited-duration opportunity to catch up with the West, then China would fall by the wayside, a has-been nation. Deng, as the Huangfu Ping articles pointed out, was critical of the party for failing to take advantage of openings to the West in the past.

Yang next discussed what made a nation strong. According to him, only when the state was prosperous could the Army be strong. Enhancing national defense and increasing modernization of the Army both depended on a sound economic foundation. He concluded, like Deng, that only by concentrating China's strength to advance toward a new scientific and technological revolution and concentrating its energy on economic construction could it become invincible in world competition and achieve a strategic position to survive beyond the century. When economic development was promoted, the people would be rich and the comprehensive national strength would be enhanced, which would provide a solid foundation for national defense construction.

Lest anyone miss the point, Yang explained: "The strength of national defense is also an important aspect of the comprehensive national strength.

To promote our modernization drive, there must be a powerful army to serve as a guarantee. It is the common duty of the people of the whole nation to show concern for and support army building. At a time when the international political environment was governed by hegemons and power politics, the nation must not relax its defense construction efforts. Only when we have boosted the economy and built up a powerful army and firm national defense can we acquire the proper position of a big country in the international community. Thus, no one will look down on us and dare to rashly offend us."

Yang instructed the PLA on what constituted socialism. There had been a battle raging between the leftists and the reformers for over a year on the issue of what was a socialist phenomenon, and what was a capitalist one. Quoting from Deng's southern tour speeches, Yang laid out Deng's major positions that the more serious problems facing the party were from leftists, not rightists. As far as Deng and the reformers were concerned, some of the leftists would have problems with reform measures, never being certain if they were socialist or capitalist. To make matters and decisions easier, Deng had a simple key for determining which it was, based on three aspects: was a measure conducive to the development of the productive forces of a socialist society; to the growth of the comprehensive national strength of a socialist country; and to the improvement of living standards. Thus, anything in the modernization efforts meeting those three requirements would be considered a good practice, including Western capitalist methods. Yang issued a warning to the PLA: They had to be ready to absorb new ideas, support them, and implement them.

The role for the Army in reform and opening and economic construction also demanded that it respond to Deng's new strategic directive to streamline, optimize and modernize. Yang offered the PLA Deng's criteria:

1. It is necessary to uphold the party's absolute leadership over the army and unremittingly preserve the nature of the people's army so as to ensure that the army will truly serve as a great wall of steel guarding the motherland, a strong pillar of the people's democratic dictatorship, and an important force to build socialist material and spiritual civilization;

2. It is necessary to uphold the principle of integration of the requirements for a revolutionary, modern, and regular army, take the

modernization of the army as a key link, adhere to the combat strength criterion, attach importance to army quality, and work hard to enhance the army's fighting capability under conditions of modern warfare;

3. It is necessary to uphold the principle of crack troops, combined arms and high efficiency, constantly improve the army structure and establishment, realize the scientific combination of man and weapons, and practice a system that combines a streamlined, highly trained army with strong reserve forces;

4. It is necessary to uphold the principle of relying on oneself and being mainly geared to one's own needs, step up scientific research in national defense and strengthen reserve technical forces with the focus placed on certain aspects, and gradually enhance the modernization standard of armament and equipment;

5. It is necessary to persistently attach strategic importance to education and training, give strict training to meet rigid requirements, try our best in running military institutes, and make efforts to improve the army's military and political quality so as to ensure that army cadres and fighters will master well both military techniques and some skills useful to socialist construction;

6. It is necessary to persistently administer the army according to law and rigid requirements, develop and improve rules, ordinances and regulation, as well as systems, perfect military laws and ordinances, and ensure that work in different fields will be carried on along the development track of regular troops;

7. It is necessary to uphold the principle of building the army through thrift and hard work, subordinate army building to national economic construction, actively increase income and reduce expenditure and work hard to improve military efficiency and economic returns and to enhance the army's logistical and comprehensive supporting capability;

8. It is necessary to persistently inherit and develop Mao Zedong military thought, vigorously explore theories on the operation of the people's army and people's war under the conditions of modern warfare, and develop and perfect the Chinese system of modern military science;

9. It is necessary to uphold the principle of political work as the lifeblood of the army, give full play to the servicing and safeguarding role of political work, educate army units with Marxism-Leninism-Mao Zedong Thought, foster a contingent of cadres who are more revolutionary, younger in average age, better educated, and more professionally competent, and unremittingly enhance unity between army officers and soldiers, between the army and the government and between the army and the people;

10. It is necessary to uphold the principle of reform as the motivation of development, proceed from China's national conditions and the Chinese army's special characteristics, make use of foreign armies' valuable experience, actively, steadily, and appropriately carry out readjustment and reform, and persistently push ahead the development of the army.

In consideration of the fact that it was the sixty-fifth anniversary of the founding of the PLA, Yang spoke of its long, proud tradition and the necessity of seizing the initiative, which might not ever come again. According to Yang, "so long as the whole party, the whole army and the Chinese people of all nationalities work hard with one heart and one mind and steadfastly strive for the set goal, China would surely rank itself among other world powers by its 100th anniversary, and its army would certainly catch up with other first-rate armies in the world in terms of modernization standards in the wake of economic development."[52]

Thus, Yang presented Deng's arguments, which had not changed since 1978. Deng had succeeded in getting the PLA to support him, but at a cost. The military region commanders and political commissars had all publicly pledged support for reform and opening, and to carry out streamlining, while being sympathetic to the requirements of the state.[53] The army had further committed itself to a generational change.[54] The CMC had agreed to major personnel changes and an increased centralization of control; however, that still did not mean that Deng was totally convinced of the loyalty of the PLA. Part of the reason for the emphasis on centralization and reduction of field command prerogative was to ensure that there was not a repeat of the mess at Tiananmen, when several officers had questioned orders to crush the students and senior, retired generals had appealed the orders. In response, Deng had established a study group on the CMC, led by Liu Huaqing, to study recent coups throughout the world, with a special emphasis on Rumania and the several coups in Thailand. Deng was nervous about the rapid fall of the Ceaucescu regime, and the seeming indifference in financial circles to Thai military coups.[55]

Further proof of Deng's concern was the extraction of personal pledges of support for his policies from all the senior commanders of the PLA. There was clearly a reference to that in Deng's published views on his southern sojourn, in which he used the term *baojia*, which can be rendered as "protect the emperor" or "protect the precious gift."[56] In any case, it could not be interpreted to mean support of constitutional rule; China had had no history of democratic institutions. The term had meaning in context only: That meaning had to be interpreted as protecting the throne or the party that was responsible for such programs. It was evident that Deng was repeating an old pattern, similar to that used by Sun Yat-sen and Chiang Kai-shek, of establishing a rule based on crack troops who personally pledged to support the institution, the man. Deng was obtaining pledges of fealty from his loyal lieutenants and supporters to back the collective wisdom of the elders of the PLA—Peng Zhen, Liu Huaqing, Yang Shangkun, Yang Baibing, Zhang Zhen, Yang Dezhi, Li Desheng, and all the others who had attended the CMC meetings in December, January, April and throughout the summer as he arranged his succession. Clearly the elders of the PLA were being endowed with authority to determine succession; but just as clearly, the PLA was guaranteeing a unified state and the power of the party in return for the price of modernization and a seat on the Politburo.

By Army Day on I August, the issue of who would remain in charge of the Army had been basically determined through a series of unpublicized meetings in Beijing and Beidaihe.[57] Initially, several military region commanders had submitted letters to the CMC asking that Yang Shangkun remain on the CMC. This was after Deng had already decreed Yang's retirement, a reduction in military regions, and the retirement of most senior officers—especially all military region commanders and special arms commanders—who were to be replaced by younger officers following the party congress. Had Deng agreed, this would have defeated the generational change, since Yang could not have been expected to replace officers who were his base of support. Deng came down on the side of new blood—

commanders with professional schooling and integrated into the new horizontal and vertical interest groups—a new breed with new weapons, more
money, greater prestige, and loyal to the state.[58]

A new PLA administration was necessary to supervise the replacement of
the Yang clique with a new core, loyal to Liu Huoqing. The generals would
retire. Their loyalty, however, would be purchased by moving them into
sinecures in the industrial sector or by promoting them to a new military
advisory board to the CMC, much as Deng had engineered the retirement
of the Yenan-era party cadre at the Twelfth Party Congress in 1982 in order
to bring new talent onto the Central Committee and Politburo. Thus, by
late July, just prior to Army Day, Deng and Yang would announce their
decision that military region commanders and special arms commanders
would retire. They would, however, continue to advise the CMC on Army
reform.[59] Never one to risk party control, Deng established his advisory
councils and placed ultimate control in the hands of the few remaining field
army colleagues—the true revolutionaries, of which Yang was one.

Thus, on the eve of the Fourteenth Congress, Deng had his prize. The
Public Security Forces, under Peng Zhen and Qiao Shi, would ensure internal stability, backed by the PLA if necessary. All armed forces took
orders from the CMC, which took orders from the remaining Long March
revolutionaries, mostly Deng's supporters. The PLA—a state within a
state—plus the Public Security Forces and the elders, were prepared to
ensure stability for the future. The center of political gravity had been
shifted, definitively and for well into the future.

6 | Triumph

◈ Mechanics of the Fourteenth Congress

Deng had the cooperation of the PLA and the backing of the regional governors. The key elements of his compromise had been agreed to by the various parties, but Deng still had a long way to go. He still had to remake party organizations to ensure that his policies outlived him. Thus, Deng set out on his campaign to recapture control of the party in a deliberate manner, reminiscent of his efforts to help Mao retake control of the party and government from Lin Biao and the PLA in the aftermath of the Ninth Party Congress in 1969. Clearly, he had not lost his organizational touch or his understanding of bureaucratic infighting. To be successful, Deng had to overcome two obstacles: the de facto authority of Chen Yun and the CAC, and the real authority that Song Ping and the conservatives held over party life by virtue of their control of the Party's Organization Department, which was responsible for establishing the criteria for and the selection of delegates, in addition to controlling the personal dossiers and all assignments of party members. To be considered successful, Deng had to emerge at the congress with the ability to name the Politburo, the Standing Committee, and the Central Committee. As well, he had to place his men in charge of the PLA.

It is important to recall earlier events, to understand both the degree to which Deng was willing to go to ensure control of the congress and his ability to plan and execute a complex agenda over several months, while apparently in declining health. Deng first tackled the problem of delegate selection. Following the failed Soviet coup in August 1991, Chen Yun and his supporters had argued for selection of delegates who had supported the crackdown in Tiananmen and had more "red" than "expert" credentials. To accomplish this, Li Peng, Song Ping, and Lu Feng had to gain control over the selection process, which was in the hands of local party bureaucrats—the same people who had been promoted by Deng following his return to power in 1978. Their task was further complicated by the fact that the new reform policies had been popular with the local people, and had given local leaders a chance to claim popular legitimacy by supporting reforms in opposition to Beijing. Even Deng had gone to Shanghai to identify with the local hero, Zhu Rongji, and provide moral support for Zhu to challenge the policies then in effect. It was unlikely, therefore, that local authorities would select, as delegates and new Central Committee members, individuals who had supported retrenchment and recentralization.

As detailed above, Li Peng had launched a new Socialist Education Campaign in the provinces, much as Mao had done in the early 1960s, to overturn the conservative market-oriented policies of Chen Yun, Deng, and others who were attempting to repair the serious economic damage Mao had caused with the Great Leap Forward. At that time, Mao had used PLA work teams to examine local party members' dossiers to determine whether they were more "red" than "expert." Mao was thus able to remake all local party offices in his image. In 1991, Li and Chen were attempting to do the same thing.

Just prior to the March Plenum, Song Ping had drawn up a plan for the allocation of deputies and delegates to the upcoming party congress. It had called for an allocation that favored the central government and party apparatus. Sixty-three to 68 percent of the delegates and members of the new Central Committee were to come from among Central Committee and State Council departments, while only 26 to 32 percent were to be chosen by provincial organizations, and only 4 to 6 percent were to be chosen from the military. When Song presented his report to the Plenum, two staunch

Deng allies, Qiao Shi and Wan Li, came out in open opposition to the plan. They expressed the view that the center of gravity for economic development had shifted from Beijing to the provinces. Both men, therefore, advocated a reversal of the figures to favor the provinces.[1]

As if on cue, Jiang held a Politburo meeting right after the Plenum, on 14 March, to push through measures that would reverse Song. The seats for provincial delegates would constitute 63 percent of the total, while central seats would comprise only 32 percent, and the PLA would have a slight increase, up to 8 percent. Jiang then brought up Deng's concerns over the criteria for delegate selection: "The allocation of the number of seats for the CCP Central Committee must be arranged from the plane of the party's basic line and central work and the local leaders' role must be brought into play." Jiang continued: "Comrade Xiaoping is greatly concerned with the progress in the preparations for the 14th CCP National Congress and demands that fuller preparations be made and that the 14th CCP National Congress usher in a new stage."[2]

Clearly, Deng could not have been more forceful. He was calling for a reappraisal of all work to that point. This meant that all selections prior to April, under Lu Feng's guidance, would be reviewed and credentials rechecked. Numbers would also be reallocated. Li, Chen, and Song had lost the tactical advantage, and with it they lost the ability to control the agenda of the Fourteenth Congress. To ensure his victory, Deng removed Song and the Organization Department from all but figurative control of the delegate selection process and the drafting of policy papers. In Song's place, Jiang was put in overall charge of congress preparations. Bo Yibo, along with Jiang and Deng's ever-faithful bridge partner, Ding Guangen, and Wen Jiabao, would oversee the drafting of the documents and delegate selection.[3] Thus, in March delegate selection came under Deng's purview. There was no apparent direct opposition. The only avenue left was the informal one— the ability of the elders and the CAC to interfere in politics. This was the route that Chen took to counter Deng's initiatives.

Following the Politburo meeting, Deng ordered Jiang to communicate its decisions to the regional and local party leadership immediately. Deng could not permit the possibility that Li and Song would attempt to verify delegates favorable to their position quickly. Jiang held a nationwide telephone conference with all regional and local party leaders on 13 April, during which he relayed Deng's instructions and his concerns about the work to date on preparations for the Fourteenth Congress. Deng wanted all delegates to emancipate their minds and think of the twenty-first century. Those who were old or feeble or failed to support reform were to be forced to step down. Those sowing dissension were to step down. The emphasis would be on principles, party character, and qualifications. These would, of course, be subject to interpretation by Deng's supporters. Deng also decreed that the candidate list should include more than the number of positions, similar to the practice used at the Thirteenth Party Congress, which would allow an element of popular democracy. Not all who were nominated would be elected.[4]

Thus, it was apparent by early April that Deng had seized the initiative and gained control of the mechanics leading up to the Fourteenth Party Congress. Since this would in all probability be his last chance to influence Chinese politics, he was leaving nothing to chance. The congress would be peopled with delegates from the provinces, which had been favored by Deng's reform and opening, and, by opening the entire country with Documents 4 and 5, Deng had ensured overwhelming support for his agenda at the congress. The new balance of party power would lie with the regional leadership, not the central bureaucracy.[5] With the PLA supporting reform and opening, Deng was reshaping Chinese politics in the same way that Mao's success over the international faction in 1945 had shaped Chinese politics for the next forty years.

Even though Deng had succeeded in manipulating the mechanics of organization in his favor, the politics of influence was still a force in Chinese politics that could undercut his efforts. Deng was thus forced to wage an ideological struggle during the spring and summer leading up to the congress to ensure victory over Chen Yun and his CAC.

Early in the New Year, Chen had made an attempt to stop Deng's momentum. The first blows were struck immediately after Deng returned from his southern journey. In an effort to reverse Deng at the Politburo meetings in February and March, Chen Yun, Li Xiannian, Wang Zhen, Wang Renzhong, Chen Zuolin, Deng Liqun, Hu Qiaomu, He Jingzhi, and others from the CAC presented the Politburo and Deng with a list of demands which would check his economic plans.[6] That effort failed when Deng succeeded in getting the Politburo to distribute his views (Document 2). Again, on the eve of the NPC in March, Chen sent another message to the CAC and the State Council in an attempt to undermine Deng's new proposals on the economy. Chen asserted that several serious questions had not been resolved, including the problem of the state enterprises that continued to lose millions. (He neglected to mention that, during the previous three years of rectification, his policies had not improved the situation.) He also responded to charges that his thinking was fossilized by asserting that the only way to develop the economy was to rely on economic laws applied in a scientific manner, which meant that China could only follow a Marxist economic plan to realize a socialist economy. He gave credit to such a plan for allowing China to withstand the chaos of the Cultural Revolution.

Next, using their muscle as elders, Chen convinced fifty-six CAC members to sign a letter to both Deng and the Politburo calling for a conference to discuss whether current policy, as stated by Deng, was correct. Chen stated, "at present there is a dangerous tendency in enlivening the economy to shake off state planning. This is a grave tendency. It will certainly create chaos, affect the entire national economy and lead to social turmoil. The main cause of the 1989 political unrest was an overheated and derailed national economy, which resulted in unbearable inflation." However, Chen blamed the core leadership of the party for this. He stated that bureaucratic corruption was exploited by people with bourgeois liberalist tendencies who encouraged the students. He thus placed responsibility for the events of 1989 with the core of liberal supporters within the leadership—which meant Deng. Chen went on to declare that if China continued under Deng's guidelines, it would end up like Russia and Yugoslavia.

According to Chen, the economy needed direction—Marxist direction—or it would end up in chaos, as had happened in 1988 and 1989. He turned to his birdcage economic theory, first advanced in 1982. He called for an enlivened economy, but instead of freeing the bird—the capitalist features of an enlivened economy—he advocated making the cage larger, for without the cage the bird of modernization would lose direction.

Deng responded that those in doubt should go to the SEZ to see for themselves. They would see that the practice was correct. At the 12 March Politburo meeting, Peng Zhen, who had been one of his harshest critics, openly supported Deng's call for greater opening and economic development. He stated that Marxism-Leninism could not be separated from social development and practice. If it did not develop, it would lose its value as truth.

Chen's next move was to call a meeting of the CAC in early March, at which he proposed that, while the CAC should be abolished at the Fourteenth Party Congress, a Central Advisory Group should be established in its place, with a life of about four years. For membership on this new, transitional group, Chen proposed Song Ping, Yao Yilin, Bo Yibo, Song Renqiong, Wang Zhen, Chen Zuolin, Deng Liqun, Hu Qiaomu, and Wang Renzhong. Chen was, in fact, proposing to reduce the old CAC down to the active members who opposed current policies. Chen could not expect Deng to agree to such a proposal; indeed, Deng recognized Chen's move for what it was, and countered with a list of his own. If there was to be a new advisory group, Deng proposed to name Yang Shangkun, Bo Yibo, Song Ping, Li Desheng, and Liu Huaqing. This new group would have no formal part in policy or decision-making in the Politburo, but it would have informal power to act on central resolutions or proposals. While nothing came of the idea at the time, clearly both leaders revealed what everyone knew would be the course of future politics. China would continue to have an informal advisory body that would make decisions. This body would be the final arbiter of Chinese politics, playing a role similar to that played by the Japanese *genro* as the shogunate was transformed into imperial rule.

While Deng had seized the initiative, Chen still had his power as an elder. In an effort to patch up the growing rift with Chen, Deng called a meeting of party seniors in Zhongnanhai on 25 April. Included were Deng, Chen, Li Xiannian, Peng Zhen, Yang Shangkun, Bo Yibo, Jiang Zemin, Li Peng, Qiao Shi, and Wan Li. The lineup, with about seven in Deng's camp and three in Chen's, including Li Xiannian and Li Peng, indicated that Deng had the upper hand. This would provide the critical mass for the post-congress advisory body. Clearly Deng was winning the influence war and consensus-building campaign.

But Chen would not back down. The result was a compromise agenda. The major points agreed to were that: (1) the basic line followed since the Third Plenary of the Eleventh Congress was correct; (2) there was a need to build socialism with Chinese characteristics, and to rely mainly on China's efforts, wisdom, and financial resources in reform and opening; (3) there was a need to seize the opportunity and use favorable conditions to expedite opening up to the world in an omnidirectional manner, and to exercise control in running special economic zones; (4) Shanghai's relevant conditions for developing Pudong were ripe, and should be supported by central and local officials; (5) the State Council's 1992 Work Report was pragmatic and gave expression to the party's basic line and central task; (6) there should be a limit to the securities markets, limited to Shanghai and Shenzhen, and it was necessary to strengthen macroeconomic controls; (7) in carrying out clean government, all party members should seriously tackle corruption and bribery; (8) the Fourteenth Congress would promote a number of middle-aged and younger cadres who conformed to the conditions for successors and had made great contributions to reform and opening; and (9) in solving turmoil occurring in localities in the future, preventive work had to be done in the initial stage of an event; clear-cut, firm, powerful, and effective measures had to be taken to resolve and stop them promptly.

This program clearly ignored the central issues dividing the two camps. Chen and Deng were no closer to agreement. Chen charged that, while the past mistakes of the "left" impacted mainly on economic construction, the mistakes of the "right" had resulted in party graft, corruption, a crisis of faith in the party, and revision and downgrading of Marxism—all of which were causes of social turmoil and instability. Deng's response was that it was the influence of the "left" that prevented people from emancipating their minds and trying new ideas. Deng criticized Marxism-Leninism-Mao Zedong Thought as dogmatic; these dogmas prevented people from carrying out new policies. The outcome of the "meeting of ten" was a stalemate. Deng had the votes to continue, but Chen had the power of influence, and his troops were still in charge of the government.[7]

After the failure of the April meeting of the party elders, each faction tried to influence events by hacking away at the candidate list for the congress and the new Politburo. Deng had supervised the drafting of the list, but Chen and the other elders also produced lists that Deng had to at least consider. The CAC even submitted its own delegate list to the Politburo. While Deng would allow some vetoes of his selections, he would not compromise on two issues: the new congress would be heavily represented by the local rather than the central party apparatus; and he would make his point in the political report to the Congress on the dangers of "leftism." Deng would control the consensus vote.

Deng settled on an unlikely pair to spread his message on reform and opening between the March Plenum and the fall congress. One was the young technocrat from Shanghai, Zhu Rongji; the other was the old stalwart from his home province of Sichuan and former colleague of Zhao Ziyang, Tian Jiyun.

Born in Feicheng, Shandong province, in 1929, Tian received a second-ary education and joined the Communist Party in 1945. He was assigned to southwest China for several years, working in financial departments. With each promotion, he rose to a higher position in the party hierarchy. He had been a confidential secretary to the Military Control Commission in southwest China, an instructor in the Guiyang People's University, and eventually the director of the financial department of Guizhou province, as well as director of the general office of the department. He was later transferred to Sichuan to head that province's financial department under Governor Zhao Ziyang. Zhao had been so impressed with his abilities that, when he was elevated to the leadership circle in Beijing, he brought Tian to Beijing in 1981 to take over the day-to-day work of Zhao's State Council as secretary general. Tian was elevated to a vice-premier of the State Council in 1983, and in 1985, at the Fifth Plenum of the Twelfth Congress, he was elevated to the Politburo and the Secretariat. He was a consistent supporter of reform and opening, even after the loss of his patron Zhao Ziyang. Deng continued to protect him, and it was Tian, not Jiang, who made the coherent arguments in support of Deng's counter-attack against the Beijing leadership in 1992.

Deng chose Tian for two chief reasons. First, as a holdover from the lib-eral faction of Zhao Ziyang, Tian had credentials as a liberal. The people and the regional party bureaucracy could trust his words, since he had been a constant supporter of Deng's policies. The second reason was per-sonal trust. Over the years, Tian had worked closely with Zhao and Deng, especially on the agrarian front, which had been of critical interest to Deng since he launched his reform and opening policies in 1978. Deng could have chosen Zhu or Jiang to deliver the message. That he chose an old liberal meant he felt that Tian—unlike Zhao, who had sided with the democratic liberals around Hu Yaobang—had stayed true to the basic Marxist approach to the economy, and was therefore acceptable to the elders—even to Chen Yun and Li Peng.

Tian gave his speech in defense of Deng's accelerated reform and open-ing at the Party School on 25 April. Entitled "Questions on Agriculture and Rural Reform and Development in China," his speech traced the

development of rural agrarian policies.[8] During the preceding years—
1978 to 1992—of reform and opening up in China, the rural areas had
undergone the greatest and fastest changes. Such changes had originated
with the creativity of the peasants and with their individual choices, arrived at through actual practice. Tian traced this development to three
basic measures within the reform program.

The first, the production contract responsibility system linking output
to the household, had amounted to a second revolution in liberating labor
in the rural areas (the first being the liberation of labor with the takeover
of the Communists in 1949 and the transformation of the countryside).
Tian pointed out that everyone acknowledged that in 1978, the peasants
were still rather poor, and that rural areas across China were not being supplied with the necessary food and clothing. After the introduction of the
contract system, grain output increased from 300 million metric tons in
1978 to over 400 million metric tons in 1984. Cotton output rose from
2.17 mmt (million metric tons) to over 6.26 mmt, while oil-bearing crops
rose from 5.22 mmt to over 11.91 mmt during the same period. Clearly,
the success of the contract responsibility program was reflected in the
statistics.

Tian went on to recount how early critics of the policy of contracting
responsibility to the individual household, with payment linked to output,
had charged that it amounted to sharing the land as a precursor to a return
to individual farming; it was restoring capitalism. Only after the program
proved to be a tremendous success did the criticism cease. However, according to Tian, following the political disturbances during the spring and summer of 1989, critics again attacked Deng's rural program. They charged that
liberalization in the political field derived from liberalization in the economic field, and the latter derived from the rural contract to the household
system. The critics tried to reverse the general direction of Deng's reform
totally, using all sorts of pretexts to return to the old, failed path of cooperatives and "turning everything into a big collective."

The second reform measure was the rescission of the unified procurement and marketing system, the readjustment of and lifting of restrictions
on the prices of some agricultural products, and the permission given to
peasants to play a part in commodity circulation. As far as these measures
were concerned, such reforms still needed to go farther.

The third reform measure, based on the first two, was the allowance of a commodity-money economy to develop in the rural areas. Tian described in detail the evolution of perhaps one of Deng's greatest success stories, for it ultimately held the key to resolving China's growing population problem as well as the surplus labor population. The growth of the commodity-money economy had launched town and township enterprises that were run by peasants, financed with their own funds, and employed a labor force that was equal in number to the total labor force employed by large cities and large enterprises over the previous thirty-year period. Tian noted that while China's state enterprises employed over 100 million laborers, the rural industries employed about as many people, and the state had not invested one dime in the effort. So, Tian was skeptical of critics who raised the issue of the rural enterprises not paying sufficient taxes to the state. Over one third of the rural enterprises were earning foreign exchange. In addition, they were taking industrial profits and reinvesting them in agriculture, public works, public health, and public schools in the amount of over 20 billion yuan, as well as paying 45.4 billion yuan in taxes each year.

The most critical measure of the success of Deng's reforms in the rural areas was the income ratio between urban and rural inhabitants. In 1981, the ratio was 2.2:1; in 1984 the gap narrowed to 1.7:1, but it widened in 1990 to 2.2:1. The statistics, quoted by Tian, reaffirmed that the price ratio between industrial and agricultural products was still unbalanced. Rural retail sales accounted for 59.2 percent of all China's retail sales in 1984; however, in 1990 that figure had dropped to 55.2 percent. Tian urged that, in the future, attention should be paid to comprehensive development of forestry, animal husbandry, sideline production, and fisheries, all of which would have high yields.

In discussing peasant savings, Tian lamented that of the 1,000 billion yuan in savings deposits, over 60 percent came from urban depositors. In order to change the equation and to foster a money economy and more savings, he recommended that peasants should change from farming to industry. That did not mean that they should rush to the cities. He was calling for a massive rural development effort that would produce new industries and tie people to the rural areas, yet yield an increase in the standard of living for peasants without releasing a large floating population that would inundate the major cities and cause untold social and political problems. Tian restated that the basic policies should not change. He called for increased state investment in agriculture, from 7 to 10 percent, through the issuance of bonds or stocks.

Tian also spoke of the leftists' call for a socialist education campaign in the rural areas, and the efforts of Deng and his supporters to head it off into a harmless press campaign. Tian noted that, at an enlarged Politburo meeting on the eve of the Eighth Plenary Session of the Thirteenth Congress, Song Ping, who was actively working with Li Peng to push the movement to counter peaceful evolution and replace reform supporters with their own, to control the formation of the Fourteenth Party Congress, had openly challenged Tian Jiyun's authority to speak for party policy in the rural areas. At that meeting Tian, following Deng's instructions that there would be no widespread campaign and any that was pursued would only affect high-level party officials, had insisted that any socialist education movement had to be implemented in accordance with reform and opening. Song had countered: "Tian, you are wrong. The aim of rural socialist education is to ensure the absence of peaceful evolution in the rural areas," meaning a mass campaign. Wan Li, the other former liberal from Zhao's days on the State Council, rose to Tian's defense and pointed out that Tian had authority in agriculture, so he could prevent any movement in the rural areas that interfered with agriculture productivity.[9]

To demonstrate the absurdity of the arguments of the "leftists," Tian proposed during his speech the establishment of a special leftist zone, where no foreign investments would be allowed and no foreigners would be permitted. Neither the inhabitants of the zone nor their children would be allowed to go overseas. The zone would be run by leftist policies; thus, everything would be done through central planning. This would mean that people would have to queue up for food and other needs. He also challenged the view that Deng Liqun had begun to circulate in his efforts to portray Mao's rule as a golden age. He said that in the 1950s, in Sichuan, he and his wife had had to stand in line to get their ration of meat, available only on holidays. Tian wondered out loud if the leftists, who had been benefiting from reform and opening, really would be anxious to implement a leftist zone that would follow the old policies.[10]

Tian gave his speech in various versions as he visited regional party centers. Its importance lay in the fact that it had been authorized by Deng, and that key lines were the same as those Deng had used during his southern tour and which would show up in later documents, especially those from the Fourteenth Party Congress. Tian had said in his speech that Deng had come out of retirement to point out critical problems at a critical moment in the party's history. The guiding principle in Deng's speeches, according to Tian, had been the basic line of "one center, two basic points." Deng had traced the line's history from its formulation at the Third Plenary Session of the Eleventh Party Congress to the Thirteenth Congress. According to Deng, the line "should not be changed for 100 years. Anyone who wants to change the line should be driven out of office. Anyone who wants to change the line should be overthrown."[11]

Quoting Deng, Tian replied to those who questioned the reason for such an edict, which in essence was justifying a revolt against the party and government. According to Tian, Deng had said that "the basic line, mapped out at the Third Plenary of the 11th Congress was correct. It was correct because it conformed to the national conditions of China and the aspirations of the people of the nation. It represented the will of the party and broad masses of the people. It was the fundamental line on which China would build a strong nation. Without it, according to Deng, there was no other way, there was only a "blind alley." Deng had spoken out for two major reasons. First, as mentioned, it was the only way—without his economic modernization plan, the nation would stagnate. Equally important, however, was the need to warn his critics, who were openly and covertly trying to sabotage, negate, and change his policy, that he would not tolerate any deviation from the basic line. Tian addressed what he and Deng considered to be the basis of the continuing charges and counterattacks against his policies. Tian stated that while Deng was concerned with rightist tendencies, he was more concerned with leftist tendencies. According to Tian, "left concerns are seriously binding up people hand and foot." He pointed out that when people had wanted to borrow foreign money, the critics had responded that such a venture to establish a foreign-invested enterprise would result in one more portion of capitalism, which would be a threat to China's socialist nature. When people wanted to let a foreigner contract to develop a piece of land, critics had charged that China's sovereignty had been bartered away, and China had been humiliated. Tian continued: "When township and town enterprises had grown, critics charged that they were the source of unhealthy tendencies, which would corrode the party and cadre. Such critics regarded the township enterprise system as a threat to socialism. More private development and individual enterprises would change the nature of socialism." Similarly, when a plant director assumed full responsibility for the success or failure of his enterprise, it was a threat to party control. Deng's critics charged that more reform and opening would damage China's already favorable situation. However, Tian responded that such critics failed to understand how China had obtained such an excellent situation.

Tian summed up the situation that had brought Deng out of retirement: "Critics charged that the contract responsibility to households was taking the road to individual farming and was a detriment to the collective and prosperity. The three kinds of foreign-owned enterprises were a hotbed of peaceful evolution; town and township enterprises were a source of unhealthy tendencies."[12] Such charges, which forced people to stop and consider if every move was capitalist or socialist, resulted in no action. This was the result of the "left" thinking which, according to Tian and Deng, existed among leading cadre. Tian stated that if such thinking was not changed, reform and opening was only empty talk. Tian concluded: "If this problem is not thoroughly solved, whether reform and opening can last long will remain a big problem."

The attack on the "leftists" continued as Deng, after providing a theoretical basis for his attack, turned to the mechanics of the upcoming congress. At the 12 May meeting of his team were Jiang, Qiao Shi, Li Peng, Li Ruihuan, Yang Baibing, Chi Haotian, Wen Jiabao, Ding Guangen, Yang Shangkun, Wan Li, and Qin Jiwei.[13] Deng emphasized his belief that the long-term threat to the party and reform and opening would be the "leftism" that strangled innovation and posed as Marxism. Thus, it was to be expected that, since Deng was controlling the agenda, the work report would include a large dose of criticism of "leftism."

Deng had laid down the law in May to the drafting committee, and he had reviewed the candidate list. Thus, it was obvious by June that Deng had determined the agenda of the congress, approved the basic documents, including the work or political report, provided the theoretical justification, and determined the membership of the Politburo, CMC, and Central Committee. However, Deng had not been able to win over Chen Yun.

With Chen still on the offensive, Deng began the process of explaining his program to his supporters, prior to the Congress, to ensure that they developed a full understanding of it so that they could counter the message Chen was trying to send via the CAC. Jiang, in a speech at the Party School in June, outlined Deng's long-range economic goals and his omnidirectional opening policy, while Qiao Shi took the message to the major government ministries and departments.[14]

As Deng had identified Tian Jiyun to spread his thoughts on agrarian reform, and Zhu Rongji to do the same for industrial reform, it was fitting for Jiang Zemin, Communist Party general secretary and president of the People's Republic, to give a perspective to China's domestic situation in light of its international setting. In a speech in June at the Central Party School for Provincial and Ministerial Leaders, Jiang expressed Deng's concern for avoiding the mistakes of the past. Just as Stalin had made serious mistakes that damaged the economic interests of the Soviet Union, so Mao had made decisions that had harmed China. It had been, according to Jiang, the intent of the party leadership in 1949 to develop relations with all nations. Unfortunately, the Cold War intervened, and China was forced to rely solely on the Soviet Bloc during the 1950s. When relations soured with Moscow at the end of that decade, China turned inward in extreme isolationism. Only at the end of the Cultural Revolution did China's policy begin to change, when the Third Plenary Session of the Eleventh Party Congress in 1978, under the direction of Deng Xiaoping, set China on a course of reform and opening.[15]

Once again, however, China was at a crossroads. Because of the collapse of the Soviet Union, Deng's "Middle Kingdom" theory was in shambles, and the "leftists" were threatening to revert to the isolationism of the past. The policy of omnidirectionalism was Deng's prescription to avoid past failures. By opening all of China to trade with all countries, regardless of ideology, he was betting that the forces of regional interests would prevent such a reversion. To succeed, however, Jiang argued that people's minds would have to be open to new ideas. According to him, China had been forced to draw on the achievements of all civilizations in order to ensure an acceleration of reform and opening. This included drawing on the experiences of the capitalist countries. Concepts such as market economy, competition, intellectual property, and shareholding were becoming commonly accepted practices in the reform and opening process. In conclusion, Jiang urged the people to be bold in breaking away from the yoke of outdated traditional concepts.

In short, the yoke of socialism had to be cast off in favor of capitalism if China was to survive. There was no sugarcoating the message. Deng had said that anything that improved the people's standard of living was acceptable to move the nation forward in relation to the rest of the nations of the world. What Jiang and Deng were calling for was nothing short of opening China to a foreign capitalist invasion. The difference, this time around, was a matter of confidence and control. This time the Chinese were in charge of their affairs, and they had the talent to supervise the foreigners and their investments. This time, they were culturally superior. In effect, Deng was advocating that China abandon Marxism, the Western doctrine they had adopted to keep the West at bay. This was no small undertaking for Deng. The conservatives understood Deng's intentions.

Jiang also expressed Deng's sense of urgency in implementing reform and opening. It was essential to China's existence that it take advantage of the interval between the collapse of the Soviet Union and its reemergence as a strong, nationalistic state or empire, based on Russia, to grow into an economically powerful nation. Deng calculated that China had about fifty years, more or less. Once Russia recovered, it would be in everyone's interest to limit China's economic and military power in the Far East. Russia would expand to control the Pacific Northeast, where its major natural resources were and its trade routes were closer to Japan and Southeast Asia than to Moscow and Europe. Clearly, the United States would also prefer a weaker China than a China intent on exercising hegemony over Southeast Asia, sitting astride the major oil lanes between the Middle East and Asia and Japan.

While Jiang had given his speech to regional and ministerial leaders, Deng called on Qiao Shi to pass the same message to the party Central Committee. According to Yang Shangkun, the members would respect Qiao.[16] Thus, Deng, through Jiang and Qiao, set out the final piece of his agenda. Interestingly, however, foreign policy was the one area in which Chen Yun, his conservatives, and the elders had always deferred to Deng. While they may not have agreed with him, none had his confidence or ability to deal with the international scene, especially after the demise of the Soviet Union. Deng consistently modulated China's internal policies in line with his perception of the international situation.

By June, the agenda for the upcoming party congress had been set and the delegates, for all intents and purposes, had been selected by Deng. Zhu, Zou, Tian, and Jiang had outlined Deng's basic agricultural, industrial, and international policies for the remainder of the twentieth century and well into the twenty-first. But while Deng had the process in hand, he did not have Chen under control; Chen's influence was such that Deng chose not to dismiss him or ride roughshod over his views. Thus, there were a series of meetings, held between August and the convening of the party congress, at which the leadership tried to iron out differences among themselves, or at least arrive at a consensus on how to move forward. The leaders, including Deng and Chen, caucused in Beidaihe in early August but failed to reach agreement on Deng's new reform and opening. Personnel arrangements for the upcoming congress must have been discussed, since numerous lists were featured in the Hong Kong press. Several individuals made it on all the lists, but it was clear there had been no real agreement on whom to add or drop from the Politburo, because immediately after the meeting the General Office of the Party—Deng's and Jiang's personal office for all intents—issued a new document: "On the Current Need to Earnestly Correct Existing Tendencies and Problems."[17] It contained the substance of several speeches made by Deng and his supporters while they toured the nation disseminating Deng's agenda. The document, coming on the heels of a meeting that had apparently failed to reach consensus, could only mean that Deng felt it necessary to again go beyond the party and preach his message to the faithful.

Deng's document struck out at twelve tendencies, which, when placed in the context of Tian Jiyun's April speech and Jiang's June speech, indicated the depth of Deng's concern. He charged that:

1. Certain people within the party were confused and asked which social system was the Communist Party adopting today;
2. Certain people were asking if Marxism-Leninism was applicable to China today;
3. Certain people had used abstract terms from Marxist works to compare the reform and opening up, which was contrary to the theories of Marxism;

4. Some people had used the two central points contained in the party's fundamental line, i.e., the Four Cardinal Principles, to shake and change the line featuring one central point, i.e., the central task of the entire party was construction;

5. Some people were resisting and distorting the resolutions, line, guidelines, and policies adopted at the Third Plenary Session of the 11th CCP Central Committee by defending the erroneous guiding ideas pursued in the latter years of Mao Zedong;

6. Some people were using bookishness and dogmatism to undermine the ideas of Comrade Deng Xiaoping, which had been proved by China's revolution and construction undertakings to be progressive, correct, and in line with China's aim of becoming a strong, modern socialist state;

7. Some were collecting, enumerating, and compiling the problems, including limited, temporary ones as well as those fairly influential ones (those already noted by the central authorities and presently being corrected, dealt with, and resolved), which had emerged in the course of reform and opening up, in order to negate the party's central task as well as the direction of reform and opening up;

8. Some, despite expressions of support for the party's fundamental line and for reform and opening up at meetings, constantly emphasized in actual work the need to pay attention to proper position, correction of ideas, and accurate focus on direction;

9. Some critics and theoretical people, as self-anointed upholders of truth, insisted on wrong viewpoints and positions, and refused to recognize changing facts, and also refused to look squarely at the objective laws concerning social development and the changes in the times;

10. Some, using the guise of opposing the rightist tendency and bourgeois liberalization, criticize correct, right, healthy, and progressive work, or honest mistakes and errors in work as bourgeois liberalization, using "leftism" to oppose so-called "rightism;"

11. Some ignored the real environment and practical conditions, and disregarded the reality of social stability, proposed launching a new political and ideological movement and conducting a class struggle movement both inside and outside the party for the purpose of

providing education on and opposing peaceful evolution as well as the intervention and infiltration of Western ideas; and

12. Some dragged up the errors and mistakes in work styles by middle-aged and young cadres who had made major contributions to the party and were correcting their errors only to discredit them."[18]

Chen Yun, however, would not surrender the field to Deng. From his summer home in Hangzhou, he answered Deng's "Twelve Points" with his own "Ten Points." This document was sent to the Politburo and was the substance of an enlarged Politburo meeting on 17 and 18 August.[19] His "Ten Points" were clearly aimed at Deng:

1. The reform and opening should have a general and class-oriented direction;

2. When calling for emancipation of the mind, greater boldness and speed, it should be integrated with scientific spirit, an attitude of seeking truth from facts, and steadfast work;

3. While the policy of opening up is part of the party's basic line, over the past 13 years there has never been a serious evaluation of that policy. Over that time, much has been said of its accomplishments, but the emerging corruption, decadence, and decline in moral climate continues to grow and spread and will lead to the destruction of society's foundation;

4. Before expanding the number of SEZ and open areas there should be a summing up of the experiences of the original ones. It will be harder to wind down the large numbers once the trend of chaos and poor results becomes evident;

5. The Pudong project in Shanghai, since it is a planned, measured development, is correct. However, since it relies on foreign investment, it is subject to external forces and is thus passive;

6. It is agreed that the state enterprises must be reformed, but the question is to which direction to pursue and with what enterprises. If it is done without a plan, only chaos will result;

7. While it is proposed to break the iron rice bowl, iron wages and iron armchair, the virtue of socialism is from each according to his ability and to each according to his work. This principle proves the superiority of socialism and has been borrowed even in the West;

8. The securities and shares market needed to be cooled and regulated or it would throw central planning into chaos;

9. Intensive investigation should be carried out before price controls are lifted, to avoid hurting families in low-income areas, areas of low economic growth and areas where problems abound;

10. The leadership and local authorities should avoid overeagerness for results. Taking bold steps, which is equated to emancipation is a manifestation of leftist tendencies, which are unscientific, contrary to the law and are rash actions. It is necessary to be concerned with this rising trend."

In his "Ten Points" Chen had called Deng's program a rightist tendency. It was always politically more correct in Chinese politics to be more leftist than rightist. Leftism in defense of socialism was still seen as rushing communism, an error in work style. Rightism in opposition to socialist principles was seen as reactionary, and the first step to doing away with the dictatorship of the proletariat and attempting to establish some form of capitalism. Chen had regurgitated the charges from the Cultural Revolution. He seemed to threaten a new mass movement along the lines of the socialist education movement that preceded the Cultural Revolution. Deng had to assume that, if Chen's line prevailed, all of his reform and opening up policies since 1978 would be reversed. The battle for the party faithful was raging right up to the congress, though Deng already had the votes and the means—the PLA—to force his vision on China. The real question was why he apparently compromised to the extent that he did, that is, leaving Li Peng on the Politburo.

Chen and Deng played the propaganda war throughout August. Chen summoned the CAC and again presented his "Ten Points." They were discussed and voted on for presentation to the Politburo, at an expanded meeting in early September. However, not all present apparently voted for the report. Since Peng Zhen, Bo Yibo, and several others had adopted Deng's viewpoint on accelerating the economy, they would have abstained, but that did not prevent Chen, as chairman, from sending his report to the Politburo. It was once again one of the issues at a contentious 4 and 5 September enlarged Politburo meeting.[20]

When Chen could not deliver a unanimous vote to the Politburo, it was apparent that his influence was waning. The clearest indicators were reports that Peng Zhen and Bo Yibo had called for the expanded Politburo meeting on 4 September. Neither individual had Politburo position, but like Deng they had informal authority. Peng actually presided over the meeting, along with Jiang. Chen presented his paper, which reiterated his charges made at the CAC in late August. He criticized Deng's socialist market economy theory, calling it unscientific, lacking any theoretical basis, and failing to provide any practical results. As his earlier paper had not spared any of Deng's basic reforms implemented since 1978, his paper to the Politburo did not spare any of Deng's policies. Chen attacked Deng's call for speeding up development, and instead called for measured, scientifically directed growth that stressed initiative and quality. In addition, Chen lashed out at Deng's intentions to do major surgery on the leadership bodies. Chen called for retaining the current leadership, with few changes, except for those too weak to carry out their tasks.[21]

While Chen announced to the gathering that he would retire from all offices following the congress, he delivered one final blow to Deng's program. He accused the leadership of selling out principle for money, that they lacked direction and lied about growth rates in the pursuit of wealth. Furthermore, he charged the leadership was ignoring theory, regionalism, and growing individualism. Deng, for his part, did not back away from a confrontation with Chen. He would agree with Chen on the charge, since he did not care if the cat was black or white, Marxist or capitalist, so long as it caught mice. He responded, "The greatest politics at the present time is construction. The greatest threat to that construction is dogmatism, bookishness and traditional old concepts and ideas that are still deeply held by many party members."[22]

The debate at the Politburo was, however, merely window dressing, since both sides knew the general outcome and had already reviewed and made comments on the draft "work report" for the congress. After the meeting, the Central Committee, under Deng's direction, issued a document to all governmental, military, and party organs greeting the opening of the Fourteenth Congress. The Ministry of Public Security issued instructions to ensure that, for the period 1 October to early November, when the Congress would be in session, there would be no untoward incidents.[23] Deng's candidate lists for the Politburo, the Standing Committee, and the Central Committee, as well as other party offices, were given to the Politburo, the CAC, and the party elders. Thus, they all, one by one, began to mouth Deng's prescription for economic development, including Li Peng, Song Ping, Lu Feng, and eventually, if not wholeheartedly, Chen Yun.

Lu Feng's "conversion" was expressed in his remarks to a national conference of provincial and municipal department directors in August, in
which he seemingly sided with Deng. In his remarks, he called on those
present to do a good job in staffing party organs so that they could carry
out the policy of one central task and two basic points. In selecting candidates, they were told to be bold and to "elect into leading bodies those
outstanding young cadres who are firm politically and bold in exploring
and blazing new trails, have made remarkable achievements in their official
careers, and are trusted by the masses."[24]

Deng, however, still offered Chen something of a compromise. While he
would not permit his plan to be subverted, he would allow some face-
saving. Li Peng was on the list of Politburo candidates, as was Zou Jiahua.[25]
Thus, as he had done since his return to power in 1978, Deng had tried to
persuade and compromise rather than vanquish his opponents. Deng had
walked away from Marxism and adopted a relativistic doctrine of utilitarian
means and ends, and he had the votes to force it through. The only action
left was for the staging of the congress to present the new compromise,
policies, and political bodies to the Chinese people.

Fourteenth Congress, Part 1

Deng finalized the "Grand Compromise" through the Fourteenth Congress. The Fourteenth and its immediate Plenums capped off a fourteen-
year effort by Deng to push China down a path of economic modernization
that can only be characterized as state capitalism. Whatever it was, it was no
longer a Marxist economy, nor was the state sustained by Marxist ideology.
Thus, it is critical to understand the outcome of the congress in order to
understand what Deng has accomplished with his last foray onto the Chinese political scene.

The lead up to the Fourteenth Congress was an important period for
China. Economic statistics showed that Deng's reforms had taken off: production was up, people were spending, inflation was in check, funds were

available for investment, and exports were up. Deng had a commanding position from which to justify putting his stamp on the new congress and future policy. In early October, the party held the Ninth Plenary Session of the Thirteenth Congress to approve arrangements—Deng's arrangements—for the Fourteenth Congress, which was to be held from 12 to 18 October.

The centerpiece of the new congress was to be Jiang's political work report, approved by the Ninth Plenum of the Thirteenth Congress.[26] Its contents were no surprise, since it had been out in draft form for several months for review and comment by various elders, advisory boards, and selected individuals. Under the guidance of Deng's lieutenants—Zhu, Ding, Wen, Jiang, and Bo—it clearly reflected all the thoughts and ideas Deng had been promulgating since his southern journey. In fact, it was the embodiment of his goals since his return to power in 1978.

Jiang opened his report with a lead-in that once again expressed Deng's overriding concern—that destiny hung in the balance and that the time to act was now, or it might forever be lost. According to Jiang, "the 13th Central Committee has comprehensively analyzed the current situation and unanimously agreed: The current domestic conditions are ripe; and the international situation is to our advantage, which provides us with both challenges and opportunities. The task of the current congress is to conscientiously sum up the practical experiences over the 14 years since the Third Plenary Session of the 11th CCP Central Committee (since Deng's return to power—author's comment), work out the strategic plan for a certain period of time to come, mobilize comrades in the entire party and the people of all nationalities throughout the country, further emancipate the mind, seize the golden opportunity, quicken the pace of reform and opening up and modernization, and win greater victories in the cause of socialism with Chinese characteristics."

At the Third Plenary of the Eleventh Congress in 1978, of course, the party had abandoned the erroneous "leftist" principle of "taking class struggle as the key link," which had become unsuitable for a socialist society, and shifted the emphasis to economics. This was the decision that initiated reform and opening up to the outside world while upholding the socialist road, the people's democratic dictatorship, the leadership of the Chinese Communist Party, and Marxism-Leninism-Mao Zedong Thought. This, according to Jiang, was also the beginnings of the "one center, two basic points" policy line that would gradually emerge as the basic line. By the Twelfth Congress in 1982, the idea of building socialism with Chinese characteristics—of integrating Marxism with the Chinese experience (culture)—had emerged as the true path for China. As part of this new formulation, the strategic goal to which Deng would frequently refer over the years was set. That goal was to quadruple the country's gross national product by the end of the century in two stages. This was later expanded to include a third step, to again double the GNP by the middle of the twenty-first century.

Jiang thus reviewed the history of reform and opening. On the rural front, he spoke of the abolition of the communes and the implementation of the contract responsibility system on a household basis, with remuneration based on output. He also pointed to the fact that the forced quota purchase of agriculture products had been abandoned. He reviewed urban reform, centered on the opening of special economic zones along the coast that involved over 200 million people. He declared irrelevant the debate over whether or not the SEZ were socialist or capitalist in nature, and in response to those critics who damned the SEZ as sources of peaceful evolution and infiltration of bourgeois liberalization, Jiang answered that, while implementing reform and opening up to the world, the party had also launched a crackdown on crime and corruption. As part of that effort, he charged the party to remain vigilant against bourgeois liberalization for the entire period of socialist modernization.

Jiang moved on to the recent history of the Thirteenth Congress, touching on the rapid, positive growth in the economy between 1984 and 1988—the period when it was under the direction of Zhao. He confessed, however, that while many aspects of the period had been favorable, serious price fluctuations and duplication of investments had necessitated a period of readjustment to bring the overall economy in line. As for the Tiananmen Incident, he reaffirmed that the party had been correct, stating that "at the turn of spring and summer in 1989, the party and government opposed turmoil with a clear-cut stand by relying on the people; pacified the counterrevolutionary rebellion which took place in Beijing; defended the political power of the socialist state; safeguarded the people's basic interests; and ensured reform and opening up and modernization, while continuing to make progress." The later decisions of the Eighth Plenum, in late 1991, on the Ten-Year and Five-Year Plans were also affirmed, as were decisions on reforming state enterprises and continued concern for agriculture.

Finally, Jiang touched on Deng's southern tour, referring to it as an inspection trip. According to Jiang, "Deng incisively analyzed the domestic and international situations and summarized the party's basic work since the Third Plenary of the 11th Congress. He had concluded that the basic line would dominate for a whole century and should never be shaken. He also demanded that the people emancipate their minds and be still bolder in reform and opening up, with a faster pace in construction so as to not lose the opportunity."

Jiang also explained the historical setting of China's socialist experiment. China was "at the initial stage of socialism, which would last for at least 100 years, with a primary goal of eliminating the contradiction between the people's increasing material demands and the backward conditions in the economy." To resolve this contradiction, "there is only one way, and that is through reform and opening. To do otherwise is to stand still. The way forward is characterized as developing the socialist market economy. This is defined as taking public ownership and distribution according to work as the main body, supplemented by other economic sectors and distribution modes. A major part of reform is opening up to the world and that is explained as a necessity in the modern world, where the international environment is characterized as one of peace and development, with capitalism and socialism in competition on one level, and mutually absorbing on another level. This being the case, China had chosen, actually been forced by historical trends, to open to the world to assimilate and utilize all the advanced civilizations and achievements created by various countries, including capitalist ones, to develop socialism." According to Jiang, a closed China would only perpetuate backwardness, but in opening China would insist on an independent foreign policy, based on peace with all nations. He praised Deng's theoretical additions to Marxism. Deng, he said, "had demonstrated tremendous political courage in opening up new paths in socialist construction and a tremendous theoretical courage to open up a new realm in Marxism, thereby making an important and historic contribution to the establishment of the theory on building socialism with Chinese characteristics."

Jiang then went on to the real reason that Deng had come out of retirement and challenged the party leadership: to make economic construction the party's basic line. Class warfare was out, unless there was a foreign invasion. Jiang, and Deng, could not be more explicit: "problems would occur, of a class nature, over time, but this would never have the weight that the center line had. Even international issues would not be allowed to interfere with economic construction."

In a very revealing statement, Jiang acknowledged that, in the past, China's economic construction had suffered because it had responded to international issues with less than a cool head. These mistakes, however, were not to be repeated. For this reason, Jiang hammered away at the threat to the basic line posed by the "leftist" influence in the party, particularly among leading members (Chen Yun). As Jiang explained, "rightist" influence had led to attacks on the Four Cardinal Principles, and even to political rebellion and bourgeois liberalization, but the "leftist" influence was challenging the basic line of reform and opening. "Leftists" claimed that the source of peaceful evolution was the reform and opening policy, and they used the idea of class struggle to attack it.

Jiang warned that the mistakes of the previous twenty years had been mainly "leftist" ones, which had had a major negative impact on the economy. He urged party members to emancipate their minds to avoid the mistakes of the past. Clearly, the crux of all of Deng's ideas was this simple fact: China had made a mistake in 1950 in siding with the Soviet Union against the West. All decisions following from that had left China in a backward position in relation to the rest of the world. The only way to correct that error was through reform and opening—now, not tomorrow. Tomorrow would be too late. This raises the interesting issue that perhaps there was much debate over how to treat the West on the eve of the Chinese Communist victory in 1949. Deng seems to imply that they were all aware of the issues that surfaced back then. In any event, this time Deng would permit no turning back. The elements of the "Compromise" would prevent turning back and turning inward.

Jiang explained the task for the remainder of the 1990s: expedite reform and opening. He said, "History had shown that the current international competition was based on a nation's comprehensive economic and scientific strength. For China this meant that the planned growth rate of six percent was insufficient to allow China to catch up with the leading nations of the West. The rate had to be adjusted upwards, to at least nine or ten percent. Moreover, the time to act was now. Development must be accelerated, in a balanced way. The key to China's development was the integration of the planned economy and market regulation."

Jiang reiterated Deng's conclusion—that capitalism included some planning, and socialism included some market mechanisms. That being the case, it did not matter if a thing was tagged as "socialist" or "capitalist." What mattered was whether it raised the people's living standards and improved production levels.

As part of the new policy of pursuing a socialist market economy, Jiang enumerated the ten major objectives that the Fourteenth Party needed to undertake:

1. Develop the socialist market economy, to include a thorough implementation of the operational mechanism in state enterprises; accelerate development of the market economy to include money and securities markets, price, distribution, and taxation reform, and removing the government from microeconomics.

2. Further extend opening up to the world; utilize more and better foreign funds, resources, technologies, and managerial experiences.

3. Adjust and optimize agriculture, to include increased inputs to agriculture and efforts to develop tertiary industries to absorb surplus labor and peasant savings and increase revenues to the state.

4. Expedite scientific and technological progress, develop education, and give full rein to the role of intellectuals, for without a large and contributing scientific and technological class, China would not be able to compete in international markets, and it would not be able to attract foreign investment, since its labor force would not be educated enough to provide the job skills.

5. All localities should give full play to their strengths, which meant that the economy should be in balance nationwide, but that the benefits of chance location, rich natural resources, favorable lines of communication, and other factors could predispose a given area to be a leader in a given commodity or service. These benefits should be developed to the fullest, and integrated into the overall economic picture to realize the economies of scale.

6. Promote the restructuring of the political system. The political structure would need to be changed to reflect the changing economic situation. However, China absolutely would not promote

the multiparty and parliamentary systems of the West. The PRC would uphold the principle of democratic centralism.

7. Reform administrative systems, eliminating party and government organs that overlapped, and improve efficiency.

8. Raise the level of the socialist spiritual civilization. The party should attach great importance to protecting academic freedom, integrate theory and practice, and let One Hundred Flowers bloom. At the same time, they should continue to crack down on the evils associated with reform and opening that limit modernization.

9. Continue to improve living standards, strictly control population growth, and strengthen environmental protection.

10. Strengthen army building, enhance national defense, and ensure the smooth progress of reform, opening up to the outside world and economic construction.[27]

Jiang described the PLA as "the strong pillar of the people's democratic dictatorship, a great wall of steel for the defense of the socialist motherland, and an important force in building socialism with Chinese characteristics. At present, and for a considerable time to come, our country's socialist modernization will continue to proceed within a complicated and changing international environment. It is necessary to act in accordance with Deng Xiaoping's thought on army building in the new period; to take the distinctively Chinese road of building a better army; to build the PLA into a powerful, modern, and regular revolutionary army; and to constantly seek to strengthen our country's national defense strength so as to provide a strong security guarantee for reform and opening up to the outside world, and economic construction. The army should adapt itself to the needs of modern warfare by enhancing combat strength in an all-around manner, and thus shoulder the mission of defending the country's territorial sovereignty over the land and air as well as its rights and interests on the sea, and should safeguard the unification and security of the motherland."

Jiang also discussed China's foreign policy in a changing international environment. Deng's view, voiced by Jiang, was that "the world was undergoing a historic period of tremendous change. The bipolar pattern had ended, and various forces were redividing and recombining, and the world had become increasingly multipolarized. This new pattern will be complex and take some time to form, and in the interim it will be possible to avoid war. However, the new world will be a tumultuous one. For its part,

China would continue to make positive efforts to promote ties with foreign countries; strive to create an international environment more favorable to China's reform and opening, and modernization; and to contribute its part to world peace and development." As Jiang stated: "China is firm in opening up our country to the outside world. China is willing to constantly strengthen and expand economic, scientific, and technological cooperation with other countries on the basis of equality and mutual benefit, and they were willing to increase exchanges. However, China would always uphold its independent and peaceful foreign policy. Safeguarding China's independence and sovereignty as well as promoting world peace and development are the basics of China's foreign policy. China will never concede to outside pressure; it will not form alliances with any country or bloc; and it will not join any military alliance. Furthermore, China will oppose hegemonism and power politics, but is willing to develop friendly relations with any nation on the basis of the Five Principles of Peaceful Coexistence."

Jiang, never the creative mind on foreign affairs, which were strictly under Deng's personal supervision, spent little more time on the issue. He concluded the report with a section on party life and party building. In this final section, he discussed the need to choose successors who were more revolutionary, younger, better educated and more competent professionally, and who possessed both ability and political integrity. The latter was to be judged by how well one performed in implementing the party's basic line.[28] Jiang's "Report" left no room for compromise with Chen's opposition. Slow growth was not an avenue. There was no room for "leftist" ideas, disruptive mass movements, and threats of class warfare. The congress would settle old scores and stack the deck to ensure that there would be no chance of reversing the "one center and two basic points" policy line of the party. Deng would set up a structure to facilitate his policies.

The personnel selected by the new congress for the Central Committee, the Politburo, the Standing Committee, and the CMC represented a major victory for Deng in his effort to make broad institutional changes. The new Central Committee included 189 full members and 130 alternate members, totaling 319, of which 46.7 percent were new faces. It was a mix of veterans from the revolutionary era, middle-aged persons, and promising younger cadre. The average age was 56.3 years, and over 83 percent had received a college degree. True to his earlier promises to the provincial leaders prior to the congress, regional and municipal members constituted 62 percent of the body, accounting for the most strategic institutional change to come out of the congress. This also sealed Deng's promise, made back in the spring of 1992, that the regional leadership would be able to thwart any policy changes in Beijing that interfered with reform and opening.[29] In addition, the career backgrounds of the members were split about evenly between party bureaucrats and those from technical professions, thus establishing the link between red and expert. But in no case were there any political liberals.

Politburo membership was increased to twenty members, to include Ding Guangen, Tian Jiyun, Zhu Rongji, Qiao Shi, Liu Huoqing, Jiang Zemin, Li Peng, Li Lanqing, Li Tieying, Li Ruihuan, Yang Baibing, Wu Bangguo, Zou Jiahua, Chen Xitong, Hu Jintao, Jiang Chunyun, Qian Qichen, Wei Jianxing, Xie Fei, and Tan Shaowen. Alternate members were Wen Jiabao and Wang Hanbin. The Standing Committee included Jiang Zemin, who retained his position as party general secretary, Li Peng, Qiao Shi, Li Ruihuan, Zhu Rongji, Liu Huaqing, and Hu Jintao. The Secretariat included Hu Jintao, Ding Guangen, Wei Jianxing, Wen Jiabao, and Ren Jianxin. Deng had settled an old score: Song Ping and Yao Yilin were out. Also gone were the "leftists" who had prevented his message from getting out over the past year. Dropped from office and membership were Wang Renzhi, head of the Propaganda Department; He Jingzhi, Minister of Culture; and Gao Di, head of *People's Daily.*

On the new Politburo, the regional or municipal leaders constituted 25 percent of the members, representing Beijing (Chen Xitong), Shanghai (Wu Bangguo), Tianjin (Tan Shaowen), Shandong (Jiang Chunyun), and Guangdong (Xie Fei). One must also include in this number the added weight of Zhu Rongji for Shanghai, Li Ruihuan for Tianjin, Li Lanqing for Tianjin, and Hu Jintao for Tibet. In short, almost 50 percent of the Politburo had roots that strongly suggested that they would be sympathetic to the problems associated with running a major municipality or province. Yang Baibing, the former secretary of the CMC, represented the PLA, though he was without a major constituency by virtue of his loss of a CMC position and General Staff job as chief commissar. Ding Guangen, Deng's bridge partner, who had helped put together the victory for Deng, was there to ensure that the grand compromise was adhered to by all parties. Zou Jiahua was there to appease Chen Yun, but he also reflected Deng's attempt to put economic technocrats in key positions. He would also help with re-centralization efforts, which fell to Zhu, who had become economics czar after the Eighth NPC in the spring of 1993.[30] Li Peng was a holdover, a reward for faithfully carrying out the martial law orders in 1989. (He retained the premiership at the Eighth, but when his second and final statutory term is over, he will be retired.) Along with Zou, his expertise in central planning would be used to balance the center against the regions. Wei Jianxing, Qiao Shi's protégé and representative of the powerful public security office, lent weight to the compromise. Qian Qichen, who was experienced in fighting on the international scene to implement Deng's foreign policy, was there to guide the inexperienced Jiang and to ensure that the "Middle Kingdom" or "Independent" policy was followed. Li Lanqing, a technocrat with regional experience, was there to support reform and opening. Li Ruihuan represented regional power, as well as the alter ego of Deng on the propaganda front. Li Tieying, the education minister, was Deng's concession to the intellectuals. Finally, Tian Jiyun, Deng's trusted lieutenant, who had handled the agriculture sector of the economy with such skill, was retained in the new congress. Ideologically, the lineup on the Politburo was almost 75 percent for reform and opening and oriented toward the regions.

The new Standing Committee consisted of seven members: Jiang, Li Ruihuan, Zhu Rongji, Hu Jintao, Li Peng, Qiao Shi, and Liu Huaqing. In this new lineup, only Li Peng remained from Chen Yun's faction of central planners of the Marxist school. Jiang was a lightweight, the compromise candidate that Deng had chosen in a hurry in 1989. Deng had little faith in him, but to avoid admitting that he had made a mistake, Deng had developed the concept of a "core" leadership built around him. Jiang was part of the old, traditional party bureaucracy, but had no powers. He had been forced to make several self-criticisms, and had offered to resign several times. Deng had refused, choosing instead to surround him with individuals of strong will who would keep him in line, as well as avoid the embarrassment of sacking another of his chosen successors. Li, Zhu, and Hu could be counted as the core of the reformers pushing Deng's market socialism. Qiao Shi, who saw the utilitarian purpose of reform, would cooperate to ensure that the regions prospered and the party remained in power. Finally, Liu Huaqing, the aging PLA veteran, was on the Standing Committee to ensure the compromise and, along with the staff of the

CMC, which by secret agreement was allowed to sit in on Politburo discussions, to protect the interests of the PLA.

Analysis of these lists (see charts below) reveal two salient points: Representing over 60 percent of the Central Committee, as opposed to only 25 percent at the Thirteenth Party Congress, the regional leaders had the majority vote in any future enlarged Politburo meeting or at any plenary.[31] This had not been a major issue at the previous congress, since Deng was still in charge and his handpicked lieutenants were in control of critical state and party offices. However, as Deng and his lieutenants had not had effective control since November 1989, it was all-important to reestablish institutional control over the party and state at the Fourteenth, as well as implement a long-term plan to maintain that control.

Finally, the last of the major policy boards, the CMC, was named: Jiang Zemin, chairman; Liu Huaqing, vice-chairman; Zhang Zhen, vice-chairman; and members Chi Haotian, Zhang Wannian, Yu Yongbo, and Fu Quanyou.

POLITBURO (STANDING COMMITTEE)

Market Socialists	Central Planners	Law and Order
Li Ruihuan	Li Peng	Qiao Shi
Zhu Rongji		Liu Huoqing
Hu Jintao		Jiang Zemin

POLITBURO

Regional/Market	Central Planners	Law and Order
Li Ruihuan	Li Peng	Qiao Shi
Zhu Rongji	Zou Jiahua	Liu Huoqing
Hu Jintao		Yang Baibing
Ding Guangen		Wei Jianxing
Li Lanqing		
Wu Bangguo		
Chen Xitong		
Qian Qichen		
Jiang Chunyun		
Xie Fei		
Tan Shaowen		

The PLA was also repaid for supporting Deng. Representation on the Central Committee was increased to 22 percent from the 18 percent it had held at the Thirteenth Congress. True to his pledge to represent all military factions, in order to achieve a political balance that he referred to as "five seas and four oceans," the Fourth and Third Field Armies had the largest representation, followed by the First and Second, respectively.[32] Thus, while the field army system still influences Chinese politics, new contravening relationships are emerging that perhaps have greater currency when deciding the factional politics of the PLA.[33] In any case, the PLA was assured of money for modernization, and the provinces were assured of independence vis-à-vis the center. Thus, two of Deng's promises had been kept.

As a final act, Deng had the CAC dissolved, eliminating any formal advisory body that could interfere with the Standing Committee. In China, however, informal power is everything. In place of the CAC, Deng established two informal policy supervisory bodies (see following chart for supposition of makeup of the two bodies). One represented the PLA, an informal group of senior officials, mainly from the CMC. These PLA elders, who represented the founding generation of the PRC and the PLA, would constitute the core of Deng's ad hoc "advisory body," to ensure that the "Grand Compromise" was honored by all parties. Their continued dominance at the peak of the informal power structure, however, did not change the fact that operational control of the PLA had also passed to the next generation, the post–Korean War generation, characterized by professional and technical school ties. But, along with Liu and Yang Baibing on the Standing Committee and Politburo, respectively, they will ensure that PLA interests are protected. This arrangement also extends to the regional and local levels, with PLA representatives sitting in on local decision-making bodies.

The second informal body, however, is the most powerful. This is the remaining group of elders of the party—the active members of the defunct CAC and others who still exercise informal authority. Of these, Peng Zhen, Bo Yibo, and Yang Shangkun remain the most influential. They will advise the leadership, mainly through the PLA CMC, which in turn will advise the Standing Committee, or more directly through consultation with their protégés on the Standing Committee. The important point is that the decision-making process is now more remote and removed from formal mechanisms. The elders will control policy through the PLA, which is the guarantor of Deng's compromise, and the PLA will advise the Politburo by its informal and formal presence.

ELDERS *(GENRO)*

Jiang Zemin (Standing Committee)
Peng Zhen
Bo Yibo
Yang Shangkun
Liu Huoqing (Standing Committee)
Zhang Zhen
Qiao Shi (Standing Committee)
Yang Dezhi
Song Renqiong
Tian Jiyun (Politburo)
Wan Li (Politburo)
Yang Baibing (Politburo)

MILITARY ADVISORS

Jiang Zemin (Standing Committee)
Peng Zhen
Qiao Shi (Standing Committee)
Liu Huoqing (Standing Committee)
Zhang Zhen
Yang Dezhi
Yang Shangkun
Li Desheng

The locus of the Communist Party's power has thus returned to its roots—the PLA. It is necessary to discuss the changes Deng has made in the role of the PLA to measure the significance of changes in the power structure at the Fourteenth Congress. The elders who ruled were aging PLA veterans. Prior to the congress, there was much speculation in Hong Kong and overseas about the prospects of the Yang brothers. Many expected Yang Baibing to take over on the CMC as a vice-chairman. Instead, the position of permanent secretary general of the CMC was abolished. He also lost his General Staff position. It was speculated that he got the Politburo job as a consolation prize for accepting the demotion.[34]

It is important to recall that, in April 1992, Deng and the CMC had agreed on a major restructuring of the PLA. The goal was to build a modern, centralized army that was totally under party control. As with past restructurings, beginning in 1985 and especially in 1990 and 1991, Deng had shuffled military regional commands to avoid mountaintopism, to ensure central control, and to avoid any charges of favoritism—his reference to "five seas and four oceans" in his letter to Jiang on the eve of the Fourteenth Congress asking for the resignation of Yang Baibing. The increased emphasis on an educated military command meant more change.

Once the congress was over, there was a major changing of the guard; initially over three hundred officers were retired. By the end of the year, more than one thousand were relieved of command and replaced by younger, more technically qualified officers.[35] While it did eliminate the influence of the Yangs and their protégés throughout the PLA, it was part of the overall plan to centralize control to eliminate the regional-based command structure and gradually replace it with a centralized, functionally defined command structure that would ensure total party control over the PLA.[36] This latter plan would require a younger, more educated, more professional force that was committed to a unified China, not one that relied on patronage from above.

Deng obviously had to have had the agreement of Yang Shangkun and Yang Baibing to implement this change. He had decided to remove the Yangs in April, when he announced Liu Huaqing's promotion. He merely waited for the appropriate moment to implement it, at the Fourteenth Party Congress. After all, their subordinates had backed Deng in his move on the party over the months leading up to the Fourteenth Congress. Had they been aware that they were to lose their jobs so quickly, they might have tried to rally around another figure, perhaps Chen and Li Peng. Thus, Deng had moved quickly after the Fourteenth Congress to replace them with a new generation in command, owing allegiance to the new order under Liu. His move also facilitated the removal of several officers who had commanded troops during the bloody Tiananmen Incident. Their removal mitigated lingering popular resentment of the PLA and internal resentment at being ordered to march on the students. Deng's move opened up the prospect of upward mobility in the PLA. In effect, he bought the loyalty of the next generation of commanders.

From a legalistic standpoint, when Deng retired in 1989 he clearly left in place an arrangement with Yang Shangkun, who took over as permanent first vice-chairman of the CMC, whereby Yang could authorize, on his signature alone, or perhaps with that of the permanent secretary, his brother Yang Baibing, troop movements. Previous to his retirement, in 1989, Deng had had control over the PLA, ever since his comeback in 1978. Mao had never allowed operational control to pass down to an authority outside the senior leadership, that is, the Politburo Standing Committee. Deng's arrangement with Yang, however, placed the PLA technically under the command of someone without such ranking, since Yang, while a Politburo member, was not on the Standing Committee. This implied that the party general secretary had no authority to direct the PLA. Deng thus reasserted senior party control when he named Liu Huaqing, a member of the Politburo Standing Committee, to the post as first vice-chairman of the CMC in April 1992, and announced that Yang Shangkun would resign at the Fourteenth Party Congress.

Deng, however, was not content with just institutional change to ensure party control over the PLA. He was aware of the fact that he had utilized his personal authority and close relationship with the Yangs, especially Yang Shangkun, to mobilize the PLA against his conservative opposition in the party. If he could do this, others could also. To prevent this from splitting the PLA and giving it a decision in an internal party debate, Deng established an informal control group over the CMC, discussed above, that consisted of the remaining PLA revolutionary-generation elders, such as Yang Shangkun, Yang Baibing, Li Desheng, Yang Dezhi, as well as the CMC leadership and the leadership of the internal security organs, Peng Zhen and Qiao Shi.

Under this arrangement, any internal policy debate will be resolved by the informal military/security council, which will then present a unified position to the CMC and instruct it on how to mobilize the PLA. This explains Deng's decision to allow the CMC to participate informally on Politburo discussions. As the guardian and guarantor of the "Grand Compromise," the PLA must have knowledge of economic policy to prevent backsliding on modernization. This also explains the massive replacement of senior officers in the aftermath of the congress. Those fired or retired had been promoted to command positions by the Yangs to support Deng's continued hold over the PLA. Once he was resigned to relinquishing power in 1992, Deng had to allow the replacement of that core group with a new generation of commanders assigned by the legitimate CMC authority, Liu Huaqing.

The restructuring of the PLA had been completed, on paper, on the eve of the Fourteenth Party Congress. Immediately after the First Plenum on 23 October, an expanded CMC meeting was convened to endorse the new leadership. Liu Huaqing and Chi Haotian outlined the new policy, which implicitly answered the question that had been raised in December 1991: how to make the PLA and China rich and powerful. The answer, of course, was to have a sound, efficient, expanding national economy. That line carried through the speeches the PLA leaders made. During the congress, Liu was quoted as saying, "the PLA must not fail the glorious mission entrusted by the 14th Party Congress and the army should build itself into a powerful, modern, regular, and revolutionary one in accordance with the thinking of Deng Xiaoping."[37] Liu was also quick to point out how this would benefit the PLA: "Our country enjoys a stable political situation and economic development. The people's living standard is improving. Our country's situation is excellent. It is necessary for us to seize the favorable opportunity and strive to raise the nation's overall national strength."

Liu made other comments for the press that laid out the new leadership's thoughts on modernization and what was important. "Modernization of the army was not limited to modernization of weaponry. But without this modernization, nothing else was possible. I believe that, along with economic development of the country, our army will make a giant step forward in its modernization. This effort was grounded in an increased appreciation of the value of science and technology. Modernization would be an empty word if there were no advanced science and technology and no people armed with such knowledge. That is why the PLA should strengthen education in science and technology."[38]

The new CMC vice-chairman and PLA chief of staff, Chi Haotian, also shared his thoughts on modernization. Quoting from Sun Tze, he stated, "National defense is a major state affair, which has a direct bearing on the life and death of a nation. It should not be left unattended." He continued: "The faster China develops its economy, carries out reform and opens its doors to the rest of the world, the more necessary it is to strengthen national defense. In that case, we can create a safe and stable environment as well as stand up against bullying, humiliation and oppression from the outside."[39]

Deng had placed the PLA last in his modernization priority scheme in 1978. In the end, to ensure that his long-term goal was successful, he had had to turn his dream over to the care of the PLA to escort it to its successful conclusion once Deng had departed the scene. In the process, Deng stabilized society. The effects will only become evident with the passage of time. Deng's "Grand Compromise" should survive his death, though at the end of the congress there were still a few planks left to be inserted in the infrastructure. Those planks would be quickly added in a series of plenums that followed the restructuring of the policy bodies.

Fourteenth Congress, Part 2

At the Fourteenth Congress, Deng put all his lieutenants into position. He left it up to them to carry out the final elements of the Grand Compromise. It took his lieutenants, Zhu Rongji and Liu Huaqing, some time, but by the Third Plenum in the fall of 1993, only one year after the congress had established the new power structure, they had basically succeeded.

The linchpin of the Grand Compromise was a promise by the provinces to resolve the problem of insufficient revenue returns to the center. Early in the modernization drive, Zhao Ziyang had allowed the favored provinces to retain the lion's share of revenues earned, as a reward for their efforts and as part of his attempt to break the ironfisted control the central ministries had over the economy. This led to uneven returns to the center, as provinces such as Guangdong retained 90 percent of earned revenues and remitted a mere 10 percent in taxes to the national treasury.

The low tax rates were designed to favor rapid growth and attract foreign investments. Cities and regions outside of the initial open areas, such as

Shanghai, on the other hand, had to remit over 50 percent of earned revenues to the center. Thus, Guangdong earned over 22 billion yuan in 1992 and remitted only 7.5 billion, whereas Shanghai earned 37 billion yuan and was forced to remit 27 billion yuan to Beijing.[40] The net result was that central revenue as a percentage of the GDP had declined from 37 percent at the start of reform in 1978 to 19 percent in 1992. If that trend continued, Beijing's share of revenue by the year 2000 would drop to 10 percent.

It was Zhu Rongji's task to tackle the problems of shrinking revenue and an inflationary economy. To that end, he drew up a sixteen-point plan to curb the inflationary tendencies in the economy and to reestablish the center's control over revenue. In general, Zhu's program proposed reforms in banking, finance, taxation, and investment. He focused on curtailing loans for speculative projects, ensuring that funds were sufficient and properly used for agricultural and infrastructure projects, instituting government bond sales through compulsory purchases, increasing interest rates for savings, strengthening the central bank, and sending work teams to the provinces to ensure compliance.

He also initiated a new taxation system to reform the government's fiscal policy.[41] Previously, the center had been forced to negotiate annually with each province to determine the percentage of revenue they would return to Beijing. Revenues generated over the agreed amount remained with the provinces. If rates were not increased, and they were not, the effect of increased economic activity resulted in more and more wealth remaining under provincial control. Zhu proposed a dual-tax system to replace the annual bargaining sessions. The new system would divide taxes between the center and the provinces in a 60:40 split, with Beijing claiming the major share. The agreement, however, guaranteed the provinces that their revenues would not dip below the level earned in 1993, while the poorer regions were assured of revenue transfers through the year 2000. Zhu, Jiang, and other senior leaders traveled throughout China in order to ensure that local officials signed on to the new system.[42]

While the tax rates were not established in the policy, it was specific in assigning the tax base. Taxes required for safeguarding and promoting national interests and the exercise of macroeconomic control were assigned to the center. Taxes directly related to economic development were to be shared between the local and national governments. Beijing, however, reserved thirty-three kinds of taxes for itself, to include customs duties, consumption tax, profit taxes from state enterprises, levies on financial services, and duties on liquor and cigarettes. Regional taxes included personal profit taxes, city construction levies, several agricultural-related taxes, and business and profit taxes on local enterprises, excluding banking, finance, insurance, mail, electricity, and railway transportation. In addition, some taxes were split between the province and the center, including the value added tax, split 75 percent to 25 percent for center and province respectively, duties on stock transfers, and taxes on resources. Thus, the wealthier provinces—those that had benefited from the opening policy—would pay more to Beijing. The new taxation system also established a uniform 33 percent tax rate on all enterprise activity not covered, and levied the same on state enterprises, cutting their rates from 55 percent to make them competitive with non-state enterprises.[43] That the provinces would agree to the plan had been ordained the previous year during Deng's southern tour. Jiang's visit to promote the new policy, prior to presentation at the fall plenum, was clearly to remind the local leaders of their responsibility to honor their agreements with Deng. The point was made by Sichuan Governor Xiao Yang in an interview in Chengdu. "Of course I'd like to give less money to Premier Li Peng. But Li Peng has to think of the whole country, and he will think 'Xiao Yang, you should give more.'"[44] Xiao continued to explain that declining revenues were hampering Beijing's ability to invest in major projects such as railroads, airports, and highways. That in turn, according to Xiao, would slow down regional development.

Clearly indicative of the "compromise," the tax system was agreed to at the Third Plenum in November.[45] The new Politburo and Central Committee, though overwhelmingly composed of provincial members, agreed to Zhu's new policies, effectively surrendering provincial autonomy. Thus, the congress agreed to implement the "Grand Compromise," specifically, the promise to increase and regularize revenue remittances to the center—revenues that would be used to fund the regional developments mentioned by Xiao Yang and modernize the PLA.

Taxation or fiscal reform addressed only half the problem facing Beijing as a result of Deng's devolutionary policies. Though Zhu's fiscal reform was perhaps the single most important policy to emerge with long-term implications, the problem of controlling the money supply continued to hamper efforts at controlling inflation, which raised its ugly head each time the economy started to take off. The major problem was the political control over the banking system exercised by the party. The banks in China were political instruments, not financial. Thus, the authorities in Beijing would order the central banks to print money if they ran short. If enterprises ran short of funds for wages as a result of poor sales, the central bank would be expected to make loans to meet the payroll. Such loans were never repaid. As a result of devolution, provincial officials were also able to order branch banks to issue loans or increase the money in circulation to meet local needs.

Once Zhu Rongji was comfortably installed in his position as economic czar following the Fourteenth Congress and the NPC meeting in March 1993, he seized operational control of the People's Bank of China (PBOC). He ruled that the banks would be separated into policy banks and financial ones, similar to the practice in the West. The commercial or financial banks would issue loans strictly based on credit worthiness. The policy banks, on the other hand, would grant loans to projects favored by the central government. Zhu reserved for himself, as economic czar, the job as governor of the People's Bank, which he established as the central bank of China, similar to the role played by the central banks in the West. The vice-governor of the bank, Chen Yuan, explained that its role would be to pursue Western-style monetary policy, especially the control of the money supply and the stabilization of the currency.

Zhu decreed that only the PBOC could authorize loans, and he placed strict limits on interbank fund transfers. Finally, he unified the foreign exchange rate as a step towards making the yuan convertible on the international currency markets.[46] Thus, Zhu was able to reassert control over provincial financial matters. The military-industrial complex was alive and well, with Chen Yun's son cooperating with Zhu, to ensure that the center held its own against the provinces, which is what Deng wanted with his compromise.

The results of Zhu's first year at the helm of economic policy, while encouraging, were less than a solid success. When he took over in early 1993, the economy had already registered a 13 percent real growth rate for 1992. For the first half of 1993, it was a record 14 percent annualized rate; industrial production was 25 percent higher than 1992, and fixed investments were 70 percent higher. In addition, price rises and money supply increases were accelerating. Zhu took immediate action. He halted fixed-asset investment, and ordered millions to be invested in infrastructure bottlenecks such as telecommunications, energy, and transportation. By early 1994 investment had dropped to 30 percent, industrial production to 19 percent. Overall inflation, however, excluding food costs, which peaked at over 20 percent in 1993, dropped to a level of 9 to 10 percent. Zhu was able to cut the money supply growth rate to the planned rate of 20 percent in 1995, successfully reducing the 35 percent inflationary growth from 1994 and 1993.[47] Thus, Zhu has been able to restore a modicum of central control over the economy through fiscal and monetary policies.

In addition to reforming the monetary and fiscal systems, Zhu had to tackle the issue of inefficient state enterprises. While in Shanghai, Zhu had proposed ways to privatize these enterprises. At the national level, the Third Plenum also announced that it had several options for resolving the problem of ailing state enterprises, one of which was privatization. Other options included merging ailing enterprises with healthy ones, or entering into joint ventures with foreign firms. During 1993 and 1994, many enterprises were sold off as joint ventures or stock shareholding arrangements.

Zhu, however, while not a Stalinist central planner, did not believe that it was necessarily in the state's interest to either sell off all the state enterprises or to allow them to go bankrupt. Everyone at the center and the provincial level was aware that the state enterprises employed over 100 million workers who, released on the economy, would create chaos. So, bankruptcy would be a last resort. In addition, the ailing enterprises accounted for 50 percent of industrial output, and just as the PLA was unwilling to relinquish its hold over industrial wealth, represented by its ownership of electronics and manufacturing enterprises, the state was clearly not ready to relinquish its interests to the private sector.

Zhu, therefore, had to transform the enterprises into profitable ones, capable of competing on the world market. Thus, as early as the spring of 1994, less than six months after the Plenum, Zhu was advocating a slow-down of privatization and a search for ways to make the enterprises more responsible for their own profits and losses.[48] Some transfers had taken place, but it appears that the compromise reached between Deng and his reformers and the central planners mandating that a sizable portion of industrial production—heavy industries production along the model of

Stalin's military-industrial complex—would remain subject to the central ministries, was left intact. Instead of privatization, management would be given autonomy, and sick industries would be merged with healthy ones.

Thus, another element of the Grand Compromise was realized. The central planners would continue to control the lion's share of industrial production, of which the Three Gorges Dam is an example. A multiprovincial, multibillion yuan project, it could only be undertaken as a national project. It is confirmation that the central ministries will continue to influence large sectors of the economy.

Deng was also intent upon ensuring party control over advancement in government, the military, and in the private sector, of the nomenklatura.[49] This was evident when Jiang and Liu were able to effortlessly dismiss Yang Baibing's associates—over one thousand officers—in the immediate aftermath of the Fourteenth Congress. Liu then promoted one thousand officers, giving them a stake in preserving the current order. However, in the civilian sector, the issue of curbing local prerogative, especially that of the provincial governors heading the provinces with the greatest growth, was a constant battle during the years of rapid growth. Local officials, such as governors Ye Xuanping of Guangdong and Zhao Zhihao of Shangdong, had refused Li Peng's demands in 1990 to turn over more funds to Beijing.[50]

If Jiang's exercise of appointment and dismissal did not have an impact on local authorities contemptuous of Beijing, clearly the Politburo's decision in 1993 and 1994 to reshuffle the majority of provincial posts to eliminate growing regionalism had to demolish the prospect of local "warlordism" reappearing in China. New party and government executives were installed in at least fifteen provinces, including Jiangsu, Zhejiang, Hunan, Henan, Shanxi, Guizhou, Gansu, Liaoning, Heilongjiang, Xinjiang, Fujian, and Hubei, during 1993 and 1994. Zhu Rongji even dismissed the governor and secretary of Heilongjiang because of their failure to implement central directives.[51] Finally, the decision to remove the party secretary of Beijing, Chen Xitong, a Politburo member, for corruption is the clearest indication of the center's determination to govern, since it could not have been done without the concurrence of the Politburo.

Not to be left out, the PLA, as guarantor of the Grand Compromise, has continued to reap its rewards in the form of ever increasing yearly budgets. Since 1988, its budget has grown by 200 percent.[52] Between 1988 and 2000, the budget grew at double-digit rates; in 1994 it increased 22 percent over 1993, and in 2001 it is scheduled to grow by over 17 percent.[53] As a result of the December 1991 agreement with Deng, the PLA will continue to garner its share of the budget pie. One estimate calculates that budget figure at close to 3 percent of China's GNP, which would make it five times the United States' estimate of $6 billion. In any case, if defense spending continues as promised by Deng, as a fixed percentage of yearly GNP, then with the economy growing at 9 or 10 percent per year, the PLA will experience significant growth in its budget. Again, the Grand Compromise is at work. The PLA, apparently flush with cash, has been on a buying spree. It has purchased advanced fighters, the Su-27 and the Su-30, as well as Kilo-class diesel submarines and *Sovremmeny*-class destroyers equipped with supersonic antiship cruise missiles, from Russia, and the Lavi fighter design from Israel. The Russian deal will become a licensed production venture for the fighters, and the Israeli blueprints were used to produce the indigenous J-9 single-seat fighter. The PLA continues to modernize its forces with Western high-technology equipment.

The PLA is also becoming a powerful force in Asia. Its leadership had sufficient clout on the Politburo to force a confrontation with the United States in early 1996 over Taiwan. In that confrontation, Beijing was trying to block Taiwan leader Lee Teng-hui's popular election. Failing that, the PRC hoped to limit his margin of victory and deny him a mandate to continue Taiwan's independent policy. The exercise in the Taiwan Strait involved all the armed forces, and included the launching of missiles into the sea near Taiwan's two major ports. The PLA was announcing to Asia and Taiwan that it could, and would, blockade the island if it declared independence. However, fearful of its impact on overall economic growth, the PLA, which had no intention of starting a war, quickly lowered the exercise tempo and language once the negative impact on the economy began to be reported from the key coastal centers in southern China.

Of course, all this is not to suggest that the course of Chinese politics will proceed smoothly. The debate over what constitutes a "communist" state, and China's image of itself in that context, has still to be settled, especially in light of societal changes being wrought by a rapidly expanding economy. However, Deng's practical solution to maintaining national cohesion, while making China a world power, should keep it on a steady course. It should emerge as an Asian economic powerhouse early in the twenty-first century. Perhaps his final instructions to the party are to be his legacy:

> The policy of taking economic construction as the key link must never be challenged; the reform and open-door policy must never be altered. The party's basic line must not be shaken for 100 years. We must properly draw the lesson from the former Soviet Union and handle well the relationship between the party center and localities. We must uphold the leadership of the CCP. The CCP's status as the ruling party must never be challenged. China cannot adopt a multiparty system. . . . CCP leadership is unshakable. . . . Nothing can be accomplished if central authority is weakened.[54]

Conclusion

A rehabilitated Deng returned to the political scene in 1978 with an agenda—to set China on a path of economic modernization to make it a prosperous and powerful nation by the middle of the twenty-first century. He resigned from public office in 1989, believing that all parties agreed that retrenchment of his reform polices following Tiananmen would be temporary. By 1991, however, the framework for Deng's master plan began to crumble, again, as events in the Soviet Union reached crisis proportions. When the Soviet Army failed to support the Communist Party of the Soviet Union in August 1991, the party collapsed, as did communism in Russia and, earlier, in its client states. Fearing a similar fate, Chen Yun and the conservatives in the Chinese Communist Party again rallied around the old ideas of a strong party, with an even stronger commitment to ideology. This meant continued retrenchment of Deng's liberal economic policies. Thus, Deng was forced to return to the political fray to save his grand design.

With the backing of the PLA, the security forces, and the remaining reformers among the elders, Deng rallied the provincial officials in a grand effort to prevent economic retrenchment and a return to the discarded and disproved policies of Mao's era. However, this time he would not rely on individuals to carry out his policies. Instead he made institutional and personnel changes to ensure broad-based support.

Since his return in 1978, Deng had been methodically replacing the Yenan generation on the Central Committee and the Politburo in order to engineer the inevitable leadership succession in line with his objectives. Rather than permit party stalwarts, who had grown up and assumed middle-level positions in the party, government, and army during the revolutionary era and immediate post-1949 years, to assume power, he sought out a new type of individual, better educated and technically qualified. In other words, he chose the "expert" over the "red." By the Fourteenth Party Congress, he had succeeded in transforming the Army's character and outlook from that of the peasant-soldier to that of the technocrat, and the party leadership from a narrow clique with revolutionary experience to a broad-based coalition of provincial, military, and government bureaucrats and technocrats, all of whom were firmly committed to market socialism and a unitary state under the control of the Chinese Communist Party. Perhaps the best indication of that transformation was the abolition by the Fourteenth Congress of the last legal vestige of the old generation's influence, the Central Advisory Commission.

Deng also fixed policy for this new leadership, so that they could not stray under the pressure of external or internal events. By opening all of China to reform during the last months of 1992, he ensured strong institutional support for his modernization policies from the provinces, which were heavily represented on the Fourteenth Central Committee, also by his design. Thus, the predominant sympathies of any expanded gathering of the party would lie with provincial interests, and that would mean support for reform and modernization.

Deng also took steps to ensure that the party remained the unchallenged ruler of China. He brought the public security forces into an informal elders "advisory group" of PLA veterans and economic reformers with strong provincial ties, like Tian Jiyun and Wan Li. Qiao Shi and his protégés, representing Public Security and State Security, sit on the "advisory group" in order to ensure that, in future Tiananmen-like incidents or in instances where a local disturbance gets out of hand, there will be a coordinated response by the People's Armed Police and the PLA.

The PLA veterans of the group, including Yang Shangkun, Yang Baibing, Yang Dezhi, Li Desheng, Zhang Zhen, and Liu Huaqing, and other sitting CMC members, will exercise supervision over the PLA. They will also be allowed to sit in on Politburo discussions to ensure that the "Grand Compromise" is adhered to by all parties. In effect, Deng has brought all parties—the PLA, public security, the provincial officials, and the central leaders into a mutual surveillance body, and tied the fate of all to the modernization effort. In so doing, he made Qiao Shi, Yang Shangkun, and Liu Huaqing, and their anointed successors, the final arbitrators of policy for the immediate future.

In looking back, it can be said that the Third Plenum of the Eleventh Central Committee in December 1978 and the Third Plenum of the Fourteenth Central Committee in November 1993 form the "bookends" of Deng Xiaoping's efforts at modernizing China. It was his vision during those years that was the impetus for the economic policies and institutional changes that will be his legacy. In the beginning, Deng advocated modernization with minimal central control in order to break the bonds of central planning, which had led China to its predicament in 1978.[1] In the end, the focus was still on modernization, but with macrocontrol from the center. Deng had effectively broken the hold of the central planners, who had tried to minimize, sabotage, and derail his Western-style market socialism in the intervening years between 1978 and 1993. In the end, the party settled for a general direction of change. It would control inflation, regulate the money supply, attack corruption, and guide the economy in close alliance with industrial leaders, much like the Japanese bureaucracy guides its economy through the mechanism of powerful state organizations like the Ministry of International Trade and Industry (MITI).

Deng was the only senior leader who forcefully pushed a vision of a new China. Looking at the record over the period from 1978 to 1994, it appears that the others were more inclined to restore the status quo ante, which meant to a time before Mao pushed his radical policies after the Eighth Congress in 1956, and naturally, to a time before he launched his Cultural Revolution.[2] Deng was quite explicit in his indictment of Mao and his policies. The party had made mistakes:

It is true that in the 38 years since then (1949) we have made a lot of mistakes. Our basic goal—to build socialism—is correct, but we are still trying to figure out what socialism is and how to build it. The primary task of socialism is to develop the productive forces. . . . But we did a poor job of developing the productive forces. That was chiefly because we were in too much of a hurry and adopted "Left" policies, with the result that instead of accelerating the development of the productive forces, we hindered it. We began making "Left" mistakes in the political domain in 1957; in the economic domain those mistakes led to the Great Leap Forward of 1958, which resulted in much hardship for the people and enormous damage to production. From 1959 through 1961 we experienced tremendous difficulties—people didn't have enough to eat, not to mention anything else. In 1962 things began to look up, and production was gradually restored to its former level. But the "Left" thinking persisted. Then in 1966 came the "cultural revolution," which lasted a whole decade, a real disaster for China. . . . We were told we should be content with poverty and backwardness and that it was better to be poor under socialism and communism than to be rich under capitalism. That was the sort of rubbish peddled by the Gang of Four. The Gang of Four's absurd theory on socialism and communism led only to poverty and stagnation.

In the first couple of years, after we had smashed the Gang of Four, not all the "Left" mistakes that had been made were corrected. The years of 1977 and 1978 were a period of hesitation in China. It was not until December 1978, when the Eleventh Central Committee convened its Third Plenary Session that we began to make a serious analysis of our experiences in the thirty years since the founding of new China.[3]

Deng resolved to offer China an alternative, and so, he and his supporters

formulated a series of new policies, noticeably the policy of reform and the policy of opening up both internationally and domestically. We set forth a new basic line, which was to shift the focus of our work to economic construction, clearing away all obstacles and devoting all our energies to the drive for social- ist modernization. To achieve modernization and to implement the reform and the open policy we need political stability and unity at home and a peaceful international environment. With this in mind, we have established a foreign policy, which in essence comes down to opposition to hegemonism and pres- ervation of world peace.[4]

Deng clearly was separating himself and his policies from those of Mao. Marxism was out; capitalism, with a heavy dose of state control (bureaucratic capitalism), was in. It was called socialism with Chinese characteristics, but Deng had, in reality, walked away from Mao and his ideologues to redefine China. In the future, theorists will have to speak of Marxism, Leninism, Mao Zedong Thought, and Deng Xiaoping's theories—pragmatic socialism with Leninist, single-party rule.[5] However, Deng no doubt went to his grave believing that he, like Mao, had merely refined Marxism.

In conclusion, Deng saw the moment to act in the collapse of the Soviet Union, but, blocked by his erstwhile friends and colleagues, he made a compact with the PLA to seize the initiative from the conservatives allied with Chen Yun. He was successful, since he, like Mao, had never for- gotten that the party's success was due to the PLA. Without it, there would have been no Communist Party of China, and no People's Republic. Thus, Deng had faithfully tended to the care and feeding of the PLA since his return to power in 1978. So, when he asked for its assistance in 1991 with an offer to increase its role in politics and a plan to make it into a modern force, it was quick to respond. All other agreements, whether among the regional leadership or the central leaders, were based on the fact that Deng controlled the gun. What is unclear is to what extent the PLA will be a force for modernization and stability in China and Asia.

While the military and the public security factions are the key players in the "Grand Compromise," the elders are the cement.[6] They hold the suc- cession and generational transition agreement together. Deng obviously gambled that the elders would survive long enough for the coalition to be institutionalized and be able to "confer" their factional influence and lead- ership to younger protégés. If that does not happen, the transition years will witness greater factional conflict, though the result will be the same: the party, the Army and the public security forces will be the dominant forces in Chinese society.

With a general consensus, then, among the factions of the "Grand Compromise"—the PLA, the regional officials, the elders, the public security forces, and the economic technocrats—on the need for economic growth and stability, it is quite likely that China will transition to a post-Deng era with little of the chaos associated with past changes in government, as in 1912 and 1949. This is not to suggest, however, that there will not be succession battles. Indeed, there has already been one such incident, when Jiang Zemin attempted to restore the role of party chairman at the Fifteenth Party Congress in 1997.[7] His efforts failed, in part, because he did not have a power base—which was the reason he was chosen as the compromise candidate of Deng and Chen in 1989—but also because his efforts to resurrect the chairmanship and gain added power did not sit well with the various factions of the party, and would have resulted in a realignment of the balance of power. However, the point is that the incident remained an internal party affair. There will be no more mass movements, like the Cultural Revolution or the Tiananmen demonstrations, to threaten social stability.

Likewise, the consensus among coalition members does not rule out policy lurches to the left and right.[8] The growing problems of crime, official corruption, unemployment, surplus labor, the invasion of "bourgeois liberalism," and the fate of state enterprises have the potential to cause significant fissures and realignments among all the factions, including the current leadership coalition.[9] This point is evident in the rising tide of nationalism that China is using to mobilize popular support in the wake of flagging interest in Communist ideology.[10]

In recent years, the leadership has focused on regaining control over Taiwan. Hard-liners in the party and PLA have pushed the buildup of missile forces opposite the island, and military exercises near the strait in an attempt to coerce and intimidate the Taiwanese, who, they fear, are moving towards a declaration of independence. However, they have refrained from an outright invasion or a blockade that could result in a confrontation with the United States. In this regard, the economic reformers, led by Zhu Rongji, have been successful in their argument that militant demonstrations and rhetoric have a negative effect on the economy and, therefore, escalation would be disastrous. Thus, nationalistic saber rattling and jingoism have been kept within an agreed limit. So long as the consensus about national priorities prevails, nationalism will be held in check, barring miscalculation.[11]

Likewise, economic considerations prevailed in 1999, when the U.S. accidentally bombed the Chinese embassy in Belgrade during NATO's Kosovo operation. At the time, China was in discussions with the U.S. over World Trade Organization (WTO) issues preliminary to membership. Outraged over what they viewed as a deliberate act, China broke off negotiations and initiated anti-American demonstrations that resulted in the destruction of U.S. property in China. (The consulate in Changsha was torched, and the embassy in Beijing was severely damaged.) When these demonstrations began to get out of hand, however, the party terminated them. They could not allow rampant nationalism to derail WTO membership, whose open markets China needs to fuel its economic growth and modernize its domestic industries. Thus, after extracting $32.5 million in compensation for the accident, China moderated its outrage and resumed negotiations.

Although these incidents demonstrate the economic imperative at work, the possibility exists that nationalism could undermine Deng's pragmatic and long-term approach to foreign policy, as there is no one in the current leadership with his experience and vision, and his protégés, like Qian Qichen in the Foreign Ministry, have little or no voice in any of the decision-making bodies. Given his belief in the necessity of a stable international environment for economic growth, this was a major oversight on his part.[12]

Whereas Deng had stressed the need to avoid an alliance with one superpower against the other, Li Peng and Jiang Zemin are talking of a "strategic partnership" with Moscow to counter U.S. power in Asia. They have sided with Russia in opposing NATO's expansion in Europe and U.S. intentions to deploy national and theater missile defenses.[13] The partnership has developed to the point where, in 2001, the two countries signed a 20-year friendship treaty, which can only serve to antagonize the United States.

When China's hard-line defense minister, Chi Haotian, who commanded the troops at Tiananmen in 1989, visited the United States in December 1996, he told American audiences that no students had been killed. Though he may have been referring to Chinese leadership reports that no students had been killed within the perimeter of the square, his dismissive and arrogant statement was guaranteed to enrage many Americans, including congressmen.[14] Similarly, Chi's comments to Secretary of Defense William Cohen during his visit to China in July 2000, that the coastal arms buildup opposite Taiwan was an internal affair and not the business of the United States, point to the blatant disregard China has for Western sensitivities, and to the possibility of miscalculation by the Chinese as to how far they can push America.

The United States, however, is not without recourse. By recognizing China's vulnerability—its economy—it has a range of options to pursue in furthering its national interests. China's continued economic growth is fueled by access to foreign markets and capital, mainly American or American-influenced. Approximately 30 percent of its exports are to the United States alone. It would be a severe blow to their modernization effort if this trade were disrupted. Why, then, should America allow unconditional access to U.S. markets, while China denies U.S. companies similar access? Likewise, if China continues in its refusal to curtail support of missiles and nuclear weapons technology in Iran, Libya, North Korea, and Pakistan, why shouldn't the United States and its allies link China's continued proliferation activities with access to Western markets and capital? Additionally, it should be made clear to China that any attempt to forcibly reunite Taiwan with the mainland will have economic consequences.

So, while the transition to a post-Deng leadership will likely be a turbulent time in Sino-American relations, it is incumbent upon the United States to focus on long-term objectives, such as the global environment, weapons sales to sensitive areas, nuclear proliferation, and stability in South Asia and on the Korean peninsula. It should not allow any single policy issue, such as human rights, to define Sino-American relations. The United States should look to, and encourage, those factions and policies that have the desired long-term goal of improving China's economy, supporting its domestic stability, and drawing it into the international political arena.

Thus, knowledge of Deng's "Grand Compromise" and its economic imperative is an invaluable tool for analysts and policymakers for interpreting China's priorities, strategies, and objectives. U.S. relations with China need no longer be a one-way street, with China the perennial offended party, dictating the terms of the dialogue. This does not mean that the United States should take a hard line or anti-Chinese posture; rather, it should recognize that it has options to use in exchange for greater cooperation on key issues and for formulating effective policy in the U.S. national interest. Such an approach will, ultimately, benefit China, Asia, and the world.

NOTES

Chapter I: REFORM AND OPENING

1. Deng Xiaoping, *Deng Xiaoping Wenxuan (Selected Works of Deng Xiaoping)*, 1975–1982, vol. 2 (Beijing: Xinhua Press, 1983), pp. 130, 142–43. The Four Modernizations were drafted by Deng Xiaoping and Zhou Enlai and announced by Zhou at the Fourth National People's Congress in January 1975. They called for modernizations, in priority order, in the fields of agriculture, industry, science and technology, and national defense. However, it was not to be implemented until late 1978, after the death of Zhou and Mao, the overthrow of the Gang of Four, and Deng's return to power. Since then, Deng has been the guiding force behind the program.

2. Richard C. Thornton, *China: A Political History, 1917–1980,* (Boulder, Colo: Westview Press, 1982), pp. 411–16, 425–31.

3. Ibid., p. 425.

4. Deng, *Wenxuan*, pp. 119–20.

5. Zeng Jianhui, "The Birth of an Important Decision—A New Step in Opening the Country to the World," *Liaowang* no. 24 (11 June 1984); *Xinhua*, 11 June 1984, Foreign Broadcast Information System-China (hereafter FBIS-CHI) -84-118(18 June 1994), p. K1.

6. Deng Xiaoping, *Fundamental Issues in Present-Day China*, (Beijing: Foreign Language Press, 1987), pp. 172, 177.

7. Chen Qimao, "New Approaches in China's Foreign Policy," *Asian Survey* no. 37 (1993), p. 239.

8. Zhao Xiaowei, "The Threat of a New Arms Race Dominates Asian Geopolitics," *Global Affairs* (Summer 1992), p. 29.

9. Deng, *Fundamental Issues,* pp. 99, 116, 178.

10. Ibid., p. 116.

11. Thornton, *China,* pp. 397–98.

12. Ibid.

13. Ibid., p. 412

14. Ibid., p. 411.

15. Ibid., pp. 434–35.

16. Ibid., p. 412.

17. Ibid., p. 429.

18. Ibid., p. 430. This is only a general lineup, but supports the author's view that Deng had emerged as the dominant faction in charge of Chinese politics.

19. Kenneth Lieberthal, *Governing China: From Revolution Through Reform* (New York: W.W. Norton, 1995), p. 187.

20. See Parris H. Chang, "Chinese Politics: Deng's Turbulent Quest," *Problems in Communism,* January–February 1981, pp. 6–8, for factional groupings; see also Michael Oksenberg, "China's 13th Party Congress," *Problems in Communism,* November–December 1987, p. 3, for a more general grouping; and Thornton, *China,* p. 430, for the major factional groupings.

21. Ibid.

22. David Shambaugh, *The Making of a Premier* (Boulder, Colo.: Westview Press 1984), p. 81.

23. Deng was referring to one of the Communist-controlled areas of China during the Revolutionary War between the Communists and the Nationalists, fought from 1937 to 1949.

24. Zeng, "The Birth of an Important Decision," *Xinhua,* 11 June 1984, FBIS-CHI-84-118 (18 June 1984), pp. K2–3.

25. Ibid.

26. Ibid., p. K3.

27. Jan Prybyla, "China's Economic Dynamos, *Current History,* September 1992, p. 265.

28. Shambaugh, *The Making of a Premier,* pp. 81, 105.

29. "No Change in China's Special Economic Zone Policies," *Wen Wei Po,* 25 April 1982, p. I, FBIS-CHI-82-083 (29 April 1982), p. W2.

30. "CCP in Hot Pursuit of Economic Criminals: Party Members and Cadres to Make Three Examinations," *Ming Pao,* 25 April 1982, p. 6, FBIS-CHI-82-083 (29 April 1982), p. WI.

31. Deng, *Wenxuan,* p. 357.

32. Ibid., p. 358.

33. The new Politburo, made up of his rehabilitated colleagues, could be expected to support Deng's policies to reverse the excessive attention to class warfare.

34. Deng, *Fundamental Issues of Present-Day China* (Beijing: Foreign Language Press, 1987), p. 3.
35. Ibid.
36. Ibid.
37. Thornton, *China,* pp. 418–19.
38. Ibid., pp. 400–07, for an analysis of international geopolitical environment involving China, the Soviet Union, and the United States on the eve of normalization of relations between Beijing and Washington; and pp. 417–22 for analysis of the Vietnam invasion.
39. Ibid., pp. 422–27, for discussion of failed overture to Moscow; see also Richard C. Thornton, "Chinese-Russian Relations and the Struggle for Hegemony in Northeast Asia," *Problems of Post-Communism* no. 1, January–February 1995, pp. 29–34.
40. See Harry Harding, *A Fragile Relationship: The United States and China Since 1972,* (Washington, D. C.: The Brookings Institution, 1992), chapter 4, for a review of Taiwan's role in Sino-American relations and the Communiqué of August 1982, which resolved the impasse. For Reagan and U.S. positions, see George P. Shultz, *Turmoil and Triumph* (New York: Charles Scribner's Sons, 1993), pp. 381–85; and Ronald Reagan, *An American Life* (New York: Simon and Schuster, 1990), p. 361.
41. Schultz, *Turmoil and Triumph,* p. 385.
42. Thornton, "Chinese-Russian Relations," p. 30.
43. Mao had used the United States to balance Moscow when he was threatened with a nuclear strike, in 1969. This led to the opening with Washington, in 1971. However, it became evident after 1973 that America would no longer support South Vietnam, leaving North Vietnam, a client state of Moscow, to consolidate political control over Indochina, in effect scuttling Beijing's policy of keeping the region splintered and encircling China with hostile neighbors. Recognizing that his policies had failed, Mao called on Deng to construct a rationale and policy to respond to the new geopolitical situation. Thus, Deng had given his famous "Three Worlds" speech at the United Nations in 1974 in order to distance China from Washington and attempt reconciliation with Moscow.
44. Deng, *Fundamental Issues,* p. 3.
45. Since Deng's return to power in 1978, and a reassessment of Soviet expansionist potential in the late 1970s and the early 1980s, the defense budget decreased continuously from 1979 until the Tiananmen Massacre in 1989 and events in the Middle East in 1991 convinced Deng and others that the budget needed to be increased. For general review of budget during these years, see Chong Pin-Lin, "Red Fist: China's Army in Transition," *International Defense Review* no. 28 (February 1995), pp. 30–34; Ellis Joffe, "The PLA and the Chinese Economy: The Effect of Involvement," *Survival* no. 2 (Summer 1995), pp. 24–43.
46. Zeng, "The Birth of an Important Decision," p. K2.
47. Ibid., p. K4.
48. Ibid.
49. Ibid., pp. K4–6.

50. Ibid., pp. 81, 105.
51. Steven Mufson, "China's Global Grain of Difference," *Washington Post*, 9 February 1996, pp. AI, A31.
52. "Communiqué of the Third Plenary Session of the 12th Central Committee of the Chinese Communist Party," *Xinhua*, 20 October 1984, FBIS-CHI-084-205, 22 October 1984, p. KI.
53. Ibid., p. KI5.
54. Nicholas R. Lardy "Chinese Foreign Trade," *China Quarterly* no. 131 (September 1992), p. 715.
55. Deng, *Fundamental Issues*, p. 118.
56. Lardy, "Chinese Foreign Trade," p. 694.
57. Deng, p. 142.
58. William H. Overholt, "China After Deng," *Foreign Affairs* no. 3 (May/June 1996), p. 72.
59. Ibid.; Lieberthal, *Governing China*, p. 274.
60. Deng, *Fundamental Issues*, p. 142.
61. Ibid., pp. 145–53, for a general discussion of the problems.
62. Ibid., pp. 113–15.
63. Ruan Ming, *Deng Xiaoping*, pp. 56–57.
64. Ibid., pp. 154–55,
65. Richard C. Thornton, "Deng's 'Middle Kingdom' Strategy," in George Hicks, ed., *The Broken Mirror: China After Tiananmen* (Chicago: St. James Press, 1990), pp. 390–91.
66. See Harding, *A Fragile Relationship*, pp. 364–66, for figures on growth of Sino-American trade.
67. Thornton, "Deng's 'Middle Kingdom' Strategy," pp. 392–96. See chapters on normalization strategies behind U.S. and China moves in Thornton, *China*, and Harding, *A Fragile Relationship*, for general discussion of political forces behind Chinese, Soviet, and American movements in Asia in general, and towards China, in particular.
68. See Ramesh Thakur and Carlyle A. Thayer, eds., *The Soviet Union as an Asian Power* (Boulder, Colo.: Westview Press, 1987), pp. 201–27, for the text of Gorbachev's speech. See Richard C. Thornton, *The Grand Strategy Behind Renewed Sino-Soviet Relations and Detente II—SALT III: American Dream or Nightmare?* (Washington: Institute for Sino-Soviet Studies, Reprint Series no. 120), for discussion of Soviet strategy behind normalization with China.
69. Richard Nixon, *In The Arena* (New York: Simon and Schuster, 1990), p. 58.
70. Ibid., p. 59.
71. Ibid.
72. Ibid. pp. 59–60.
73. Ibid. p. 60.
74. Ibid.
75. Ibid.
76. Thornton, "Deng's 'Middle Kingdom' Strategy," p. 394.

77. Ibid., pp. 161–73.
78. Ibid., pp. 171–72.
79. Wu Wenmin, "Xing Ban Jingji Te Chu Zheng Zhi Bu Hui Shou Su Yao Ba Te Chu Ban De Gen Kui Xie Geng Hao Xie" (More Effectively Manage the Special Economic Areas; Don't Allow Evil Practices to Develop), *Renmin Ribao*, 7 February 1987, p. I.
80. Deng, *Fundamental Issues*, p. 196.
81. "Zhongguo Gongchan Dang De Shi San Zi Quan Guo Dai Biao Da Hui Kai Mu" (The Opening of the 13th Congress of the Communist Party), *Renmin Ribao*, 26 October 1987, p. I.
82. Ibid.
83. Oksenberg, "China's 13th Party Congress," pp. 4–5.
84. Ibid., p. 14.
85. A. Doak Barnett, *The Making of Foreign Policy in China* (Boulder, Colo.: Westview Press, 1985), pp. 10–11.
86. The Politburo lineup is the author's attempt to portray the general factional lineup, which included many Deng allies in his faction since they could presumably be counted on to support him.
87. Li Yunqi, "China's Inflation," *Asian Survey* no. 7 (July 1989), p. 665.
88. Central Intelligence Agency, *The Chinese Economy in 1989 and 1990: Trying to Revive Growth While Maintaining Social Stability* (Washington, D. C.: Central Intelligence Agency, 1990), p. 17; Lardy, "Chinese Foreign Trade," pp. 715–17.
89. Andrew G. Walder and Xianxia Gong, "Workers in the Tiananmen Protests: The Politics of the Beijing Workers' Autonomous Federation," *Australian Journal of Chinese Affairs* no. 29 (January 1993), p. 2.
90. Ibid.
91. Ibid.
92. Ruan Ming, *Deng Xiaoping: Chronicle of an Empire* (Boulder, Colo.: Westview Press, 1994), pp. 205–10. This was also a charge against Zhao by the elder, Wang Zhen, at a meeting of Deng and the party elders at Deng's home at the height of the crisis, on 21 May. See Zhang Liang (comp.), Andrew J. Nathan and Perry Link, eds., *The Tiananmen Papers* (New York: Public Affairs, 2001), pp. 258–59.
93. "Deng Xiaoping Nanxun Jiang Huo De Er Hao Wen Jian 'Wan Wen'" (Full Text of Document no. 2 on Deng's Remarks During His Southern Tour) *Cheng Ming*, 1 April 1992, pp. 23–27.
94. Steven Mufson, "A Tiananmen Symbol," *Washington Post*, 3 June 1995, p. A18. For a version of Zhao's testimony, as recorded in the recently released *The Tiananmen Papers*, that, while true to Zhao's sentiments quoted at the time, show some variation in translation, see Zhang, Nathan, and Link, *The Tiananmen Papers*, p. 442.
95. Central Intelligence Agency, *The Chinese Economy in 1989 and 1990*, p. I.; Thornton, "Deng's 'Middle Kingdom' Strategy," p. 395.
96. Zhang, *The Tiananmen Papers*, p. 26.

97. Central Intelligence Agency, *The Chinese Economy in 1989 and 1990*, pp. 1–2.

98. Mufson, "A Tiananmen Symbol," p. A18.

99. Zhang, *The Tiananmen Papers*, pp. 256–64.

100. "Communiqué of the Fourth Plenary Session of the 13th CCP Central Commit- tee," FBIS-CHI-121-89, 26 June 1989, p. 15; for a discussion of the charges against Zhao, without naming him, see "Zhuan Da Deng Xiaoping Tong Zhi De Zhong Yao Jiang Hua Jiang Diao Ba Si Xiang Tong Yi Dao Jiang Hua Shang Lai (Trans- mit the Important Instructions of Comrade Deng Xiaoping on Emphasizing Uni- fying Thought), *Renmin Ribao*, 14 Jun 1989, p. 1. The meeting is also covered in the documents included in the recently released book of documents on senior leadership discussions in Zhang Liang et al., *The Tiananmen Papers*. *The Tiananmen Papers*, in addition to the official documents on party meetings, includes the records of informal dis- cussions among the leadership over how to handle the protestors. These informal records, the after-the-fact memos of what was said at the meetings, present a vivid picture of a leadership united in its efforts to prevent a reoccurrence of the wide- spread violence that accompanied the Cultural Revolution, though the authenticity of the documents presents a problem.

101. Jim Hoagland, "Senior Chinese Official Who Fled Emerges from Hiding," *Washing- ton Post*, 4 September 1989, p. A1.

102. Ibid., pp. 324, 420–32.

Chapter 2: LOSING CONTROL

1. See Robert Delfs, "Power to the Party," *Far Eastern Economic Review*, 7 December 1989, pp. 23–25; Louise de Rosario, "Quick Step Back," *Far Eastern Economic Review*, 19 October 1989, pp. 47–48; Central Intelligence Agency, *The Chinese Economy in 1989 and 1990: Trying to Revive Growth While Maintaining Social Stability*; and David L. Shambaugh, "The Fourth and Fifth Plenary Sessions," *China Quarterly* no.118 (December 1989), pp.860–61, for a discussion of the steps taken in the economic field to reverse the direction and pace of Deng's and Zhao's liberalizations.

2. de Rosario, "Quick Step Back," p. 47.

3. Ibid.

4. Louise de Rosario, "Three Years' Hard Labor," *Far Eastern Economic Review*, 30 November 1989, p. 68.

5. de Rosario, "Quick Step Back," p. 48.

6. Shambaugh, "The Fourth and Fifth Plenary Sessions of the 13th CCP Central Committee."

7. Deng Maomao, *Deng Xiaoping: My Father* (New York: Basic Books, 1995), p. 470.

8. Central Intelligence Agency, *The Chinese Economy in 1991 and 1992: Pressure to Revisit Reform Mounts* (Washington, D. C., 1992), p. 3.

9. de Rosario, "'Three Years' Hard Labor," p. 69.

10. See Tai Ming Cheung, "Policy in Paralysis," *Far Eastern Economic Review*, 10 January 1991, pp. 10–11; and K. C. Yeh, "Macroeconomic Issues in China in the 1990s," *China Quarterly* no. 132 (December 1992), pp. 542–44, for interesting analysis of

effect of new programs; see "Zhong Gong Zhong Yang Guan Yu Zhi Ding Guo Min Jing Ji He She Hui Fa Zhen Shi Nian Guai Hua He 'Ba Wu' Ji Hua De Jian Ji" (Chinese Communist Party Central Committee's Proposals for the Ten-Year Development Program and the Eighth Five-Year Plan), *Renmin Ribao*, 29 January 1991, pp. 1–4, for text of documents.

11. K. C. Yeh, "Macroeconomic Issues," p. 543.

12. Tai Ming Cheung, "Policy in Paralysis," p. 10.

13. The Politburo members likely to support Deng, but not on the Standing Committee and thus not able to control an agenda, included Tian Jiyun, Wu Xueqian, Li Tieying, Wan Li, Li Ximing, Yang Shangkun, Qin Jiwei, and Ding Guangen.

14. Ibid.

15. Lena H. Sun, "Moderate to Become Chinese Vice Premier," *Washington Post*, 3 April 1991, p. A20.

16. "Commentator Huangfu Ping's Identity Viewed," *Ta Kung Pao*, 7 October 1992, p. 14, FBIS-CHI-92-201 (16 October 1992), p. 19.

17. Huangfu Ping, "New Lines of Thought Needed in Reform and Opening," *Jiefang Ribao*, 2 March 1991, p. 1, FBIS-CHI-91-047 (11 March 1991), p. 64.

18. "Commentator Huangfu Ping's Identity Viewed," *Ta Kung Pao*, 7 October 1992, p. 14, FBIS-CHI-92-201 (16 Oct 1992), pp. 18–21; Zhao Suisheng, "Deng Xiaoping's Southern Tour," *Asian Survey* no. 8 (August 1993), p. 749. For a discussion of Deng Xiaoping's and his daughter Deng Nan's role in directing "Huangfu Ping," see He Bin and Gao Xin, *Zhong Gong 'Tai Zi Dang'* (The Communist Party's Princely Party), (Taibei: Shi Bao Wen Huo, 1992), pp. 74–78.

19. "Commentator Huangfu Ping's Identity Viewed," *Ta Kung Pao*, p. 18.

20. Ibid. pp. 18–21.

21. "Grasp the Key Points in the Crucial Period—On Investigating State-Owned Large and Medium-sized Enterprises," *Jiefang Ribao*, 8 February 1991, p. 1, FBIS-CHI-91-034 (20 February 1991), p. 49.

22. Ibid.

23. Ibid.

24. Ibid.

25. Ping Huangfu, "Reform and Opening Requires a Large Number of Cadres With Both Morals and Talent," *Jiefang Ribao*, 12 April 1991, p. 1, FBIS-CHI-91-074, 17 April 1991, p. 61.

26. Ibid.

27. Ibid, p. 62.

28. Ibid, pp. 61–62.

29. Wei Yung-cheng, "Reveal the Mystery of Huangfu Ping," *Ta Kung Pao*, 8 October 1992, p. 14, FBIS-CHI-92-201 (16 October 1992), p. 21.

30. Zhao Susheng, "Deng Xiaoping's Southern Tour," p. 749.

31. Sun, "Moderate to Become Chinese Vice Premier."; Lincoln Kaye, "Avoiding the Issues," *Far Eastern Economic Review*, 12 December 1991, p. 12.

32. Shambaugh, *The Making of a Premier*, pp. 115–16.

33. Tai Ming Cheung, "Marking Time," *Far Eastern Economic Review*, 8 August 1991, p. 25.
34. "NPC: Stability and Development," *China News Analysis* 1433, 1991, p. 3.
35. Tai Ming Cheung, "The Last Post," *Far Eastern Economic Review*, 23 November 1989, p. 10.
36. Shambaugh, "The Fourth and Fifth Plenary Session," pp. 854–57.
37. Wei Yung-cheng, "Reveal the Mystery of Huangfu Ping," FBIS-CHI-92-201 (16 October 1992), p. 21.
38. Liu Pi, "Evil Wind of Praising Chen, Speaking Ill of Deng, Criticizing Zhao Prevails in Beijing: Difficulties in Implementing Deng Xiaoping's Three Policy Decisions," *Ching Pao*, October 1991, pp. 26–28, FBIS-CHI-91-198 (11 October 1991), p. 15.
39. Lincoln Kaye, "Bitter Medicine," *Far Eastern Economic Review*, 5 September 1991, p. 10.
40. "Jiang Zemin Di Da Su Lian Jin Xing Zheng Zhi Fang Wen"(Jiang Zemin Arrives in the Soviet Union for an Official Visit), *Renmin Ribao*, 16 May 1991, p. 1.
41. Ibid.
42. Ibid.
43. See *Renmin Ribao*, 16 May 1991, p. 1 and 17 May 1991, p. 8, for reporting on Jiang's trip, official speeches and news conference comments.
44. Jiang Zemin, "Building Socialism the Chinese Way," *Beijing Review*, 8–14 July, 1991, pp. 15–32.
45. "Sulian Zhengbian Chendiao Beijing" (Overthrow of Soviet Government Shakes Beijing), *Pai Hsing*, 1 October 1991, pp. 3–4.
46. Jiang Zemin, "Building Socialism," p. 22.
47. Ibid., p. 23.
48. Ibid.; Liu Pi, "Evil Wind," p. 15.
49. "Sulian Zhengbian," *Pai Hsing*, 1 October 1991, pp. 3–4.
50. For an understanding of these earlier campaigns and why Chinese feared the start of another mass campaign, see Thornton, *China: A Political History, 1917–1980*, especially chapters XI and XII; and Maurice Meisner, *The Deng Xiaoping Era* (New York: Hill and Wang, 1996), pp. 39–41, 48–55.
51. Jiang Zemin, "Building Socialism," p. 25.
52. Ibid., p. 26.
53. Ibid.
54. Ibid.
55. "Sulian Zhengbian," p. 3.
56. The campaign against bourgeois liberalization was nothing new; there had been earlier campaigns that Deng had allowed when it did not interfere with his economic reforms. For an excellent discussion of the ideological campaigns during Deng's tenure, see Merle Goldman, *Sowing the Seeds of Democracy In China* (Cambridge: Harvard University Press; 1994), especially chapters 3, 4, 5, and 8.
57. Lu Yu-sha, "Deng Xiaoping Jiu ErWu Jianghuo Fadong Gaige Er Gongshi"

(Deng's September 25 Speech Launches the Second Wave of Reform), *Tangtai*, 15 January 1992, p. 35.

58. "Sulian Zhengbian," p. 3.

59. Ibid.

60. He Po-shih, "Sulian Bianzheng, Zhonggong Dui Nei Ru He Shuo?" (What Does CPC Say Internally in Wake of Changing Situation in Soviet Union?), *Tangtai* no. 10 (January 1992), p. 43.

61. Liu, "Evil Wind."

62. He, "What Does the CCP Say," p. 42.

63. Ibid., pp. 44–45.

64. Ibid.

65. Ibid. pp. 43–44.

66. Liu, "Evil Wind," p. 16.

67. Gao Di, "Problems Posed by the Soviet Situation," *China Quarterly* no. 130 (June 1992), pp. 482–91. Gao was a hard-line ideologue named as vice-president of the Party School in 1988. In 1989 he took over control of *People's Daily* as part of the conservative reaction to the Tiananmen incident. He pushed Deng Liqun's policies to suppress intellectual dissent.

68. Ibid., pp. 482–83.

69. Ibid., pp. 487–89.

70. Ibid. p. 490.

71. Liu, "Evil Wind," p. 16. Party members would recall that the widespread chaos and suffering resulting from the Cultural Revolution had its beginning in the Leading Group Mao established to lead his assault on the party in 1967.

72. Liu, "Evil Wind," pp. 14–16.

73. Chen Yeping, "De Sai Jian Ye Yi De Wei Shu" (Have Both Political Integrity, Ability, Stress Political Ability: On Criterion for Selecting Cadres), *Renmin Ribao*, 1 September 1991, p. 5.

74. "Sulian Zhengbian," pp. 3–4.

75. Chi Ma, "Fan He Ping Yan Bian Gao De Cao Mu Jie Bing Jiang Ju Deng Xiaoping Ming Pao Zhong Xuan Bu" (Instructed by Deng Xiaoping, Jiang Zemin Bombards Central Propaganda Department for Being in State of Extreme Nervousness in Opposing Peaceful Evolution), *Ming Bao*, 8 October 1991, p. 2.

76. Lo Ping, "Wang Meng Shi Jain Yu He Jingzhi Xin Zheng Shi" (Wang Meng Event and He Jingzhi's New Offensive), *Cheng Ming* no. 170 (1 December 1991), pp. 18–21.

77. Chung Hsiao, "Li Ruihuan Goes to Shanghai to Promote Reform Vigorously as Deng, Jiang, and Zhu Hit by Sniper's Shot," *Cheng Ming* no. 173 (5 December 1991), pp. 18–20, FBIS-CHI-91-234 (5 December 1991), p. 19.

78. Ibid.

79. Zhao, "Deng Xiaoping's Southern Tour," p. 743.

80. He Po-shih, "Ba Zhong Chuanhui Qianxi Wang Zhen Dangmian Da Ma Deng Xiaoping, Deng Xiaoping Yuan Chengdan 'Liu Si' Ze Ren, Yang Shangkun Biaotai

Wan Jun Ting Jiang Zemin" (Wang Zhen Reproaches Deng Xiaoping on Eve of 8th Plenum as Deng Shows Willingness to Assume "4 June" Responsibility and Yang Shangkun Openly Supports Jiang Zemin's Direction in Army Work), *Tangtai,* 15 December 1991, p. 16.

81. Lu Yu-sha, "Deng Xiaoping's '25 September' Speech," *Tangtai,* January 1992, pp. 35–37.

82. Ibid.

83. "Evolution Toward Multipolar Global Pattern Seen," *Joint Publications Research Service,* 27 September, 1991, pp. 2–3.

84. Ibid.

85. Chi Ma, "Instructed by Deng Xiaoping, Jiang Zemin Bombards Central Propaganda Department for Being in State of Extreme Nervousness in Opposing Peaceful Evolution," *Ming Pao,* 8 October 1991, p. 2.

86. Ibid.

87. Lo Ping and Li Tzuching, "Jie Mi Wen Jian Zhong De Bu Wen Di Chu" (Unstable Regions Set Forth in Top Secret Document), *Cheng Ming,* 1 January 1992, pp. 8–9.

88. Guan Chuan, "Nung Cun Heping Yanbian Chongji Shejiao" (Peaceful Evolution in Rural Areas Thwarts 'Socialist Education Movement), *Cheng Ming,* 1 January 1991, pp. 24–25.

89. "Realities To Be Faced in China in the Wake of the Dramatic Changes in the USSR and Strategic Choices," *Zhongguo Qingnian Bao,* 1 September 1991, FBIS-CHI-92-050-A (13 March 1992), p. 8.

90. Cheng Ying, "CCP's Internal Propaganda Outline in Perspective," *Chiushih Nientai,* 1 September 1991, pp. 34–35, FBIS-CHI-91-177 (12 September 1991), pp. 29–31.

91. Guan Chuan, "Nung Cun," pp. 24–25; Lo Ping, "Ji Mi," p. 9.

92. Li Ming, "Deng Says That Failure to Boost Economy Will Lead to Collapse of Communist Party," *Ching Pao,* 5 December 1991, p. 34, FBIS-CHI-91-237 (10 December 1991), p. 24.

93. Ibid.

94. Ibid.

95. Ibid.

96. Ibid.

97. Lin Painiao, "Zhong Gong Xin Xing Dui Mei Zheng Ce" (CCP Formulates New Policy Toward United States), *Cheng Ming,* 1 December 1991, pp. 17–19.

98. Ibid.

99. Ibid.

100. Ibid.

101. Ibid.

102. Liu Ying, "Deng Personally Decided on Tactics for Talks with Baker," *Ching Pao* (Hong Kong) 5 December 1991, pp. 30–31, FBIS-CHI-91-237 (10 December 1991), p. 6.

103. Lin Painiao, "Zhong Gong," pp. 8–9.

104. Lena H. Sun, "Baker Says Gains Made with China," *Washington Post*, 18 November 1991, p. AI.

105. Lo Ping and Li Tzuching, "Deng Chen Liang Pai Jiao Feng Yu Ba Zhong Chuan Hui" (Contest Between Deng and Chen Factions and Eighth Plenary Session), *Cheng Ming*, 1 December 1991, pp. 6–8.

106. FBIS-CHI-91-234 (5 December 1991), p. 20; *Renmin Ribao* carried a report of the conference, but only a general reference to Deng's speech. See "Fa Zhan Dang De Shi Ye Yao Xie Xi Dang Shi Dang Jian Li Lun" (Study the Theory of Party Building), *Renmin Ribao*, 21 November 1991, p. 8.

107. Li Peng, "Guan Yu Dang Qian Jing Ji Xing Kuan He Jin Yi Bu Gao Hao Guo Ying Da Zhong Xing Qi Ye De Wen Ti" (The Current Economic Situation and the Issue of Further Improving State-Owned Large and Medium-Sized Enterprises), *Renmin Ribao*, 11 October 1991, p. I.

108. Ibid.

109. Ibid.

110. "Ba Shen Zhen Te Chu Jian She De Geng Hao" (Make Greater Efforts to Develop the Special Economic Areas), *Renmin Ribao*, 6 December 1991, p. I.

111. Ibid.

112. Ibid.

113. "Nu Li Kai Qiang Nung Ye He Nung Cun Gong Zuo Xin Ju Huo"(Work Hard to Create a New Situation for Agriculture and Rural Work), *Renmin Ribao*, 30 November 1991, p. I.

114. "Zhong Gong Shi San Jie Zhong Gong Wei Yuan Hui Jian Kai Quan Hui " (Communiqué of the Eighth Plenary Session of the Thirteenth CCP Central Committee), *Renmin Ribao*, 30 November 1991, p. I.

115. Ibid.

116. Ibid.

117. Li Renzhu, "Da Li Jia Qiang Ge Ji Ling Dao Ban Zi Jian She" (CCP Organization Chief Outlines 1992 Tasks), *Renmin Ribao*, 10 December 1991, p. I.

118. Ibid.

119. Tsen Shan, "Kuanglung Kai Ming Pai De Fan Chi Xuan" (Anticyclone of Frenzied Attack on Group of the Enlightened), *Cheng Ming*, 1 February 1992, pp. 16–17.

120. Lo Ping, "Wang Meng Shi Jian Yu He Jingzhi Xin Zheng Shi" (Wang Meng Event and He Jingzhi's New Offensive), *Cheng Ming*, 1 December 1991, pp. 11–13.

121. Ibid., p. 20.

122. Geoffrey Crothall, "Deng, Chen Yun 'Plotting' Strategy in Shanghai," *South China Morning Post*, 19 December 1991, p. 14, FBIS-CHI-91-244 (19 December 1991), p. 18.

Chapter 3: STRIKING BACK

1. "CCP To Set Directives on Personnel Changes," *Kyodo*, 3 December 1991, FBIS-CHI-91-232 (3 December 1991), p. 32. Willy Wo-lap Lam, "PLA Prepares for 'High-Level' Personnel Changes, *South China Morning Post*, 10 December 1991, p. 10,

states that the meeting started on 2 December; Tang Chia-liang, "Zhonggong Junwei Guangda Huiyi Mi Liang Renshi Biange Jianxiao Yezhang Jun, Qi Ta Jun Chu Bu Biandong" (The CMC Meets in a Secret, Expanded Session to Discuss Personnel Cuts, Reduction in Field Armies, But Seven Military Regions Will Remain the Same), *Kuang Chiao Ching*, 16 May 1992, pp. 12–16.

2. Tang Chia-liang, "Central Military Commission Enlarged Meeting Secretly Discusses Personnel Changes," *Kuang Chiao Ching*, 16 May 1992, pp. 12–13.
3. For a discussion of PLA international arms sales, see Eric Hyer, "China's Arms Merchants: Profits in Command," *China Quarterly* no. 132 (December 1992), pp. 1101–18.
4. Ibid.
5. People's Radio Network, 17 December 1991, FBIS-CHI-91-243 (18 December 1991), p. 41.
6. "Chief of General Staff Calls for Modernization," *Agence France-Presse*, 17 December 1991, FBIS-CHI-91-243 (18 December 1991), p. 41.
7. Ibid.
8. "Deng Calls for Maintaining Powerful Army," *Agence France-Presse*, 20 December 1991, FBIS-CHI-91-245 (20 December 1991), p. 20.
9. Ibid.
10. Li Tzu-ching, "Deng Xunshi Wu Sheng Shi Fan Ji Chen Yun" (Deng Xiaoping on Inspection Tour of Five Provinces; Strikes Back at Chen Yun), *Cheng Ming*, 1 February 1992, pp. 9–12.
11. Ibid., p. 10.
12. Ibid.
13. Ibid., p. 11.
14. Liu Donggeng, "Jiao Ta Shi Di, Zhen Zhuo Shi Gan, Li Shi Xing Shi Zhu Yi" (While Inspecting Troops Stationed in Jiangsu, Jiang Zemin Urges Whole Army to Uphold Principles of Building Army Through Hard Work and Thrift and Stresses Practical Results in Work), *Jiefang Junbao*, 26 January 1992, pp. 1, 4.
15. Lu Tai, "Yang Shangkun Dao Xinjiang Buzhi Fang Tubian" (Yang Shangkun Inspects Xinjiang, Makes Arrangements to Prevent Sudden Changes), *Cheng Ming*, 1 February 1992, pp. 27–28.
16. Ibid.
17. Li Tzu-ching, "Deng Xunshi," *Cheng Ming*, 1 February 1992, pp. 9–12.
18. Ibid.
19. Wang Yihua, "Jun Dui Sheng Chan Jing Ying Wen Si Liu" (What Is Seen Regarding Troops' Production and Economic Activities and Thoughts Provoked Thereby), *Jiefang Junbao*, 12 December 1991, p. 2.
20. Ibid.
21. "Zhuan Jun She Hui Zhu Yi Xin Nian Jiao Yu Chu De Chen Ji" (PLA Concentrating on Socialist Education), *Renmin Ribao*, 5 December 1991, p. 7; "Gai Ge Kai Fang Shi Tui Jin Bu Dui Jian She De Jiang Da Dong Li" (Reform, Opening Up Said to Promote Army Building), *Jiefang Junbao*, 20 November 1991, p. 3.
22. Ibid., p. 3.

23. Lei Feng was the hero of the party's 1960s socialist education campaign. A soldier, he died in an accident, but his diary recorded his love for Mao and the party. In the 1990s, the image has been modernized to fit the requirements of the electronic age.

24. Ibid., p. 7.

25. Ibid.

26. Geoffrey Crothall, "Deng, Chen Yun 'Plotting' Strategy in Shanghai," *South China Morning Post*, 19 December 1991, p. 14, FBIS-CHI-91-244, 19 December 1991, p. 18; *Lien Ho Pao*, 10 May 1992, p. 2, FBIS-CHI-92-091 (11 May 1992), p. 16.

27. Chou Tieh, "Zhong Ceng Wei Lian Ming Cu Qu Xiao Jing Ji Te Chu" (Some Central Advisory Commission Members Submit Written Statement to Central Committee Calling for Abolition of Special Economic Zones), *Ming Pao*, 6 March 1992, p. 2.

28. Hsia Yu-hung, "Deng Xiaoping Says Army Must Serve as Guarantee for Reform and Opening Up," *Lien Ho Pao*, 10 May 1992, p. 2, FBIS-CHI-92-091 (11 May 1992), p. 16.

29. "Deng Xiaoping Tan Guangdong Cheng Lung Tou Yao Qi Hao Cuo Yong" (Deng Xiaoping Tours Zhuhai, Saying That Guangdong Economy Should Play Leading Role in China's Economic Development), *Ta Kung Pao*, 26 January 1992, p. 1.

30. Wen Li, "Instill Sense of Urgency on Reform and Opening Up," *Wen Wei Po*, 28 January 1992, p. 2, FBIS-CHI-92-018 (28 January 1992), p. 22.

31. Ibid; Lei Zhonyu, "Geng Fang Kuan Xie Geng Da Dan Xie,"(Open Wider and Faster), *Renmin Ribao*, 26 January 1992, p. 1.

32. Ibid. p. 1; Lei Zhongyu, "Yang Shangkun Dao Cha Zhu Hai Shen Zhen"(Yang Shangkun Inspects Zhuhai and Shenzhen), *Renmin Ribao*, 2 February 1992, p. 1.

33. Ibid.

34. Ibid.

35. Ibid.

36. Pang Xiecheng, "Jiang Zemin Hui Lai Shanghai" (Jiang Zemin Returns to Shanghai), *Renmin Ribao*, 26 January 1992, p. 1; Ying Yi, "Jiang Zemin Recently Returns to Shanghai to Encourage Local Officials, *Ming Pao*, 30 January 1992, p. 8, FBIS-CHI-92-20 (30 January 1992), p. 21.

37. "Tian Jiyun In Hainan; Notes Urgency of Opening," *Xinhua*, 28 January 1992, FBIS-CHI-92-018 (28 January 1992), p. 27.

38. Cary Huang, "Bo Yibo Supports Shenzhen Price Reform Program," *Standard*, 24 January 1992, p. A6, FBIS-CHI-92-016 (24 January 1992), p. 15.

39. Wu Duanze, "Gaige Kaifang Bi Xu Jia Qiang Zheng Fa Gongzi" (Strengthen Legal Work in Support of Reform and Opening), *Renmin Ribao*, 29 January 1992, p. 8.

40. Ibid.

41. Lu Yu-shan, "Deng Xiaoping Yi Jun Gan Gaige" (Deng Xiaoping Uses Army Instead of Party to Promote Reform), *Tangtai*, 15 May 1992, pp. 19–20; Lin Wu, "Zhu Hai Yuan Lin Jun Wei Huiyi Neiqing" (Intelligence from the Zhuhai Yuan Lin CMC Meeting), *Cheng Ming*, 1 March 1992, pp. 15–16, 89; Tang Hsio-chao, "Jiang Zemin Shi Lung Nei Mu" (Inside Story of Jiang Zemin's Loss of Favor), *Kai Fang*, 18 March 1992, pp. 16–17.

42. Ibid.

43. Yang Baibing, "Zhun Dui Yao Wei Gaige Kaifang 'Bao Jia Hu Hang'" (PLA to "Escort" Reform, Opening), *Renmin Ribao*, 24 March 1992, p. 2.
44. Ibid.
45. Luo Yuwen, "More on Yang's Remarks," *Xinhua*, 23 March 1992, FBIS-CHI-92-057 (24 March 1992), p. 15.
46. Willy Wo-lop Lam, "Jiang, 'Shanghai Faction' Expanding Influence," *South China Morning Post*, 2 January 1992, p. 10, FBIS-CHI-92-001 (2 January 1992), pp. 25–26.
47. Chen Chieh-hung, "Deng Xiaoping Puts Forward the 'Eight Shoulds,' Says 'Three Kinds of People' Must Step Down," *Ching Pao*, 5 March 1992, pp. 45–46, FBIS-CHI-92-045 (6 March 1992), pp. 14–16.
48. Ibid., p. 15.
49. Ibid.
50. Ibid.
51. Lo Ping, "Chen Yun Xiang Deng De Xin Tiao Zhan" (Chen Yun Responds to Deng's New Challenge), *Cheng Ming*, 1 February 1992, pp. 6–8.
52. Ibid., p. 31.
53. Ibid.
54. Ibid.
55. Ibid.
56. Ibid., p. 27.
57. Ibid.
58. Ibid., p. 28.
59. Lo Ping, "Liang Jutou Shanghai Jiao Feng Ji" (Records of the Shanghai Meeting between the Two Leaders), *Cheng Ming*, 1 March 1992, pp. 6–11.
60. Tan Xiancai, "Qiao Shi Inspects Guangxi," *Xinhua*, 6 February 1992, FBIS-CHI-92-028 (11 February 1992), p. 21; Lu Tai, "Yang Shangkun," pp. 27–28; Lu Donggeng, "Jiao Ta Shi Di, Zhen Zhuo Shi Gan, Li Shi Xing Shi Zhu Yi" (While Inspecting Troops Stationed in Jiangsu, Jiang Zemin Urges Whole Army to Uphold Principles of Building Army Through Hard Work and Thrift and Stresses Practical Results in Work), *Jiefang Junbao*, 26 January 1992, pp. 1,4; Huo Szu-fang, "Three Main Points in Deng Xiaoping's Remarks Delivered During Southern China Tour, Principles Set for Personnel Arrangements at 14th National Congress," *Ching Pao*, 5 March 1992, pp. 34–37, FBIS-CHI-92-060 (27 March 1992), p. 34.
61. Willy Wo-lap Lam, "Sources Report 'Intensified' Factional Strife," *South China Morning Post*, 11 March 1992, p. 13, FBIS-CHI-92-048 (11 March 1992), p. 15.
62. Cheng Te-lin, "Chen Yun Says There Are Two Major Dangers Inside CCP," *Ching Pao*, 5 March 1992, p. 47, FBIS-CHI-92-054 (19 March 1992), p. 39.
63. Ibid.
64. Lo Ping, "Deng Chen Jiao Feng De Xin Zhan Yi" (A New Chapter in the Battle Between Deng and Chen), *Cheng Ming*, 1 April 1992, pp. 8–12. Information in the next paragraphs was drawn from this source.
65. Ibid.

66. Zhao Suishen, "Deng Xiaoping's Southern Tour," *Asian Survey* no. 8 (August 1993), p. 754.
67. Lo Ping, "Deng Chen," pp. 8–9.
68. Ibid., pp. 10–11.
69. Ibid., p. 11.
70. Wally Wo-lap Lam, "Politburo Session Upholds 'Deng Xiaoping Line,'" *South China Morning Post*, 13 March 1992, pp. 1, 10, FBIS-CHI-92-050 (13 March 1992), p. 18. Information in the next paragraphs was drawn from this source.
71. Ibid.
72. "Deng Xiaoping Nanxuan Jianghuo Di Er Hao Wen Jian"(Full Text of Document No. 2 on Deng Remarks) *Cheng Ming*, 1 April 1992, pp. 23–27. Information in this paragraph was drawn from this source.
73. Ibid.
74. Ibid.
75. Ibid.
76. Shih Chun-yu, "Zhong Yang Bu Zhi Jia Su Gaige Kaifang" (Central Authorities Make Arrangements To Speed Up Reform and Opening Up), *Ta Kung Pao*, 4 March 1992, p. 2; "Zhua Zhu You Li Shi Ji Jia Kuai Gaige Kaifang Ji Zhong Shen Li Ba Jing Ji" (Accelerate the Pace of Reform and Opening and Reforming Administrative Organs in Response to Economics), *Renmin Ribao*, 3 March 1992, p. 1. Information in the next paragraphs was drawn from this source.
77. Ibid.
78. Wally Wo-lap Lam, "Deng Puts Bo Yibo in Charge of Appointments," *South China Morning Post*, 4 April 1992, p. 12, FBIS-CHI-92-064, 2 April 1992, p. 38.
79. _____, 25 March 1992, FBIS-CHI-92-058, 25 March 1992, p. 12.
80. Ibid.
81. "Zhu 'Leading Voice on Reform,'" AFP, 25 March 1992, FBIS-CHI-92-058, 25 March 1992, p. 13; "Guo Wu Yuan Cheng Li Jing Ji Mao Yi Ban Gong Shi" (State Council Establishes Trade and Economics General Office), *Renmin Ribao*, 12 June 1992, p. 1; "State Planning Commission to Transform Function in Five Areas," *Ching-chi Tao-pao*, 15 June 1992, p. 11, FBIS-CHI-92-120, 22 June 1992, p. 31.
82. Ibid., p. 13.

Chapter 4: MORE, BETTER, FASTER

1. "Jiang Zemin Jie 'Si Hao Wen Jiang' Biao Tai" (Jiang Zemin Declares Stand Through "Document No. 4"), *Tangtai*, 15 June 1992, p. 10.
2. Tien Fu, "Bo Yibo Nuli Kaolung Deng Xiaoping" (Bo Yibo Tries to Close Ranks with Deng Xiaoping), *Tangtai*, 15 June 1992, p. 21.
3. "Zhong Gong Jue Ding Cai Chu Yi Xie Xin Zheng Ci Xin Zuo Shi Li Zheng Chuan Guo Jing Ji Geng Hao Geng Kuai Shang Xin Tai Jie" (The CCP Decides to Adopt a Series of New Policies to Speed Up the Economic Situation), *Renmin Ribao*, 8 June 1992, p. 1; "The CCP Issues Document Number Four, Fully Expounding Expansion of Opening Up," *Ta Kung Pao*, 18 June 1992, p. 2, FBIS-CHI-92-118,

18 June 1992, pp. 19–20; "Jiang Zemin Declares Stand Through 'Document No. 4,'" *Tangtai*, 15 June 1992, p. 10; Lam, *China After Deng Xiaoping*, (Singapore: Wiley, 1995), pp. 76–78; *China Quarterly* no. 131, September 1992, p. 848.

4. Ibid., p. 19.

5. "Guo Wu Yuan Cheng Li Jing Ji Mao Yi Ban Gong Shi" (The State Council Establishes the General Office for Economics and Trade), *Renmin Ribao*, 12 June 1992, p. 1. Information in the next paragraphs is drawn from this source.

6. Ibid.

7. "State Planning Commission To Transform Functions in Five Areas," *Ching-chi Tao-pao*, 15 June 1992, p. 11, FBIS-CHI-92-120, 22 June 1992, p. 31.

8. Sun Kuo-han, "Deng Delivers Long Speech at Shoudu Iron and Steel Company, Advocates Promoting Talent in Economic Management to Run Government," *Ching Pao*, 5 July 1992, pp. 31-35, FBIS-CHI-92-129, 6 July 1992, pp. 21-24; Yen Shen-tsun, "Deng Xiaoping's Talk During His Inspection of Shoudu Iron and Steel Complex," *Kuang Chiao Ching*, 16 July 1992, pp. 6-7, FBIS-CHI-92-138, 17 July 1992, pp. 7–8. Information in the next paragraphs is drawn from this source.

9. Ibid.

10. Zhu Rongji, "Excerpts," *Zhongguo Jingji Tizhi Gaige*, 23 February 1992, pp. 7-9, FBIS-CHI-92-107, 3 June 1992, pp. 29–31.

11. Ibid.

12. Ibid.

13. "Guo Wu Yuan Pi Zhuan Jin Nian Jing Ji Ti Zhi Gaige Yao Dian" (The State Council Publishes the Main Points for This Year's Reform of the Economic System), *Renmin Ribao*, 29 March 1992, p. 7.

14. Zhu Rongji, "Excerpts," *Zhongguo Jingji Tizhi Gaige*, 23 February 1992, pp. 7-9, FBIS-CHI-92-107, 3 June 1992, pp. 29–31.

15. Ibid.

16. Ibid.

17. Lam, *China*, p. 79.

18. Bao Xin, "A New Important Formulation in China's Reform," *Liaowang Overseas Edition*, 17 August 1992, p. 2, FBIS-CHI-92-184, 22 September 1992, p. 36.

19. Zou Jiahua, "Chuan Guo Ren Da Chang Wei Hui Zhu Xing Chuan Ti Hui" (The Standing Committee of the People's Congress Holds a Special Enlarged Meeting), *Renmin Ribao*, 2 September 1992, p. 1–2. Information in the next paragraphs is drawn from this source.

20. Ibid.

21. "Gui Ding Qi Yi Na Xie Jing Ying Zi You Chuan" (Establish a Few Regulations over Economy), *Renmin Ribao*, 11 September 1992, p. 2; "Da Lu Jing Ji Ceng Zhang Shi Tou Zhu Rongji Jiang Qian Shi Du Kongzhi" (Zhu Rongji Calls for Appropriate Controls over China's Economic Growth Momentum), *Ming Pao*, 9 September 1992, p. 8.

22. "Prices of Primary, Basic Products to be Raised," Xinhua, 10 September 1992, FBIS-CHI-92-177, 11 Sep 1992, p. 55; Tian Huiming, "China's Price Reform Is

Moving from the 'Realm of Planning' to the 'Realm of Market,'" *Zhongguo Xinwen She*, 1 September 1992, FBIS-CHI-92-177, 11 September 1992, p. 55.

23. Ibid.

Chapter 5: THE PLA AS "PROTECTOR AND ESCORT"

1. For a general discussion of changing perceptions of Soviet threat, see Wang Chongjie, "Acute Economic Troubles," *Beijing Review* no. 4, 26 January 1981, pp. 15–16; Mu Youlin, "Focus on Soviet Strategy," *Beijing Review* no. 20, 18 May 1981, p. 3; Chen Ci, "1980 in Retrospect," *Beijing Review* no. 1, 5 January 1981, pp. 11–13; Qi Ya and Zhou Jirong, "Expansionist Soviet Global Strategy," *Beijing Review* no. 23, 22 June 1981, pp. 22–25; Jonathan D. Pollack, "Chinese Global Strategy and Soviet Power," *Problems in Communism* January-February 1981, pp. 54–69, especially pp. 64–68; Paul H. B. Godwin, "Chinese Military Strategy Revised: Local and Limited War;" *Annals of American Academy of Political and Social Scientists*, no. 519, January 1992, pp. 191–201.

2. For background on Deng's rehabilitation, see Richard C. Thornton, *China: A Political History, 1917–1980*, (Boulder: Westview Press, 1982), Section XV; discussion on arms sales by the PLA see Eric Hyer, "China's Arms Merchants: Profits in Command," *China Quarterly* no. 132, 1992, pp.1101–1118; for a discussion of PRC strategic perceptions in the early 1980s, see Jonathan D. Pollack, "Chinese Global Strategy and Soviet Power," Problems in Communism, January-February 1981, pp. 54–69; "Soviet Military Strategy for World Domination," *Beijing Review*, 28 January 1980, pp. 15–19, 26; and "Expansionist Soviet Global Strategy," *Beijing Review*, 22 June 1981, pp. 23–25.

3. Paul H. B. Godwin, "Chinese Military Strategy Revised: Local and Limited War," *Annals of American Academy of Political and Social Scientists*, January 1992, p. 191.

4. Ibid., pp. 191–201; for a discussion of the emerging Chinese threat to Southeast Asia, as well as general details on new military strategy, see Ross H. Munro, "Awakening Dragon," *Policy Review*, Fall 1992, pp. 10–16; Chong Pin-lin, "Red Fist," *International Defense Review*, February 1995, pp. 30–34; A. James Gregor, "China's Shadow Over Southeast Asian Waters," *Global Affairs*, 1993, pp. 1–13; and John W. Garver, "China's Push Through the South China Sea: The Interaction of Bureacratic and National Interests," *China Quarterly* no. 131, December 1992, pp. 999–1029.

5. "Deng Calls for Maintaining Powerful Army," *Agence France-Presse*, 20 December 1991, FBIS-CHI-91-245, 20 December 1991, p. 20.

6. Ibid.

7. Yang Baibing, "Zhun Dui Yao Li Gaige Kaifang 'BaoJia Hu Hang'" (The PLA Must "Escort" Reform and Opening), *Renmin Ribao*, 24 March 1992, p. 2. Information in the next paragraphs was drawn from this source.

8. Ibid.

9. Chen Shao-pin, "Deng Xiaoping Fetes High-Ranking Officers of 'Three Armed Services,'" *Ching Pao*, 5 May 1992, p. 40, FBIS-CHI-92-094, 14 May 1992, pp. 32–33.

10. Ibid., p. 33.
11. Ibid.
12. Ibid.
13. Wally Wo-lap Lam, *China After Deng Xiaoping*, (New York: John Wiley and Sons, 1995), p. 197.
14. Chen Shao-pin, "Deng Xiaoping Fetes High-Ranking Officers of 'Three Armed Services,'" *Ching Pao*, 5 May 1992, p. 40, FBIS-CHI-92-094, 14 May 1992, pp. 32–33.
15. Ibid.
16. Ibid.
17. Lam, *China*, p. 197. Lam states that the secret arrangements also applied to the local military districts. At the national level, ten generals included CMC members Zhang Zhen, Chi Haotian, Zhan Wannian, Yu Yungbo, and Fu Quanyou.
18. He Po-shih, "Zhonggong Li Cu Jia Qiang Kongzhi Jun Dui" (Lamenting Changes in Soviet Union, CCP Seeks Tighter Control of Armed Forces), *Tangtai*, 15 January 1992, pp. 53–54.
19. Ibid., p. 39
20. Ibid.
21. Ibid.
22. Ibid., pp. 39–40.
23. Zeng Guangjun, "Zhi Liang: Jun Dui De Sheng Ming" (Quality: The Army's Lifeline), *Jiefang Junbao*, 3 January 1992, p. 3. Information in the next paragraphs was drawn from this source.
24. Ibid.
25. "Jia Qiang Zhi Liang Jian She, Duo You Zhong Guo Te Se De Jing Bing Zhi Lu" (Improve Quality, Take Distinctly Chinese Road of Training "Top-Notch" Troops), *Jiefang Junbao*, 1 January 1992, p. 1.
26. Ibid.
27. Jia Yong, "Zai Gai Ge Zhong Fen Jin De Ren Min Jun Dui" (The People's Army Reform Forges Ahead), *Liaowang*, 27 July 1992, pp. 4–5.
28. "West Remains Chief Enemy," *Der Spiegel*, 16 January 1995, p. 110, FBIS-CHI-92-08, 16 January 1995, p. 1.
29. He Po-shih, "Ba Zhon Chuan Hui Qian Xi Wang Zhen Dangmian Ma Deng Xiaoping, Deng Xiaoping Yuan Chengdan 'Liu Si' Zeren, Yang Shangkun Baiotai Chuan Jun Ting Jiang Zemin" (Wang Zhen Reproaches Deng Xiaoping on Eve of 8th Plenum as Deng Shows Willingness to Assume "4 June" Responsibility and Yang Shangkun Openly Supports Jiang Zemin's Direction in Army Work), *Tangtai*, 15 December 1991, p. 16.
30. Lam, *China*, p. 197.
31. Willy Wo-lap Lam, "Deng Said Securing Military's Support for Reform," *South China Morning Post*, 1 April 1992, p. 11, FBIS-CHI-92-063, 1 April 1992, p. 28.
32. Wang Yihua, "Jun Dui Sheng Chan Jing Ying Wen Si Liu" (What Is Seen Regard-

ing Troops' Production and Economic Activities and Thoughts Provoked Thereby), *Jiefang Junbao*, 12 December 1991, p. 2.

33. Ibid.

34. Ibid.

35. In the end, though, the lure of riches interfered with the professional military mission. Corruption set in and the PLA was able to avoid paying the state taxes, customs, fees, on its commercial enterprises. The senior leadership of the PLA was concerned that corruption was harming the PLA and thus, when Jiang Zemin ordered the PLA out of its commercial ventures in July 1998, the PLA complied. Though they retained their production enterprises and local enterprises to employ the soldiers, and the state compensated for the loss of revenue with a budget increase, the PLA remains a major player in some commercial areas. For an excellent discussion of the rise and fall of the PLA's commercialism, see James C. Mulvenon, *Soldiers of Fortune: The Rise and Fall of the Chinese Military-Business Complex, 1978–1998* (New York: M.E. Sharpe, 2001).

36. Lin Wu, "Zhuhai Yuanlin Junwei Huiyi Neiqing" (Inside Story of Central Military Commission's Meeting in Zhuhai's Yuanlin Guest House), *Cheng Ming*, 1 March 1992, pp. 15–16, 89.

37. Terry Cheng, "Military Changes Said Prompted by Deng's Age," *Standard*, 5 May 1992, p. A5, FBIS-CHI-92-087, 5 May 1992, p. 23; AFP, 14 September 1992, FBIS-CHI-92-178, 14 September 1992, p. 24.

38. "Document No. 26 of CCP Central Committee General Office Reveals Considerable Reduction of PLA Soldiers, Readjustment in Seven Military Regions," *Ching Pao*, 2 July 1992, p. 2, FBIS-CHI-92-128, 2 July 1992, pp. 34–35.

39. Ibid. While much of programmed change was initiated, the number of military regions remained the same, at seven. Probably for reasons of security and avoiding a political battle, the issue was shelved.

40. Lam, "Deng Xiaoping Names Liu Huaqing to CMC," *South China Morning Post*, 15 July 1992, p. 10, FBIS-CHI-92-136, 15 July 1992, p. 16.

41. Xing Laizhao, "Ba You Huo Jie Gou Fang Zai Tu Chu Wei Zhi" (Give Prominence To Structural Optimization), *Jiefang Junbao*, 15 May 1992, p. 3.

42. Ibid.

43. Yi Jianru, "Generals' Trips to Special Economic Zones," *Liaowang Overseas Edition*, 29 June 1992, pp. 4–7, FBIS-CHI-92-137, 16 July 1992, pp. 13–15.

44. *Agence France-Presse*, 14 September 1992, FBIS-CHI-92-178, 14 September 1992, p. 24.

45. Yuan Xuequan, "Qiang Gan Zi Yong Yuan Ting Dang Zhi Hui" (Gun Always Remains Under Party Command), *Jiefang Junbao*, 19 July 1992, p. 1; Hong Heping, "'Sheng Ming Xian' Geng Ju Sheng Ming Li" ("Lifeline" Has Greater Vitality), *Jiefang Junbao*, 21 July 1992, p. 1.

46. Ibid.

47. Ibid.

48. Shi Genxing, "Jian Ding Bu Yi De Shen Huo Jun Dui Gaige" (Unswervingly Deepen Reform of Army), *Jiefang Junbao*, 31 July 1992, p. 3.
49. Ibid.
50. Ibid.
51. Yang Baibing, "Bang Ze Qi Wei Guo Jia Gaige He Jian She Bao Jia Hu Hang De Zung Gao Shi Ming" (Shouldering the Lofty Mission of Escorting and Protecting China's Reform and Construction), *Renmin Ribao*, 29 July 1992, pp. 1, 3. Information in the next paragraphs is drawn from this source.
52. Ibid.
53. Kuang Pi-hua, "Zhong Gong Jun Fang Da Zheng Dun" (Large-Scale Reorganization of Chinese Armed Forces), *Kuang Chiao*, 16 August 1992, pp. 14–15.
54. Ibid., p. 28.
55. Lam, "Army Sets Up Committee to Prevent Coup Attempts," *South China Morning Post*, 14 August 1992, p. 1, FBIS-CHI-92-158, 14 August 1992, p. 27.
56. "Deng Xiaoping Nanxuan," pp. 26–27.
57. Ibid., pp. 27–28; Chen Chieh-hung, "Yang Shangkun, Wan Li Will Completely Retire from Office at the 14th Party Congress," *Ching Pao*, 5 September 1992, pp. 37–38, FBIS-CHI-92-174, 8 September 1992, p. 30.
58. Guan Chuan, "Deng Chu Mian Tiao Jie Qin, Yang Fen Zheng" (Deng Personally Mediated Disputes Between Qin Jiwei and Yang Baibing), *Cheng Ming*, 1 October 1992, pp. 19–20; "The PLA After the Fourteenth Party Congress," China News Analysis, 1 February 93, pp. 6–9.
59. Chen, "Yang Shangkun," p. 30.

Chapter 6: TRIUMPH
1. He Po-shih, "Shi Si Ta Daibiao Ben Yue Di Chansheng" (Delegates to 14th CCP National Congress Known by End of May), *Tangtai*, 15 May 1992, p. 12; Liu Li-kai, "Two Preparatory Groups for 14th CCP National Congress," *Chiu-shih Nien-tai*, 1 April 1992, p. 17, FBIS-CHI-92-066 (6 April 1992), p. 41; Shan Yueh, "Shi Si Da Ren Shi Dou Zheng Su Mu Zhan" (Prelude to Struggle for Personnel Arrangements on Eve of 14th CCP National Congress), *Cheng Ming*, (1 April 1992), p. 15.
2. Ibid.
3. Ibid.
4. Ibid.
5. Harry Harding, "'On the Four Great Relationships': The Prospects for China," *Survival*, vol. 36, no. 2 (Summer 1994), p. 33.
6. Lo Ping, "Chen Yun Pai De Da Fan Pu" (Large-Scale Counteroffensive from Chen Yun Camp), *Cheng Ming*, 1 April 1992, pp. 12–14. Information in the next paragraphs is drawn from this source.
7. Ibid.
8. Sun Chin-hui, "Tian Jiyun Reveals Background on Deng Xiaoping's Talks During His Inspection in South China," *Kuang Chiao Ching*, 16 July 1992, pp. 12–14, FBIS-

CHI-92-152 (6 August 1992), pp. 11–13; "Tian Jiyun Dang Jiao Jiang Huo Ji Yao" (Summary of Tian Jiyun's Speech Before Party School), *Pai Hsing,* 16 June 1992, pp. 4–5; Ming Chuang, "Deng Xiaoping and Chen Yun Reached a Political Agreement More Than Two Months After the Publication of Deng's Remarks Made During His Tour in Southern China," *Ching Pao,* 6 June 1992, pp. 36–38, FBIS-CHI-92-116 (16 June 1992), pp. 18–23. Information in the next paragraphs is drawn from this source.

9. Ibid., p. 20.
10. Willy Lo-Lap Lam, "Tian Jiyun Proposes 'Special Leftist Zone,'" *South China Morning Post,* 7 May 1992, pp. 1, 10, FBIS-CHI-92-089 (7 May 1992), pp. 22–23.
11. Sun Chin-hui, "Tian Jiyun Reveals Background on Deng Xiaoping's Talks During His Inspection in South China," *Kuang Chiao Ching,* 16 July 1992, pp. 12–14, FBIS-CHI-92-152, (6 August 1992), pp. 11–13; "Tian Jiyun Dang Jiao," *Pai Hsing,* 16 June 1992, pp. 4–5.
12. Ibid., p. 13.
13. Lin Wu, "Deng Xiaoping Tan Pi 'Zuo' Yu Zheng Gai" (Deng Xiaoping on Criticizing 'Leftism' and Political Reform), *Cheng Ming,* 1 June 1992, pp. 13–14.
14. Jiang Zemin, "Ba Jing Ji Jian She He Gai Ge Kai Fang Gao De Geng Kuai Geng Hao" (Reform and Opening Must Be Implemented Faster and Better), *Renmin Ribao,* 15 June 1992, p. 1; "Opening Wider," *China Daily,* 16 Jun 92, p. 4, FBIS-CHI-92-116 (16 June 1992), pp. 16–17.
15. Ibid.
16. Lo Ping, "Deng Xiaoping Cheng Ren Dang Nei Fen Ji Yan Zhong" (Deng Xiaoping Admits Serious Differences Inside CCP), *Cheng Ming,* 1 July 1992, pp. 15–17.
17. Tseng Chi, "Zhong Yang Wen Jian Lie Yu 'Zuo Qing' Cuo Wu" (Central Document Lists "Leftist" Mistakes), *Cheng Ming,* 1 September 1992, pp. 27–28.
18. Ibid.
19. Huang Ching, "Chen Yun Ti Shi Tiao Yi Jiang" (Chen Yun Forwards 10 Divergent Views), *Cheng Ming,* 1 August 1992, pp. 15–16.
20. Lo Ping, "Shi Si Ta Qian Xi Deng Chen Dui Zhen" (Deng, Chen Are Pitted Against Each Other on Eve of 14th CCP National Congess), *Cheng Ming,* 1 October 1992, pp. 6–8.
21. Ibid.
22. Ibid.
23. "CCP Issues Document to Greet 14th Party Congress; Police Mobilized to Maintain Public Order in Beijing," *Ching Chi Jih Pao,* 12 Sep 1992, p. 3, FBIS-CHI-92-178 (14 September 1992), p. 18.
24. Lu Feng, "Zu Zhi Gong Zuo Yao Geng Hao Wei Jing Ji Jian She Fu Wu" (Organizational Work Must Serve Economic Reconstruction), *Renmin Ribao,* 5 August 1992, p. 1.
25. Cheng Te-lin, "Some Inkling of Members of Political Bureau Standing Committee to Be Proposed by 14th CCP National Congress," *Ching Pao,* 5 August 1992, pp.

47–48, FBIS-CHI-92-152 (6 August 1992), pp. 8–9. This is only one of several that were appearing in Hong Kong press sources. All had the same list of candidates in general.

26. Jiang Zemin, "Jiakuai Gaike Kaifang He Xiandaihua Jianshe Bufa Duoqu Zhongguo Tese Shehui Zhuyi Shiye De Genda Shengli" (Speed Up the Pace of Reform, the Open Door and Modernization Construction in Order to Strive for Even Greater Victories for the Cause of Socialism with Chinese Characteristics), *Renmin Ribao*, 21 October 1992, pp. 1–3. Information in the next paragraphs is drawn from this source.

27. Ibid.

28. Ibid.

29. Lam, *China*, pp. 197, 364.

30. David Bachman, "China in 1993," *Asian Survey*, no. 1 (January 1994), pp. 31–33; Lincoln Kaye, "Shaping the Succession," *Far Eastern Economic Review*, 8 April 1993, pp. 10–11.

31. Harry Harding, "'On the Four Great Relationships': The Prospects for China," *Survival*, no. 36 (Summer 1994), p. 33.

32. Ibid., p. 197.

33. Li Cheng, and Lynn White, "The Thirteenth Central Committee of the Chinese Communist Party," *Asian Survey* no. 4 (April 1988), pp. 371–99; Michael D. Swaine, *The Military and Political Succession in China*. Rand Report R-4254-AF, Santa Monica, Calif.: Rand Corporation, 1992.

34. For speculation on Yang Baibing's political downfall, see especially Tai Ming Cheung, "General Offensive," *Far Eastern Economic Review*, 10 December 1992, p. 14; Wally Wo-Lap Lam, *China After Deng Xiaoping*, p. 213, ff. 72.

35. Lam, *China*, pp. 213–16; Li Cheng and Lynn White, "The Army in the Succession to Deng Xiaoping," *Asian Survey* no. 8 (August 1993), pp. 757–86.

36. For reasons of security and perhaps to avoid a political fight, the present structure of the military regions remained the same, though command was centralized, leaving the regional commands the ability to act as fronts in the event of hostilities in their region.

37. Luo Yuwen, "Army Urged to Fulfill 'Glorious Mission,'" *Xinhua*, 15 October 1992, FBIS-CHI-92-200-S (15 October 1992), p. 27.

38. Ibid.

39. Ibid.

40. Lam, *China*, p. 88.

41. Ibid.; Lena H. Sun, "Center May Reclaim Power in China," *Washington Post*, 29 October 1993, p. A33; David Bachman, "China in 1993," *Asian Survey* no. 1 (January 1994), p. 34.

42. Sun, "Center May Reclaim Power in China," p. A33.

43. Lam, p. 89.

44. Sun, "Center May Reclaim Power," p. A33.

45. "Sansi Shizi Zhongyang Zhunhui Jueding" (14th CCP Issues Decision at Third Plenum), *Renmin Ribao,* 17 November 1993, pp. 1–2.
46. Lam, *China,* pp. 91–92.
47. "China's Economy, Reined In," *The Economist,* 21 May 1994, p. 38, "China's Runaway Economy," *The Economist,* 16 May 1993, p. 16, "Economy, Wait and See," *Far Eastern Economic Review,* 31 August 1995, p. 40.
48. Lam, *China,* p. 85, Lena H. Sun, "Beijing, Fearing Unemployment, Slows Reform of State Industries," *Washington Post,* 20 April 1994, p. A15.
49. See John P. Burns, *The Chinese Communist Party Nomenklatura System: A Documentary Study of Party Control of Leadership Selection* (Armonk, N.Y.: M. E. Sharpe, 1989), for discussion of Chinese patronage system.
50. Lam, *China,* pp. 58–59.
51. Ibid., p. 406.
52. Nayan Chanda, "Fear of the Dragon," *Far Eastern Economic Review,* 13 April 1992, p. 25.
53. "Stepping Out: China's Lengthening Shadow," *International Defense Review,* February 1995, p. 35; and Craig S. Smith, "China Sends Its Army Money, And A Signal To The U.S.," *New York Times,* 11 March 2001, p. A1.
54. Lam, *China,* pp. 28, 286.

CONCLUSION

1. Deng was always the pragmatist. He is noted for his famous statement in 1962 that it did not matter if a cat was white or black, so long as it caught mice. In 1962, Deng and Chen Yun advocated family plots to help the economy recover from the disastrous Great Leap Forward. However, throughout his lifetime he never wavered in his commitment to the party and its right to govern China. He assisted Mao in the anti-rightist movement in 1956, when the party persecuted intellectuals that had criticized the party, and he helped Mao purge individuals at the start of the Cultural Revolution.

2. Tian Jiyun's defense of Deng's policies in 1992 were in answer to continued conservative opposition over the same issues since 1978. As noted in Deng's statement on page 118, he was willing to use pragmatic economic measures, but he would not surrender the dictatorial rule of the communist party.

3. Deng, *Fundamental Issues,* pp. 179–83.

4. Ibid., p. 183.

5. See earlier details of Deng's interviews with Nixon to further understand Deng's basic pragmatism.

6. Naturally, as Deng's generation of elders—the "second generation"—die off one by one, the "third generation," consisting of today's active leadership, that is, Jiang Zemin, Li Peng, Qiao Shi, Chi Haotian, Zhang Wannian, will move to the back bench, behind the throne, to pull strings much as Deng and colleagues did. Thus, the "genro" will evolve into the "third generation" while the active leadership will be

the "fourth generation," represented by Wen Jiabao, Zeng Qinghong, Wu Bangguo, and others. For an excellent discussion of generational politics in China, see Cheng Li, "Jiang Zemin's Successors: The Rise of the Fourth Generation of Leaders in the PRC," *China Quarterly* no. 161 (March 2000), pp. 1–40.

7. For discussions of possibility of restoring the party chairmanship, see "China in Transition," *Far Eastern Economic Review*, 18 July 1996, p. 26.

8. For an optimistic view of the post-Deng leadership, based on a unified, consensus-based arrangement, see H. Lyman Miller, "The Post-Deng Leadership: Premature Reports of Demise?" *Washington Journal of Modern China* no. 2, (Fall–Winter 1994), pp. 1–16.

9. For a general discussion of China's current economic problems as well as a review of the domestic issues growing out of Deng's policy of economic growth, see Steven Mufson, "China's Growing Inequality," *Washington Post*, 1 January 1997, pp. A1, A26–A27.

10. For a general discussion of the rising tide of nationalism in China, see Nayan Chanda and Karl Huus, "The New Nationalism," *Far Eastern Economic Review*, 9 November 1995, pp. 20–26; Karl Huus, "The Hard Edge," *Far Eastern Economic Review*, 9 November 1995, p. 28; and Liu Binyan, "Against the Wind," *Far Eastern Economic Review*, 9 November 1995, p. 26.

11. See Nigal Holloway, "No Ordinary General," *Far Eastern Economic Review*, 12 December 1996, for a discussion of PLA miscalculation on Taiwan exercises.

12. Ibid.

13. Steven Mufson, "China, Russia Swap Support, Sign Array of Agreements," *Washington Post*, 26 April 1996, p. A27; Lee Hockstader, "Russia, China Affirm 'Strategic Partnership,'" *Washington Post*, 26 December 1996, p. A19.

14. Julian Baum, "A Case of Nerves," *Far Eastern Economic Review*, 26 December 1996 and 2 January 1997, p. 20.

BIBLIOGRAPHY

NEWSPAPERS AND NEWS AGENCIES

The *New York Times, Washington Post,* and *Wall Street Journal* in the United States; the *South China Morning Post, Ming Pao, Ta Kung Pao* in Hong Kong; and *People's Daily, Liberation Army Daily* and *Liberation Daily* in China all provided valuable daily information.

MONOGRAPHS AND PERIODICALS

"A Visit That Will Open Up the Future." *Wen Wei Pao,* 15 May 1991, p. 2.

"Ba Shen Zhen Te Chu Jian She De Geng Hao" (Do Better in Economic Reform in Shenzhen and Zhuhai). *Renmin Ribao,* 6 December 1991, p. I.

Bachman, David M. *Bureaucracy, Economy, and Leadership in China: The Institutional Origins of the Great Leap Forward,* New York: Cambridge University Press, 1991.

―――. "China in 1993." *Asian Survey* no. I (January 1994): 31–34.

Baker, James A., III. "America in Asia: Emerging Architecture for a Pacific Community." *Foreign Affairs* vol. 70, no. 5 (Winter 1991–92): 1–18.

Barnett, A. Doak. *The Making of Foreign Policy in China,* London: I. B. Tauris, 1985.

Baum, Julian. "A Case of Nerves." *Far Eastern Economic Review,* 26 December 1996 and 2 January 1997

Bonavia, David. *Deng.* Hong Kong: Longman, 1989.

Brzezinski, Zbigniew. "A Plan for Europe." *Foreign Affairs* vol. 74, no. 1 (January/February 1995): 26–42.

Burns, John P. "China's Nomenklatura System." *Problems in Communism* no. 36 (September–October 1987): 36–51.

———. "Chinese Civil Service Reform: The Thirteenth Party Congress Proposals." *China Quarterly* no. 120 (December 1989): 739–70.

———. *The Chinese Communist Party Nomenklatura System: A Documentary Study of Party Control of Leadership Selection*, Armonk, N. Y.: M. E. Sharpe, 1989.

"CCP in Hot Pursuit of Economic Criminals: Party Members and Cadres to Make Three Examinations." *Ming Bao*, 25 April 1982, p. 6.

"CCP to Set Directives on Personnel Changes." *Kyodo*, 3 December 1991.

"CCP Issues Document to Greet Fourteenth Party Congress; Police Mobilized to Maintain Public Order in Beijing." *Ching Chi Jih Pao*, 12 September 1992, p. 3.

Central Intelligence Agency. *The Chinese Economy in 1989 and 1990: Trying to Revive Growth While Maintaining Social Stability.* Washington, D.C.: Central Intelligence Agency, 1990.

———. *The Chinese Economy in 1990 and 1991: Uncertain Recovery.* Washington, D. C.: Central Intelligence Agency, 1991.

———. *The Chinese Economy in 1991 and 1992: Pressure to Revisit Reform Mounts.* Washington, D.C.: Central Intelligence Agency, 1992.

Chanda, Nayan. "Fear of the Dragon." *Far Eastern Economic Review*, 13 April 1992, p. 25.

Chanda, Nayan and Karl Huus. "The New Nationalism." *Far Eastern Economic Review*, 9 November 1995, p. 28.

Chang King-yuh, ed. *Mainland China After the Thirteenth Party Congress.* Boulder, Colo.: Westview Press, 1990.

Chang, Parris H. "Chinese Politics: Deng's Turbulent Quest." *Problems in Communism* vol. 30, no. 1 (January–February 1981): 1–21.

Chen Chieh-hung. "Deng Xiaoping Puts Forward the 'Eight Shoulds,' Says 'Three Kinds of People' Must Step Down." *Ching Pao*, 5 March 1992, pp. 45–46.

———. "Yang Shangkun, Wan Li Will Completely Retire From Office at the 14th Party Congress." *Ching Pao*, 5 September 1992, pp. 37–38.

Chen Shao-pin. "Deng Xiaoping Fetes High-Ranking Officers of 'Three Armed Services.'" *Ching Pao*, 5 May 1992, p. 40.

Chen Yeping. "De Sai Jian Ye Yi De Wei Shu" (Have Both Political Integrity, Ability, Stress Political Ability: On Criterion for Selecting Cadres). *Renmin Ribao*, 1 September 1991, p. 5.

Chen Yun. *Chen Yun Wenxuan* (Selected Works of Chen Yun, 1956–1985). Beijing: Xinhua She, 1986.

Cheng Li, and White, Lynn. "The Thirteenth Central Committee of the Chinese Communist Party." *Asian Survey* no. 4 (April 1988): 371–99.

———. "The Army in the Succession to Deng Xiaoping." *Asian Survey* no. 8 (August 1993): 757–86.

Cheng Te-lin. "Chen Yun Says There Are Two Major Dangers Inside CCP." *Ching Pao*, 5 March 1992, p. 47.

————. "Some Inkling of Members of Political Bureau Standing Committee to Be Proposed by Fourteenth CCP National Congress." *Ching Pao,* 5 August 1992, pp. 47–48.

Cheng Ying. "CCP's Internal Propaganda Outline in Perspective." *Chiushih Nientai,* (1 September 1991): 34–35.

"Chief of General Staff Calls for Modernization." *Agence France-Presse,* 17 December 1991.

Chi Hsin. *Deng Xiaoping: A Political Biography.* Hong Kong: Cosmos Books, 1978.

Chi Ma. "Fan He Ping Yan Bian Gao De Cao Mu Jie Bing Jiang Ju Deng Xiaoping Ming Pao Zhong Xuan Bu" (Instructed by Deng Xiaoping, Jiang Zemin Bombards Central Propaganda Department for Being in State of Extreme Nervousness in Opposing Peaceful Evolution). *Ming Bao,* 8 October 1991, p. 2.

"China's Economy, Reined In." *The Economist,* 21 May 1994, p. 38.

China Quarterly. "Deng Xiaoping: An Assessment." Special issue no. 135, September 1993.

Chong Pin-Lin. "Red Fist: China's Army in Transition." *International Defense Review* no. 28 (February 1995): 30–34.

Chou Tie. "Zhong Ceng Wei Lian Ming Cu Qu Xiao Jing Ji Te Chu" (Some Central Advisory Commission Members Submit Written Statement to Central Committee Calling for Abolition of Special Economic Zones). *Ming Pao,* 6 March 1992, p. 2.

"Commentator Huangfu Ping's Identity Viewed." *Ta Kung Pao,* 7 October 1992, pp. 14–21.

Chuang Ming. "Deng Xiaoping and Chen Yun Reached a Political Agreement More Than Two Months After the Publication of Deng's Remarks Made During His Tour in Southern China." *Ching Pao,* 6 June 92, pp. 36–38.

Chung Hsiao. "Li Ruihuan Goes to Shanghai to Promote Reform Vigorously as Deng, Jiang, and Zhu are Hit by Sniper's Shot." *Ching Pao* no. 173 (5 December 1991): 26–28.

Crothall, Geoffrey. "Deng, Chen Yun 'Plotting' Strategy in Shanghai." *South China Morning Post,* 19 December 1991, p. 14.

"Da Lu Jing Ji Ceng Zhang Shi Tou Zhu Rongji Jiang Qian Shi Du Kongzhi" (Zhu Rongji Calls for Appropriate Controls over China's Economic Growth Momentum). *Ming Pao,* 9 September 1992, p. 8.

Delfs, Robert. "Power to the Party." *Far Eastern Economic Review,* 7 December 1989, pp. 23–25.

"Deng Instructs Leaders on Peaceful Evolution." *Ming Pao,* 8 October 1991, p. 2.

"Deng Calls for Maintaining Powerful Army." *Agence France-Presse,* 20 December 1991.

Deng Maomao. *Deng Xiaoping: My Father.* New York: Basic Books, 1995.

Deng Xiaoping. *Fundamental Issues in Present-Day China.* Beijing: Foreign Language Press, 1987.

————. *Deng Xiaoping Wenxuan* (Selected Works of Deng Xiaoping,1975–1982), vol. 2. Beijing: Foreign Language Press, 1984.

"Deng Xiaoping Nanxuan Jiang Huo De Er Hao Wen Jian" (Full Text of Document No. 2 on Deng's Remarks). *Cheng Ming,* no. 187 (1 April 1992): 23–27.

"Deng Xiaoping Tan Guangdong Cheng Lung Tou Yao Qi Hao Cuo Yong" (Deng Xiaoping Tours Zhuhai, Saying That Guangdong Economy Should Play Leading Role in China's Economic Development). *Ta Kung Pao*, 26 January 1992, p. I.

de Rosario, Louise. "Quick Step Back." *Far Eastern Economic Review*, 19 October 1989, pp. 47–48.

———. "Three Years' Hard Labor." *Far Eastern Economic Review*, 30 November 1989, p. 68.

"Document No. 26 of CCP Central Committee General Office Reveals Considerable Reduction of PLA Soldiers, Readjustment in Seven Military Regions." *Ching Pao*, 2 July 1992, p. 2.

Domes, Jurgen. "Who and What Comes Next in Communist China." *Global Affairs* (Summer 1993): 125–40.

Dreyer, June Teufel. "Deng Xiaoping: The Soldier." *China Quarterly* no. 135 (September 1993): 536–51.

"Economy, Wait and See." *Far Eastern Economic Review*, 31 August 1995. p. 40.

"Evolution Toward Multipolar Global Pattern Seen." *Joint Publications Research Service*, 27 September 1991, pp. 2–3

"Fa Zhan Dang De Shi Ye Yao Xia Xi Dang Shi Dang Jian Li Lun" (Study the Theory of Party Building). *Renmin Ribao*, 21 November 1991, p. 8.

Foreign Broadcast Information Service. *China Daily Report* (various issues). Arlington, Va.: FBIS.

Franz, Uli. *Deng Xiaoping*. New York: Harcourt, Brace Jovanovich, 1988.

"Gai Ge Kai Fang Shi Tui Jin Bu Dui Jian She De Jiang Da Dong Li" (Reform, Opening Up Said to Promote Army Building). *Jiefang Junbao*, 20 November 1991, p. 3.

Garver, John W. "China's Push Through the South China Sea: The Interactions of Bureaucratic and National Interests." *China Quarterly* no. 132 (December 1992): 999–1028.

Godwin, Paul H. B. "Chinese Military Strategy Revised: Local and Limited War." *Annals of the American Academy of Political and Social Science* vol. 519 (January 1992): 191–201.

Goldman, Marshall I. *What Went Wrong with Perestroika*. New York: W. W. Norton, 1991.

Goldman, Merle. *Sowing the Seeds of Democracy in China*. Cambridge, MA: Harvard University Press, 1994.

Goldstone, Jack A. "The Coming Chinese Collapse." *Foreign Policy* no. 99 (Summer 1995): 35–52.

Goodman, David S. *Deng Xiaoping and the Chinese Revolution*. New York: Routledge, 1994.

Goodman, David S. G., and Gerald Segal, eds. *China in the Nineties*. New York: Oxford University Press, 1991.

Gorbachev, Mikhail. *The August Coup*. New York: HarperCollins, 1991.

"Grasp the Key Points in the Crucial Period—On Investigating State-Owned Large and Medium-sized Enterprises." *Jiefang Ribao*, 8 February 1991, p. I.

Gregor, A. James. "China's Shadow over Southeast Asian Waters." *Global Affairs* vol. III, no. 3. (Summer 1992): 1–13.

Guan Chuan. "Deng Chu Mian Tiao Jie Qin, Yang Fen Zheng" (Deng Personally Medi-
ated Disputes Between Qin Jiwei and Yang Baibing). *Cheng Ming* no. 192 (1 October
1992): 19–20.
————. "Nung Cun Heping Yanbian Chongji 'Shejiao'" (Peaceful Evolution in Rural
Areas Thwarts "Socialist Education Movement"). *Cheng Ming* no. 171 (1 January
1991): 24–25.
"Gui Ding Qi Yi Na Xie Jing Ying Zi You Chuan" (Establish a Few Regulations over
Economy). *Renmin Ribao*, 11 September 1992, p. 2.
"Guo Wu Yuan Cheng Li Jing Ji Mao Yi Ban Gong Shi" (State Council Establishes Trade
and Economics General Office). *Renmin Ribao*, 12 June 1992, p. 1.
"Guo Wu Yuan Pi Zhuan Jin Nian Jing Ji Ti Zhi Gaige Yao Dian" (The State Council
Publishes the Main Points for This Year's Reform of the Economic System). *Renmin
Ribao*, 29 March 1992, p. 7.
Haass, Richard N. "Paradigm Lost." *Foreign Affairs* vol. 74, no. 1 (January/February 1995):
44–58.
Hao Yufan and Huan Guacang, eds. *The Chinese View of the World*. New York: Pantheon
Books, 1989.
Harding, Harry. *China's Foreign Relations in the 1980s*. New Haven, Conn.: Yale University
Press, 1984.
————. *A Fragile Relationship: The United States and China since 1972*. Washington, D. C.:
Brookings Institution, 1992.
————. *China's Second Revolution*. Washington, D. C.: Brookings Institution, 1987.
————. "'On the Four Great Relationships': The Prospects for China." *Survival* vol. 36,
no. 2 (Summer 1994): 22–42.
————. "China at the Crossroads: Conservatism, Reform or Decay?" *Adelphi* 275 (March
1993): 36–48.
————. "Asia Policy to the Brink." *Foreign Policy* no. 96 (Fall 1994): 57–74.
Harrison, James Pinckney. *The Long March to Power: A History of the Chinese Communist Party,
1971–79*. New York: Praeger, 1972.
He Bin and Guo Xin. *Zhong Gong "Taize Dang"* (The Communist Party's Princely Party).
Taibei: Shi Bao Wen Hua, 1992.
He Po-shih. "Ba Zhong Chuan Hui Qianxi Wang Zhen Dangmian Ma Deng Xiaoping;
Deng Xiaoping Yuan Chengdan 'Liu Si' Ce Ren; Yang Shangkun Biaotai Quan Jun
Ting Jiang Zemin" (Wang Zhen Reproaches Deng Xiaoping on Eve of Eighth
Plenum as Deng Shows Willingness to Assume "4 June" Responsibility and Yang
Shangkun Openly Supports Jiang Zemin's Direction in Army Work). *Tangtai*, 15
December 1991, p. 16.
————. "Shi Si Ta Daibiao Ben Ye Di Chan Sheng" (Delegates to Fourteenth CCP
National Congress Known by End of May). *Tangtai*, 15 May 1992 p. 12.
————. "Sulian Bianzheng, Zhonggong Dui Nei Ru He Shuo?" (What Does CCP Say
Internally in Wake of Changing Situation in Soviet Union?). *Tangtai*, January 1992,
pp. 41–52.

————. "Zhonggong Li Cu Jia Qiang Kongzhi Jun Dui" (Lamenting Changes in Soviet Union, CCP Seeks Tighter Control of Armed Forces). *Tangtai*, 15 January 1992, pp. 53–54.

Hicks, George. *The Broken Mirror: China After Tiananmen*. Chicago: St. James Press, 1990.

Hoagland, Jim. "Senior Chinese Official Who Fled Emerges from Hiding." *Washington Post*, 4 September 1989, p. AI.

Hockstader, Lee. "Russia, China Affirm 'Strategic Partnership.'" *Washington Post*, 26 December 1996, p. AI9.

Holloway, Nigal. "No Ordinary General." *Far Eastern Economic Review*, 12 December 1996.

Hong Heping. "'Sheng Ming Xian' Geng Ju Sheng Ming Li" (Lifeline Has Greater Vitality). *Jiefang Junbao*, 21 July 1992, p. I.

Hsia Yu-hung. "Deng Xiaoping Says Army Must Serve as Guarantee for Reform and Opening Up." *Lien Ho Pao*, 10 May 1992, p. 2.

Huang, Cary. "Bo Yibo Supports Shenzen Price Reform Program." *Standard*, 24 January 1992, p. A6.

Huang Ching. "Chen Yun Ti Shi Tiao Yi Jiang." (Chen Yun Forwards Ten Divergent Views). *Cheng Ming*, 1 August 1992, pp. 15–16.

Huang Yasheng. "Why China Will Not Collapse." *Foreign Policy* no. 99 (Summer 1995): 54–68.

Huo Szu-fang. "Three Main Points in Deng Xiaoping's Remarks Delivered During Southern China Tour, Principles Set for Personnel Arrangements at Fourteenth National Congress." *Ching Pao*, 5 March 1992, pp. 34–37.

Huus, Karl. "The Hard Edge." *Far Eastern Economic Review*, 9 November 1995, p. 28.

"Jia Qiang Zhi Liang Jian She, Duo You Zhong Guo Te Se De Jing Bing Zhi Lu" (Improve Quality, Take Distinctly Chinese Road of Training 'Top-Notch' Troops). *Jiefang Junbao*, 1 January 1992, p. I.

Jia Yong. "Zai Gai Ge Zhong Fen Jin De Ren Min Jun Dui." (The People's Army Reform Forges Ahead). *Liaowang*, 27 July 92, pp. 4–5.

Jiang Zemin. "Ba Jing Ji Jian She He Gai Ge Kai Fang Gao De Geng Kuai Geng Hao" (Do a Better and Faster Job of Reform and Opening). *Renmin Ribao*, 15 June 1992, p. I.

————. "Building Socialism the Chinese Way." *Beijing Review*, 8–14 July 1991, pp. 15–32.

————. "Jiakuai Gaike Kaifang He Xiandaihua Jianshe Bufa Duoqu Zhongguo Tese Shehui Zhuyi Shiye De Genda Shengli" (Speed Up the Pace of Reform, the Open Door and Modernization Construction in Order to Strive for Even Greater Victories for the Cause of Socialism with Chinese Characteristics). *Renmin Ribao*, 21 October 1992, pp. 1–3.

"Jiang Zemin Jie 'Si Hao Wen Jian' Biaotai" (Jiang Zemin Declares Stand Through "Document No. 4"). *Tangtai*, 15 June 1992, p. 10.

"Jiang Zemin Di Da Su Lian Jin Xing Zheng Zhi Fang Wen" (Jiang Zemin Arrives in the Soviet Union for an Official Visit). *Renmin Ribao*, 16 May 1991, p. I.

Joint Economic Committee, Congress of the United States. *China's Economic Dilemmas in the 1990s.* Armonk, N. Y: M. E. Sharpe, 1992.

Joffe, Ellis. *Party and Army Professionalism and Political Control in the Chinese Officer Corps, 1949–1964,* Cambridge, MA: Harvard University Press, 1971.

———. "The PLA and the Chinese Economy: The Effect of Involvement." *Survival* no. 2 (Summer 1995): 42–43.

Kau, Michael Ying-Mao and Susan H. Marsh, eds. *China in the Era of Deng Xiaoping.* Armonk, N. Y.: M. E. Sharpe, 1993.

Kaye, Lincoln. "Bitter Medicine." *Far Eastern Economic Review,* 5 September 1991, p. 10.

———. "Avoiding the Issues." *Far Eastern Economic Review,* 12 December 1991, p. 12.

———. "Shaping the Succession." *Far Eastern Economic Review,* 8 April 1993, pp. 10–11.

Kim, Samuel S. *China and the World.* Boulder, Colo.: Westview Press, 1984.

———. "China as a Regional Power." *Current History* vol. 91, no. 566 (September 1992): 247–52.

Kissinger, Henry. *White House Years.* Boston: Little, Brown, 1979.

Kristof, Nicholas D. and Sheryl Wudunn. *China Wakes.* New York: Random House, 1994.

Kuang Pi-hao. "Zhong Gong Jun Fang Da Zheng Dun." (Large-Scale Reorganization of Chinese Armed Forces). *Kuang Chiao,* 16 August 1992, pp. 14–15.

Lam, Willy Wo-lap. "Jiang, 'Shanghai Faction' Expanding Influence." *South China Morning Post,* 2 January 1992, p. 10.

———. "Sources Report 'Intensified' Factional Strife." *South China Morning Post,* 11 March 1992, p. 13.

———. "Politburo Session Upholds 'Deng Xiaoping Line.'" *South China Morning Post,* 13 March 1992, pp. 1, 10.

———. "Tian Jiyun Proposes 'Special Leftist Zone.'" *South China Morning Post,* 7 May 1992, pp. 1, 10.

———. *China After Deng Xiaoping.* Singapore: Wiley, 1995.

Lardy, Nicholas R. "Chinese Foreign Trade." *China Quarterly* no. 132 (September 1992): 691–720.

Lei Zhonyu. "Geng Fang Kuan Xie Geng Da Dan Xie" (Open Wider and Bolder). *Renmin Ribao,* 26 January 1992, p. 1.

———. "Yang Shangkun Dao Cha Zhu Hai Shen Zhen" (Yang Shangkun Inspects Shenzhen and Zhuhai). *Renmin Ribao,* 2 February 1992, p. 1.

Li Cheng. "Jiang Zemin's Successors: The Rise of the Fourth Generation of Leaders in the PRC." *China Quarterly* no. 161 (March 2000): 1–40.

Li Cheng, and Lynn White. "The Thirteenth Central Committee of the Chinese Communist Party." *Asian Survey* no. 4 (April 1988): 371–99.

———. "The Army in the Succession to Deng Xiaoping." *Asian Survey* no. 8 (August 1993): 757–86.

Li Ming. "Deng Says That Failure to Boost Economy Will Lead to Collapse of Communist Party." *China Pao,* 5 December 1991, p. 34.

Li Peng. "Guan Yu Dang Qian Jing Ji Xing Kuan He Jin Yi Bu Gao Hao Guo Ying Da Zhong Xing Qi Ye De Wen Ti" (The Current Economic Situation and the Issue of Further Improving State-Owned Large and Medium-Sized Enterprises). *Renmin Ribao,* 11 October 1991, p. 1.

Li Renzhu. "Da Li Jia Qiang Ge Ji Ling Dao Ban Zi Jian She" (CCP Organization Chief Outlines 1992 Tasks). *Renmin Ribao,* 10 December 1991, p. 1.

Li Tzu-ching. "Deng Xunshi Wu Sheng Shi Fan Ji Chen Yun" (Deng Xiaoping on Inspection Tour of Five Provinces; Strikes Back at Chen Yun). *Cheng Ming* no. 184 (1 February 1992): 9–14.

Li Yunqi. "China's Inflation." *Asian Survey* no. 7 (July 1989): 655–68.

Li Zhisui. *The Private Life of Chairman Mao.* New York: Random House, 1994.

Liang Zhang (comp.), Andrew Nathan, and Perry Link, eds. *The Tiananmen Papers* (New York: Public Affairs, 2001).

Lieberthal, Kenneth. *Governing China: From Revolution Through Reform.* New York: W. W. Norton, 1995.

Lin Painiao. "Zhong Gong Xin Xing Dui Mei Zheng Ce" (CCP Formulates New Policy Toward United States). *Cheng Ming* no. 170 (1 December 1991): 17–19.

Lin Wu. "Deng Xiaoping Tan Pi 'Zuo' Yu Zheng Gai" (Deng Xiaoping on Criticizing "Leftism" and Political Reform). *Cheng Ming* no. 185, (1 June 1992): 13–14.

———. "Zhuhai Yuanlin Junwei Huiyi Neiqing" (Inside Story of Central Military Commission's Meeting in Zhuhai's Yuanlin Guest House). *Cheng Ming* no. 182, (1 March 92): 15–16, 89.

Liu Binyan. "Against the Wind." *Far Eastern Economic Review,* 9 November 1995, p. 26.

Liu Li-kai. "Two Preparatory Groups for Fourteenth CCP National Congress." *Chiu-shih Nien-tai,* 1 April 1992, p. 17.

Liu Pi. "Evil Wind of Praising Chen, Speaking Ill of Deng, Criticizing Zhao Prevails in Beijing: Difficulties in Implementing Deng Xiaoping's Three Policy Decisions." *Ching Pao,* October 1991, pp. 14–16, 26–28.

Liu Ying. "Deng Personally Decided on Tactics for Talks with Baker." *Ching Pao (Hong Kong),* 5 December 1991, pp. 30–31.

Lo Ping. "Chen Yun Pai De Da Fan Pu" (Large-Scale Counteroffensive From Chen Yun Camp). *Cheng Ming* no. 186 (1 April 1992): 12–14.

———. "Chen Yun Xiang Deng De Xin Tiao Zhan" (Chen Yun Responds to Deng's New Challenge). *Cheng Ming* no. 184 (1 February 1992): 6–8.

———. "Deng Xiaoping Cheng Ren Dang Nei Fen Ji Yan Zhong" (Deng Xiaoping Admits Serious Differences Inside CCP). *Cheng Ming* no. 189 (1 July 1992): 15–16, 17.

———. "Deng Chen Jiao Feng De Xin Zhan Yi" (A New Chapter in the Battle Between Deng and Chen). *Cheng Ming* no. 186 (1 April 1992): 8–11.

———. "Liang Jutou Shanghai Jiao Feng Ji" (Records of the Shanghai Meeting between the Two Leaders). *Cheng Ming* no. 185 (1 March 1992): 6–11.

———. "Shi Si Ta Qian Xi Deng Chen Dui Zhen" (Deng, Chen Are Pitted Against

Each Other on Eve of Fourteenth CCP National Congess). *Cheng Ming* no. 192 (1 October 92): 6–8.

———. "Wang Meng Shi Jain Yu He Jingzhi Xin Zheng Shi" (Wang Meng Event and He Jingzhi's New Offensive). *Cheng Ming* no. 170 (1 December 1991): 11–13.

Lo Ping and Li Tzuching. "Deng Chen Liang Pai Jiao Feng Yu Ba Zhong Chuan Hui" (Contest Between Deng and Chen Factions and Eighth Plenary Session). *Cheng Ming* no. 170, (1 December 1991): 6–8.

———. "Jie Mi Wen Jian Zhong De Bu Wen Di Chu" (Unstable Regions Set Forth in Top Secret Document). *Cheng Ming* no. 183 (1 January 1992): 8–9.

Lu Donggeng. "Jiao Ta Shi Di, Zhen Zhuo Shi Gan, Li Shi Xing Shi Zhu Yi" (While Inspecting Troops Stationed in Jiangsu, Jiang Zemin Urges Whole Army to Uphold Principles of Building Army Through Hard Work and Thrift and Stresses Practical Results in Work). *Jiefang Junbao*, 26 January 1992, pp. 1, 4.

Lu Feng. "Zu Zhi Gong Zuo Yao Geng Hao Wei Jing Ji Jian She Fu Wu" (Organizational Work Must Serve Economic Reconstruction). *Renmin Ribao*, 5 August 1992, p. 1.

Lu Tai. "Yang Shangkun Dao Xinjiang Buzhi Fang Tubian" (Yang Shangkun Inspects Xinjiang, Makes Arrangements to Prevent Sudden Changes). *Cheng Ming*, no. 184, (1 February 1992): 27–28.

Lu Yu-sha. "Deng Xiaoping Jiu Er Wu Jianghuo Fadong Gaige Di Er Gongshi" (Deng Speech Seen as Launching Reform "Offensive"). *Tangtai*, 15 January 1992, pp. 35–37.

Luo Yuwen. "More on Yang's Remarks." *Xinhua*, 23 March 1992.

———. "Army Urged to Fulfill 'Glorious Mission.'" *Xinhua*, 15 October 1992.

McCormick, Barrett L., Su Shaozhi, and Xiao Xiaoming. "The 1989 Democracy Movement: A Review of the Prospects for Civil Society in China." *Pacific Affairs* vol. 65, no. 2 (Summer 1992): 182–202.

Meisner, Maurice. *The Deng Xiaoping Era.* New York: Hill and Wang, 1996.

Miller, H. Lyman. "The Post-Deng Leadership: Premature Reports of Demise?" *Washington Journal of Modern China* no. 2 (Fall–Winter 1994): 1, 16.

Ming, Ruan. *Deng Xiaoping: Chronicle of an Empire.* Boulder, Colo.: Westview Press, 1994.

Montinola, Gabbriella, Qian Yingyi, and Barry R. Weingast. "Federalism, Chinese Style: The Political Basis for Economic Success in China." *World Politics* no. 48 (October 1995): 50–81.

Mufson, Steven. "A Tiananmen Symbol." *Washington Post*, 3 June 1995, p. A18.

———. "China's Global Grain of Difference." *Washington Post*, 9 February 1996, pp. A1, A31

———. "China, Russia Swap Support, Sign Array of Agreements." *Washington Post*, 26 April 1996, p. A27

———. "China's Growing Inequality." *Washington Post*, 1 January 1997, pp. A1, A26–A27

Mulvenon, James C., *The Rise and Fall of the Chinese Military-Business Complex, 1978–1998.* Armonk, N. Y.: M. E. Sharpe, 2001.

Munro, Ross H. "Awakening Dragon." *Policy Review* no. 62 (Fall 1992): 10–16.

Nelsen, Harvey W. *The Chinese Military System: An Organizational Study of the Chinese People's Liberation Army,*. 2nd. ed. Boulder, Colo.: Westview Press, 1981.

Ning Ma. "Deng Xiaoping Yi Jun Gan Zheng" (Deng Xiaoping Uses Army Instead of Party to Promote Reform). *Tangtai*, 15 June 1992, p. 12.

Nixon, Richard. *In The Arena.* New York: Simon and Schuster, 1990.

"No Change in China's Special Economic Zone Policies." *Wen Wei Pao*, 25 April 1982, p. 1.

"Nu Li Kai Qiang Nung Ye He Nung Cun Gong Zuo Xin Ju Huo" (Work Hard to Create a New Situation for Agriculture and Rural Work). *Renmin Ribao*, 30 November 1991, p. 1.

Oksenberg, Michael. "China's Thirteenth Party Congress." *Problems in Communism* vol. 36, no. 6 (November–December 987): 1–17.

"Opening Wider." *China Daily*, 16 June 1992, p. 4.

Overholt, William H. *The Rise of China.* New York: W. W. Norton, 1993.

Pang Xiecheng. "Jiang Zemin Hui Lai Shanghai" (Jiang Zemin Returns to Shanghai). *Renmin Ribao*, 26 January 1992, p. 1.

Ping Huangfu. "New Lines of Thought Needed in Reform and Opening." *Jiefang Ribao*, 2 March 1991, p. 1.

———. "Reform and Opening Requires a Large Number of Cadres with Both Morals and Talent." *Jiefang Ribao*, 12 April 1991, p. 1.

Pollack, Jonathan D. "Chinese Global Strategy and Soviet Power." *Problems in Communism* vol. 30, no. 1 (January–February 1981): 54–69.

Pye, Lucian W. "An Introductory Profile: Deng Xiaoping and China's Political Culture." *China Quarterly* no. 135 (September 1993): 412–44.

Reagan, Ronald. *An American Life.* New York: Simon and Schuster, 1990.

"Realities to Be Faced in China in the Wake of the Dramatic Changes in the USSR and Strategic Choices." *Zhongguo Qingnian Bao*, 1 September 1991.

Saich, Tony. "The Fourteenth Party Congress: A Programme for Authoritarian Rule." *China Quarterly* no. 132, (December 1992): 1136–60.

"Sansi Shizi Zhongyang Zhunhui Jueding" (Fourteenth CCP Issues Decision at Third Plenum). *Renmin Ribao*, 17 November 1993, pp. 1–2.

Schell, Orville. *Mandate of Heaven.* New York: Simon and Schuster, 1994.

Segal, Gerald. "China Changes Shape: Regionalism and Foreign Policy." *Adelphi* 287, March 1994.

———. "China and the Disintegration of the Soviet Union." *Asian Survey* no. 9 (September 1992): 848–868.

Shambaugh, David L. *The Making of a Premier.* Boulder, Colo.: Westview Press, 1984.

———. "The Fourth and Fifth Plenary Sessions of the Thirteenth CCP Central Committee." *China Quarterly* no. 118, (December 1989): 852–62.

———. "Regaining Political Momentun: Deng Strikes Back." *Current History* vol. 91, no. 566 (September 1992): 257–261.

———. "Introduction: Assessing Deng Xiaoping's Legacy." *China Quarterly* no. 135 (September 1993): 409–412.

———. "Deng Xiaoping: The Politician." *China Quarterly* no. 135 (September 1993): 457–91.

———. "Growing Strong: China's Challenge to Asian Security." *Survival* vol. 36, no. 2 (Summer 1994): 43–59.

———. "China's Changing Shape." *Foreign Affairs* vol. 73, no. 3 (May/June 1994): 44–58.

Shan Yueh. "Shi Si Da Ren Shi Dou Zheng Su Mu Zhan" (Prelude to Struggle for Personnel Arrangements on Eve of Fourteenth CCP National Congress). *Cheng Ming,* 1 April 1992, p. 15.

Shi Genxing. "Jian Ding Bu Yi De Shen Huo Jun Dui Gaige" (Unswervingly Deepen Reform of Army). *Jiefang Junbao,* 31 July 1992, p. 3.

Shih Chun-yu. "Zhong Yang Bu Zhi Jia Su Gaige Kaifang" (Central Authorities Make Arrangements to Speed Up Reform and Opening Up). *Ta Kung Pao,* 4 March 1992, p. 2.

Shirk, Susan L. *The Political Logic of Economic Reform in China,* Berkeley: Unversity of California Press, 1993.

Shultz, George P. *Turmoil and Triumph.* New York: Macmillan, 1993.

Smith, Craig S., "China Sends Its Army Money, and a Signal to the U.S." *New York Times,* 11 March 2001, p. A1.

"State Planning Commission to Transform Function in Five Areas." *Ching-chi Tao-pao,* 15 June 1992, p. 11.

"Stepping Out: China's Lengthening Shadow." *International Defense Review,* February 1995, p. 35.

"Sulian Zhengbian Chendiao Beijing" (Overthrow of Soviet Government Shakes Beijing). *Pai Hsing,* 1 October 1991, pp. 3–4, 22–23.

Sun Chin-hui. "Tian Jiyun Reveals Background on Deng Xiaoping's Talks During His Inspection in South China." *Kuang Chiao Ching,* 16 July 1992, pp. 12–14.

Sun Kuo-han. "Deng Delivers Long Speech at Shoudu Iron and Steel Company, Advocates Promoting Talent in Economic Management to Run Government." *Ching Pao,* 5 July 1992, pp. 31–35.

Sun, Lena H. "Moderate to Become Chinese Vice-Premier." *Washington Post,* 3 April 1991, p. A20.

———. "Baker Says Gains Made with China." *Washington Post,* 18 November 1991, p. A1.

———. "Center May Reclaim Power in China." *Washington Post,* 29 October 1993, p. A33.

———. "Beijing, Fearing Unemployment, Slows Reform of State Industries." *Washington Post,* 20 April 1994, p. A15.

Swaine, Michael D. *The Military and Political Succession in China.* Rand Report R-4254-AF. Santa Monica, Calif.: Rand Corporation, 1992.

Tai Ming Cheung. "The Last Post." *Far Eastern Economic Review,* 23 November 1989, p. 10.

———. "Policy in Paralysis." *Far Eastern Economic Review,* 10 January 1991, pp. 10–11.

————. "Marking Time." *Far Eastern Economic Review,* 8 August 1991, p. 25.

————. "General Offensive." *Far Eastern Economic Review,* 10 December 1992, p. 14

Tang Chia-liang. "Zhonggong Junwei Guangda Huiyi Mi Liang Renshi Biange Jianxiao Yezhang Jun, Qi Ta Jun Chu Bu Biandong" (The CMC Meets in a Secret, Expanded Session to Discuss Personnel Cuts, Reductions in Field Armies, but Seven Military Regions Will Remain the Same). *Kuang Chiao Ching,* 16 May 1992, pp. 12–16.

Tan Xianci. "Qiao Shi Inspects Guangxi." *Xinhua,* 6 February 1992.

Tang Hsiao-chao. "Jiang Zemin Shi Lung Nei Mu" (Inside Story of Jiang Zemin's Loss of Favor). *Kai Fang,* 18 March 1992, pp. 16–17.

Taylor, George E. "China as an Oriental Despotism." *Problems of Post Communism* no. 1 (January–February 1995): 25–28.

Thakur, Ramesh and Carlyle A. Thayer, eds. *The Soviet Union as an Asian Power.* Boulder, Colo.: Westview Press, 1987.

Thornton, Richard C. *China: A Political History, 1917–1980.* Boulder, Colo.: Westview Press, 1982.

————. *The Nixon–Kissinger Years.* New York: Paragon Press, 1989.

————. *The Carter Years.* New York: Paragon Press, 1991.

————. "Deng's 'Middle Kingdom' Strategy." In *The Broken Mirror,* ed. George Hicks. Chicago: St. James Press, 1990. 390–400.

————. "Mikhail Gorbachev: A Preliminary Strategic Assessment." *The World and I* (January 1993): 583–93.

————. "Chinese-Russian Relations and the Struggle for Hegemony in Northeast Asia." *Problems of Post Communism* no. 1, (January-February 1995): 29–34.

————. "Russo-Chinese Detente and the Emerging New World Order." (Unpublished Paper, 1995).

"Tian Jiyun in Hainan; Notes Urgency of Opening," *Xinhua,* 28 January 1992.

"Tian Jiyun Dang Jiao Jiany Huo Ji Yao" (Summary of Tian Jiyun's Speech Before Party School). *Pai Hsing,* 16 June 1992, pp. 4–5.

Tien Fu. "Bo Yibo Nuli Kaolung Deng Xiaoping" (Bo Yibo Tries to Close Ranks with Deng Xiaoping). *Tangtai,* 15 June 1992, p. 21.

Tsen Shan. "Kuanglung Kai Ming Pai De Fan Chi Xuan" (Anticyclone of Frenzied Attack on Group of the Enlightened). Cheng Ming no. 184 (1 February 1992): 16–17.

Tseng Chi. "Zhong Yang Wen Jian Lie Yu 'Zuo Qing' Cuo Wu" (Central Document Lists "Leftist" Mistakes). *Cheng Ming* no. 191 (1 September 1992): 27–28.

Walder, Andrew G. and Xianxin Gong. "Workers in the Tiananmen Protests: The Politics of the Beijing Workers' Autonomous Federation." *Australian Journal of Chinese Studies* no. 29 (January 1993).

Wang Yihua. "Jun Dui Sheng Chan Jing Ying Wen Si Liu" (What Is Seen Regarding Troops' Production and Economic Activities and Thoughts Provoked Thereby). *Jiefang Junbao,* 12 December 1991, p. 2.

Wei Yung-cheng, "Reveal the Mystery of Huangfu Ping" *Ta Kung Pao,* 8 October 1992, p. 14.

Wen Li. "Instill Sense of Urgency on Reform and Opening Up." *Wen Wei Pao*, 28 January 1992, p. 2.

Whitson, William W., with Huang Chen-hsia. *The Chinese High Command: A History of Communist Military Politics, 1927–1971*. New York: Praeger, 1973.

Wu Duanze. "Gaige Kaifang Bi Xu Jia Qiang Zheng Fa Gongzi" (Strengthen Legal Work in Support of Reform and Opening). *Renmin Ribao*, 29 January 1992, p. 8.

Wu Wenmin. "Xing Ban Jingji Te Chu Zheng Zhi Bu Hui Shou Su Yao Ba Te Chu Ban De Gen Kui Xie Geng Hao Xie" (Manage the Special Economic Areas Better and More Openly). *Renmin Ribao*, 7 February 1987, p. I.

Xing Laizhao. "Ba You Huo Jie Gou Fang Zai Tu Chu Wei Zhi" (Give Prominence to Structural Optimization). *Jiefang Junbao*, 15 May 1992, p. 3.

Yahuda, Michael. *Towards The End of Isolationism: China's Foreign Policy After Mao*. London: Macmillan Press, 1983.

———. "Deng Xiaoping the Statesman." *China Quarterly* No. 135 (September 1993): 551–73.

Yang Baibing. "Zhun Dai Yao Wei Gaige Kaifang 'Bao Jai Hu Hang'" (PLA to "Escort" Reform Opening) *Renmin Ribao*, 24 March 1992, p. 2.

———. "Bang Ze Qi Wei Guo Jia Gaige He Jian She Bao Jia Hu Hang De Zung Gao Shi Ming" (Shouldering Lofty Mission of Escorting and Protecting China's Reform and Construction—In Commemoration of 65th Anniversary of Founding of People's Liberation Army). *Renmin Ribao*, 29 July 1992, pp. I, 3.

Yeh, K. C. "Macroeconomic Issues in China in the 1990s." *China Quarterly* No. 131 (September 1992): 501–44.

Yen Shen-tsun. "Deng Xiaoping's Talk During His Inspection of Shoudu Iron and Steel Complex." *Kuang Chiao Ching*, 16 July 1992, pp. 6–7.

Ying Yi. "Jiang Zemin Recently Returns to Shanghai to Encourage Local Officials. *Ming Pao*, 30 January 1992, p. 8.

Yueh Shan. "Shi Si Da Ren Shi Dou Zheng Su Mu Zhan" (Prelude to Struggle for Personnel Arrangements on Eve of Fourteenth CCP National Congress). *Cheng Ming* no. 186 (I April 1992): 15.

Yuan Xuequan. "Qiang Gan Zi Yong Yuan Ting Dang Zhi Hui" (Gun Always Remains Under Party Command). *Jiefang Junbao*, 19 July 1992, p. I.

Zeng Guangjun. "Zhi Liang: Jun Dui De Sheng Ming" (Quality: The Army's Lifeline). *Jiefang Junbao*, 3 January 1992, p. 3.

Zhang Xiaowei. "The Fourteenth Central Committee of the CCP." *Asian Survey* no. 8 (August 1993): 787–803.

Zhao Suisheng. "Deng Xiaoping's Southern Tour." *Asian Survey* no. 8 (August 1993): 739–56.

Zheng Yi. *Zhong Gong Zhun Tou Dian Jiang Lu* (The Top Generals of the PLA). Taibei: Kaijin Wenhua, Ltd. 1995.

"Zhonggong Fachu Si Hao Wen Jian Chuan Mian Chan Shu Guang Da Kaifeng" (CCP Issues Document Number Four, Fully Expounding Expansion of Opening Up). *Ta Kung Pao*, 18 June 1992, p. 2.

"Zhong Gong Jue Ding Cai Chu Yi Xie Xin Zheng Ci Xin Zuo Shi Li Zheng Chuan Guo Jing Ji Geng Hao Geng Kuai Shang Xin Tai Jie" (The CCP Decides to Adopt a Series of New Policies to Speed Up the Economic Situation). *Renmin Ribao*, 8 June 1992, p. I.

"Zhong Gong Shi San Jie Zhong Gong Wei Yuan Hui Jian Kai Quan Hui" (Communiqué of the Eight Plenary Session of the Thirteenth CCP Central Committee). *Renmin Ribao*, 30 November 1991, p. I.

"Zhong Gong Zhong Yang Guan Yu Zhi Ding Guo Min Jing Ji He She Hui Fa Zhen Shi Nian Guai Hua He "Ba Wu" Ji Hua De Jian Ji" (Chinese Communist Party Central Committee's Proposals for the Ten-Year Development Program and the Eighth Five-Year Plan). *Renmin Ribao*, 29 January 1991, pp. I–4.

"Zhongguo Gongchan Dang De Shi San Zi Quan Guo Dai Biao De Hui Kai Mu" (The Opening of the Thirteenth Congress of the Communist Party). *Renmin Ribao*, 26 October 1987, p. I.

Zhu Rongji. "Exerpts." *Zhongguo Jingji Tizhi Gaige*, 23 February 1992, pp. 7–9.

"Zhua Zhu You Li Shi Ji Jia Kuai Gaige Kaifang Ji Zhong Shen Li Ba Jing Ji" (Firmly Grasp the Principle of Speeding Up Opening Is Economics). *Renmin Ribao*, 3 March 1992, p. I.

"Zhuan Da Deng Xiaoping Tong Zhi De Zhong Yao Jiang Hua Jiang Diao Ba Si Xiang Tong Yi Dao Jiang Hua Shang Lai" (Transmit the Important Talk of Deng Xiaoping in Shanghai on Unifying Thought and Words). *Renmin Ribao*, 14 June 1989, p. I.

"Zhuan Jun She Hui Zhu Yi Xin Nian Jiao Yu Chu De Chen Ji" (PLA Concentrating on Socialist Education). *Renmin Ribao*, 5 December 1991, p. 7.

Zou Jiahua. "Chuan Guo Ren Da Chang Wei Hui Zhu Xing Chuan Ti Hui" (The Standing Committee of the People's Congress Holds a Special Enlarged Meeting). *Renmin Ribao*, 2 September 1992, p. I–2.

INDEX

ABOUT THE AUTHOR

Doctor Michael E. Marti is employed by the Department of Defense. Currently, he is a Senior Fellow at the Center for the Study of Chinese Military Affairs at the Institute for National Strategic Studies at National Defense University, specializing in Chinese national security and foreign policy. Previous assignments included a one-year tour in the Office of the Assistant Secretary of Defense for International Security Affairs as the Assistant Country Director for China, Taiwan, and Mongolia in the Office of Asian-Pacific Affairs. He is a graduate of the National War College and holds a Ph.D. in Chinese history from George Washington University. Doctor Marti is married and lives in Maryland.